The Affinity Photo Guidebook

A Step-by-Step New User's Manual

Frank Walters

This work is copyrighted material.

©**KuhlmanPublishing**

All rights reserved. No portion of this book may be reproduced in any form without written permission from the publisher, except as permitted by U.S. Copyright law. All images and text in this book have been used with permission from their original sources. All logos and depictions of the UI are copyright of Serif (Europe) Ltd. and this book is not endorsed or supported by Affinity. All images have been used with permission.

We are a self-publishing company employing several authors. We take our books very seriously and try our very best to publish high-quality books that deliver the expected results we advertise in our book descriptions. If there is ever an issue with syntax, content or book layout, please don't hesitate to contact us before you leave negative comments. We promise we will address your concerns as quickly as we can. Software develops quickly and when we publish our books we know in a short time there will be new updates. We promise to try to keep up with updates in all of our books as the software updates.

About the price of the printed versions: We apologize that our printed books cost as much as they do. Our books are full of high-quality images and these make the book file size quite large. The larger the file size, the more expensive the book becomes. We always try to keep the price as low as possible and we promise our take is not exorbitant.

For permissions, questions or to submit your own artwork, contact us at **KuhlmanPublishing@yahoo.com**

ISBN: 979-8676-0361-33

Introduction to (the revised) Affinity Photo Guidebook

Affinity Photo is fun to use with this step-by-step new user's manual. This DIY book will guide you through the first 10 skills new users need to know how to do plus twenty in-depth techniques to further increase your knowledge and skillset in using this market-leading photo editor.

We created each tutorial to be visually impressive with 4K quality screenshots as well as our unique method of *italicizing* action words and **bolding** main objects - like the **Menu bar** - **Toolbar** items, the **Studios**, and the **Tools**. We tell you with our words and show you with our screenshots exactly how to do each step for every tutorial.

As of the date of publication, we guarantee all tutorials work as they are in the book.

This New Edition

The first edition of this book was published in December 2019 and in February we invested in new computers and monitors, which allowed us to create books with a much higher image resolution. So, we unpublished The Affinity Guidebook and this new copy is a revamped edition with all new 4K quality screenshots and two new lessons.

If you have purchased the previously published book, please send us an email and we'll work something out for you.

The Images in This Book

At the end of this book is a list of all images used in this book. We have also included at the beginning of each lesson hyperlinks to the images used in that lesson.

We highly recommend you take the time and download all of the images at the back of the book and place them in an easy-to-find folder on your desktop. Then, when you are working your way through the book, you will very easily find all images.

Feel free to email us to ask for a full list of all of the images used in this book. We have a list of the images with their hyperlinks in a Word.docx that we'd be happy to send to you if you ask.

If you have any problems downloading the images, please contact us at: **KuhlmanPublishing@yahoo.com**

A Note about Hyperlinks

If the provided hyperlinks to our images don't work, please type out their webpages into your search engine and you should be able to easily find them. Most of the images are license-free from the website Pixabay.

If you would like a separate Word document with all these hyperlinks so you can simply click on them to open them up onto your screen, please email us and we'll send you this list.

A Note About Redundancy

Learning new skills take a lot of repetition. We know this, so we structured this book with lots of the same ideas and shortcuts. This is done so you learn as fast as possible. We consider we've done our job if when you are done going through this book, you're able to retain most of the main features of this software.

Version Update 1.8

In late February 2020, Serif Affinity Photo released their update 1.8. In this book we use these new updates in the chapters Basics #1 & #9. To learn more about this update, go here: https://affinity.serif.com/en-gb/1-8/

The coolest update for previous Adobe Photoshop users is the ability to edit Adobe Photoshop Smart Objects. To set Affinity Photo to be able to do this:

Go to **Menu bar** - **Affinity Photo** - **Preferences** - **General**

Check on the **box** for "Import PSD smart objects where possible"

Affinity Photo can now edit yours or your client's PSD smart objects. You can receive them from Photoshop, work on them in Affinity Photo and then export the file as a PSD file.

Free Cover Image Tutorial
If you would like a free tutorial on how to create our cover image with John Lennon, please send us an email and we'll send it to you for free. KuhlmanPublishing@yahoo.com

Be a Part of Our Growing Community

We would like to create a community feeling about out books. If we can help you in any way, please send us and email and we'll respond quickly. Our mobile phones are always on. We'd be delighted to help you get past a tough spot in your learning by sending you personalized help.

We are here for you!

Examples of Techniques Taught

Double Exposure Effect (p.55)

How to Create Realistic Shadows (p.140)

Impressive 3D Pop-Out Effects (p.111)

Water Flame Candles (p. 125)

Transparent Text Effects (p. 46)

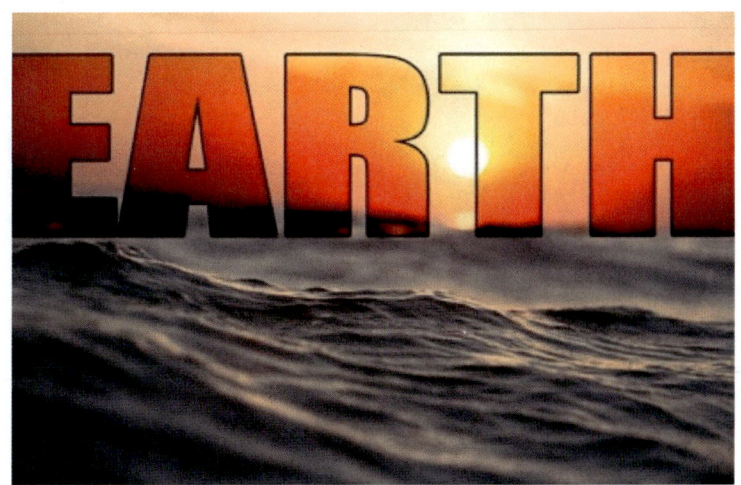

Transparent Clothing Effects (p. 146)

Realistic Reflections (p. 162)

Jumping Over Text Effects (p. 176)

Table of Contents

Introduction to (the revised) Affinity Photo Guidebook 3
Free Cover Image Tutorial 4
Examples of Techniques Taught 5
 # 1 – How to Open Images/Documents/Templates 9
 # 2 – Affinity Photo's User Interface (aka the Screen) 13
 # 3 – How to Crop Pictures 17
 # 4 – How to Remove Imperfections from a Photo 20
 # 5 – How to Use the Adjustments Layer 24
 # 6 – How to Use Masks 29
 # 7 - How to Make Selections 33
 # 8 – How to Change the Background of a Photo 35
 # 9 – How to Add Text to an Image 43
 # 10 – How to Save & Export 50
Tutorial 1: How to Create a Double Exposure Effect 55
Tutorial 2: How to Create a Color Splash Effect 63
Tutorial 3: How to Create a Stylish Duotone Effect 65
Tutorial 4: How to Create a Matte Image Effect 73
Tutorial 5: How to do a Sky Replacement 79
Tutorial 6: How to Create a High-Speed Effect 88
Tutorial 7: How to Create a Dispersion Effect 96
Tutorial 8: How to Create a Face Warp 102
Tutorial 9: How to Create a Beautiful Pop Art Effect 105
Tutorial 10: How to Create a Pop Out or 3D Effect 111
Tutorial 11: How to Create a Water Flame Candle 125
Tutorial 12: How to Create a Face Swap 132
Tutorial 13: How to Crop an Image in a Circle Shape 137
Tutorial 14: How to Make a Realistic Shadow 140
Tutorial 15: How to Make a Transparent Clothing Effect 146
Tutorial 16: How to Put a Face on the Moon 155
Tutorial 17: How to Make Realistic Reflections 162
Tutorial 18: How to Restore Old Photographs 170
Tutorial 19: How to Transform Any Image into a Pencil Drawing 173

Tutorial 20: How to Create a Jumping Over Text Effect *176*

List of Tutorials and Their Image Webpages *179*

The Five Areas on the Affinity Photo Screen *181*

The Most Common Shortcuts You Need to Know *183*

Dedication *184*

First 10 Skills for Beginners

In this first section, we will be covering the basics of Affinity Photo. Please make sure you are familiar with these first 10 skills so that you will be able to apply what you will learn to the 20 tutorials that follow. You will probably refer back to these pages often. Repetition is the best teacher.

Again, be sure to have downloaded all of the images from the preceding pages into a specific Affinity Photo folder on your desktop. Doing this will save you very much time.

1 – How to Open Images/Documents/Templates

In Affinity Photo there are several ways to open Images onto the canvas. We'll discuss how to Open Documents and Templates after we've explained how to open images.

To open images, there are 5 ways to do this:

1. Open...

Go to the **Menu bar** - **File** - **Open** (or use the shortcut **Ctrl/Cmd+O**). This will open up your computer's search pop-out window where you can choose from which folder or location the image you want is located and then when you find it, *double-click* on it and it will be opened into the Affinity Photo UI.

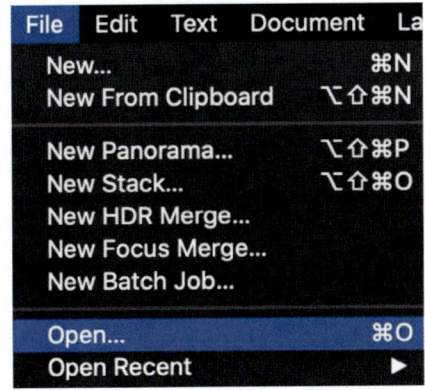

2. Open Recent

This will open a recently opened image that you may or may not have used with Affinity Photo. This is a useful option for when you need to work with multiple images over several hours.

3. Open... RAW Image

Opening images that are in RAW format will be immediately placed in the Develop Persona where you can make edits to the image before you upload it as a regular photo image (.jpg or .png). You do not need to specify that you have a RAW image, Affinity Photo will know automatically.

4. Stock Images

Affinity Photo lets you locate stock images directly inside the UI so that once you find an image you want to edit, you simply *click* on that image & *drag* it onto the canvas. There is a Stock tab located directly under the Color Wheel in the Layers Studio (see black rectangle). In order to *drag, drop* & *release* a stock photo (see yellow arrow), you need to first have an open document on the canvas.

Affinity Photo has three websites where you can use their Stock photography. Simply *click* on the vertical double-arrows (see our yellow rectangle) to *choose* between Unsplash, Pexels, and Pixabay. First *type* in the title of the image you are looking for (we typed "model").

5. *Click & Drag*

Click & *drag* also works. Simply *click* on an image someplace on your computer & *drag* it onto the Affinity Photo canvas. Be sure when doing this, be sure to place the new image and release it on a blank area of the canvas. That will cause it to be its own image separate from an existing image (if there is one already on the canvas). If you *click* & *drag* an image from your computer and release the mouse button over an existing image, the new image will become part of the underlying image. If this happens, simply *press* **Crtl/Cmd+Z** to *undo* your action. Then, go back and do it properly.

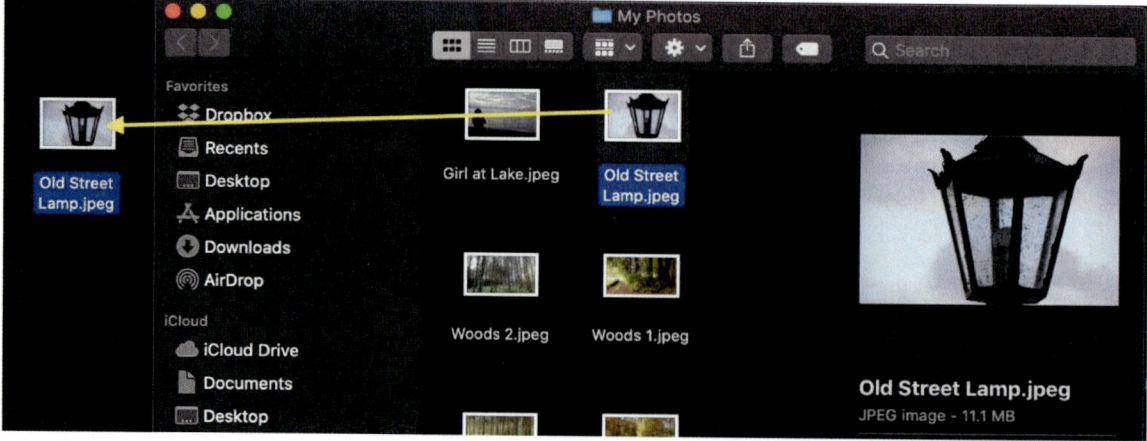

6. Open with...

Find an image on your computer and *right-click* on it and in the pop-out window choose Affinity Photo.

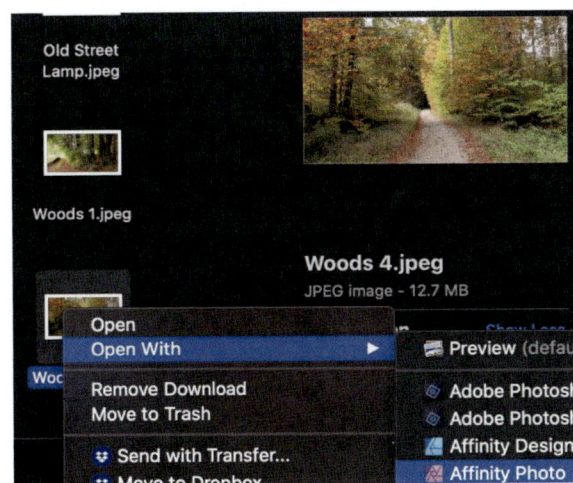

7. New... (Document)

When you *click* on **New...** (**Ctrl/Cmd+N**), a pop-out window will appear where you can choose which form of Document you want to use: A **Preset** or a **Template** (see left-side of image below).

See **Basics #9** for a full tutorial on opening new Documents and creating Presets.

First, let's discuss the Presets - There are seven categories: My Presets, Print, Print Ready, Photo, Web, Devices, Architectural.

Note: The right-side of the screen, the **Layout**, is where you can change your particularly-sized document's dimensions and DPI. Once you find a preset you like and want to keep it for later, *click* on the "circled**+**" (see yellow rectangle) at the top of the Layout area and it'll become a new Preset.

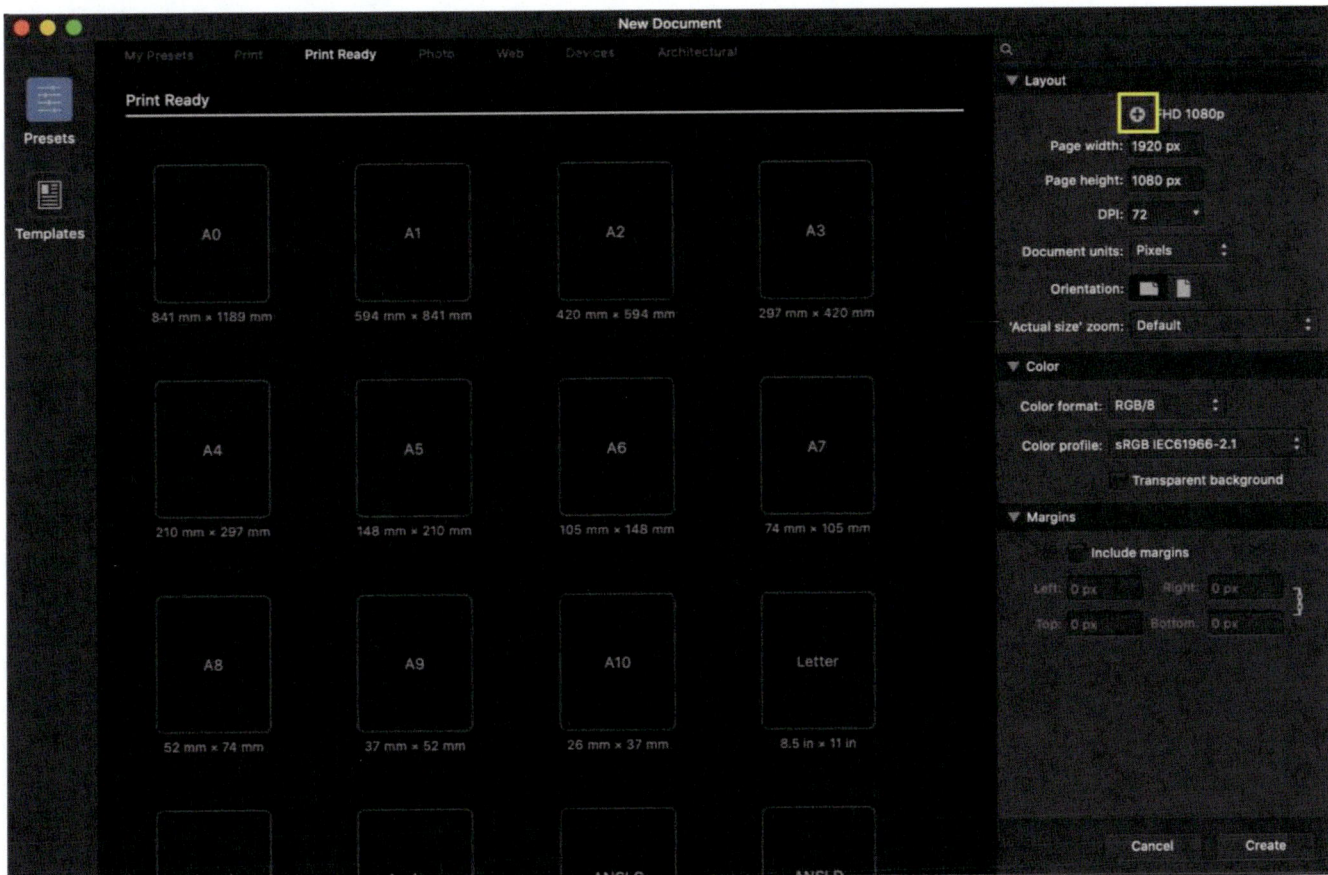

My Presets is where you'll place the specifically-sized documents you use all the time. This will be your go-to category for most of our new documents.

Print & **Print Ready** handle documents you print. **Print Ready** is calibrated for specific printers.

Photo is for photos of different sizes. This is useful when you need a specific print size.

Devices is to be used when you need to make sure your document fits perfectly within a specific device's screen.

Architectural is a preset to be used for architecture images.

Templates: These are pre-made items containing images, layers, effects, and other settings all pre-prepared for you to use. You can make your own templates or you can probably find a few freebees online.

Finished. This ends this tutorial.

2 – Affinity Photo's User Interface (aka the Screen)

The 2nd skill to learn is understanding the Affinity Photo`s **User Interface** (UI) and how Affinity Photo is organized.

To help you quickly see how it's organized, we've added the names of the different parts you need to know to get a great start in learning this software.

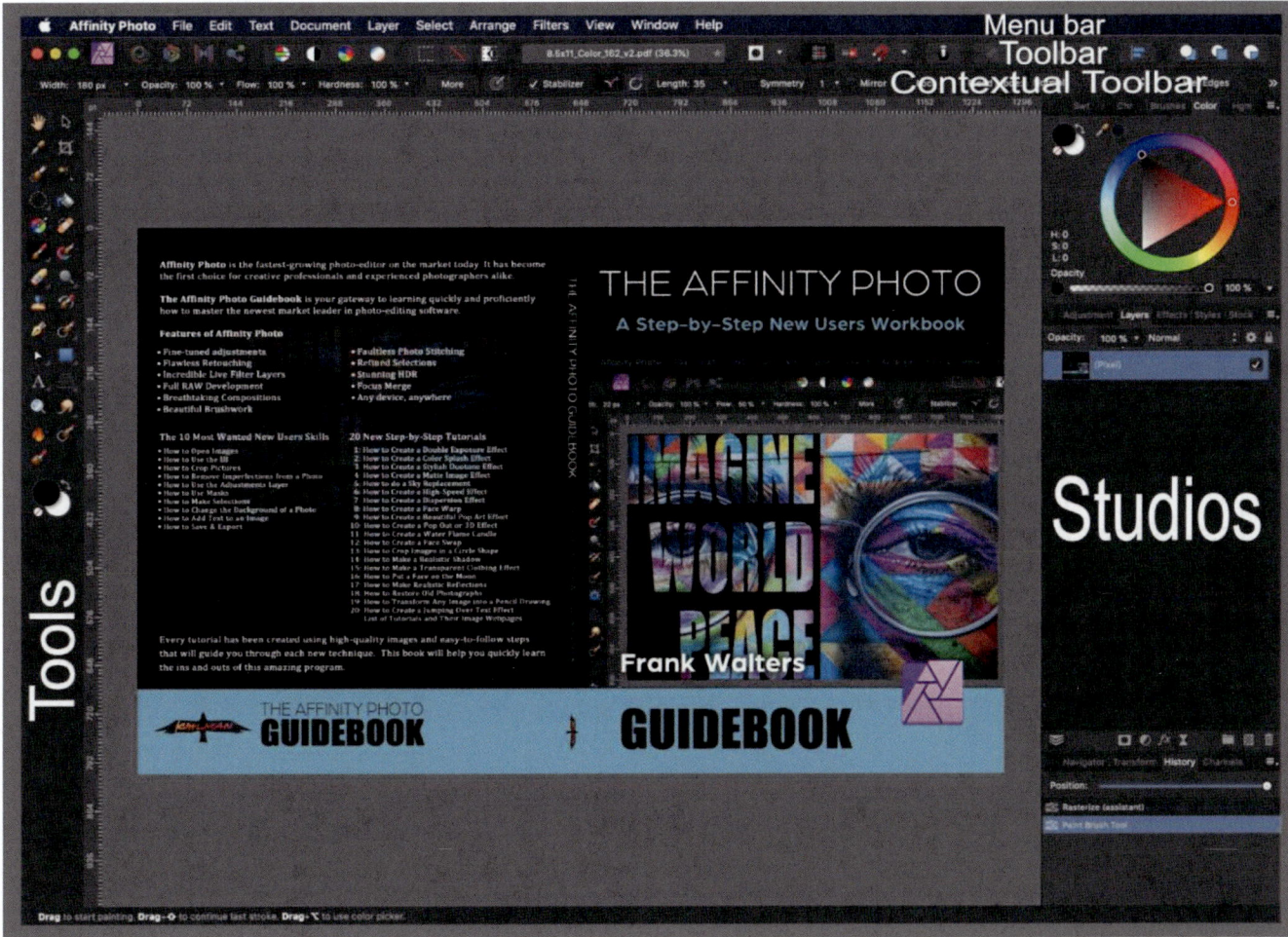

On the left side of the screen are all the **Tools** you need to edit your pictures.

Whenever you *click* on the **Tools**, different options appear at the top of the interface. This top section above the canvas and on top of the image tabs is called the Contextual Toolbar**.**

The Contextual Toolbar allows you to make different changes, like *changing* the **Width** of the **Brush**, or *adjust* the level of an image's **Opacity**.

On the right-side of the screen's interface, you have the **Studios**. At the top of the **Studios**, you can *click* on **Color**, **Histogram** (Hgm), **Swatches** (Swt), **Brushes**, and **Macro** and in the middle section of the **Studio**, you have different panels –**Adjustment, Layers, Effects, Styles, Stock.**

Here is how to use some of these panels and some of the tools.

To **Add/Delete** Studio panels:

Go to the **Menu bar** and *choose* **View**

Select **Studio** from the drop-down menu.

Check **on** the panels you want to **add**.

Check **off** the panels you want to **delete**.

Note: In this image, **Adjustments** are added while **Assets** are not added to the Studios.

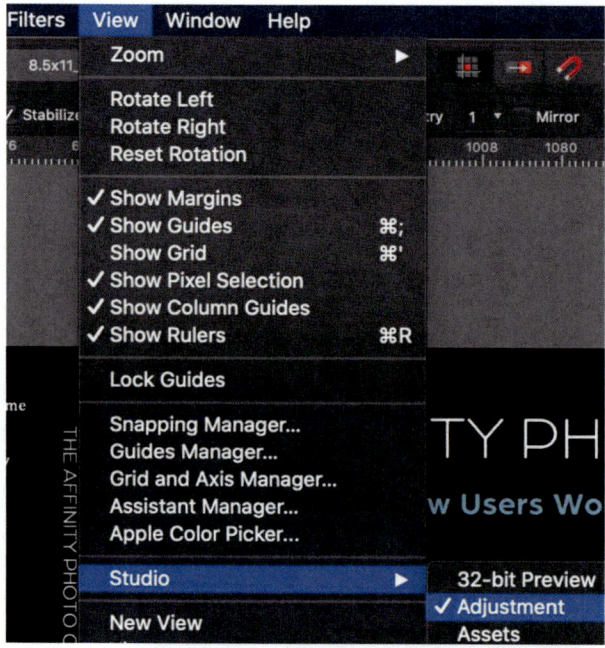

To *reset* the **Studio** options (this is important to remember if you accidently *press* the wrong buttons in the Studio):

Go to the **Menu bar** and *choose* **View**

Select **Studio** from the drop-down menu.

Click **Reset Studio** (this is located at the very bottom of the list).

Affinity Photo can customize its tools from the left side panel. To do this:

Go to the **Menu bar** and *choose* **View**.

Select **Customize Tools** (watch for a pop-out window).

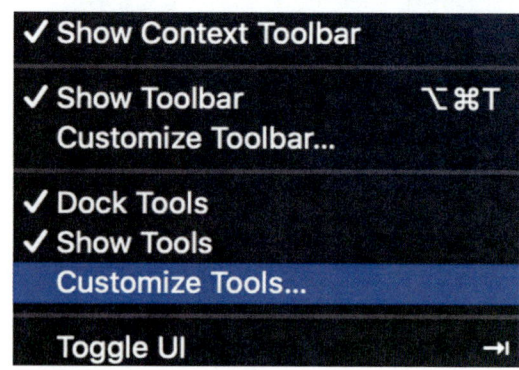

14

Use *drag* & *drop* to *move* any **Tools** you want to add to the left-side column. You can also do the opposite and remove any Tool from the left-side Tool column and place it back in the pop-out window full of tools by *click* & *drag* if you want to.

For example, you can take the **Red Eye Removal Tool** and *drag* it to the Tools column (yellow arrow).

Special Note:

The most important thing we can recommend to you is to change the Tools column from one to two columns. Why? Because with two columns, the Fore-/Background colors will be placed at the bottom of the Tools. This is extremely helpful as you increase in your mastery of this program.

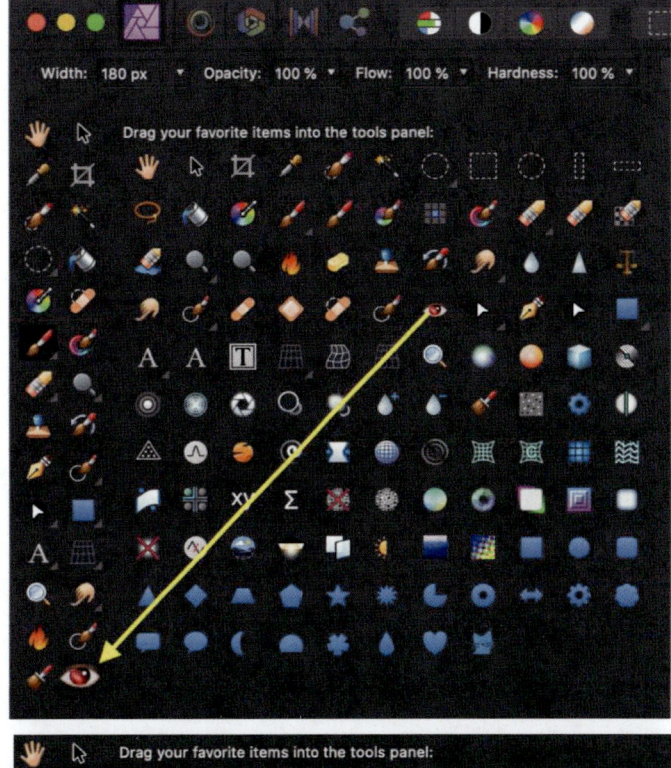

To do this:

> *Go* to the **Number of Columns** tab on the bottom left-hand portion of the pop-out window and *select* the number of the columns that you prefer (e.g. 2).

You will now have two columns of **Tools** on the left-side of the UI with the Fore-/Background color circles present as well.

When you`re done with customizing your **Tools**, *press* **Close** (see image to the right).

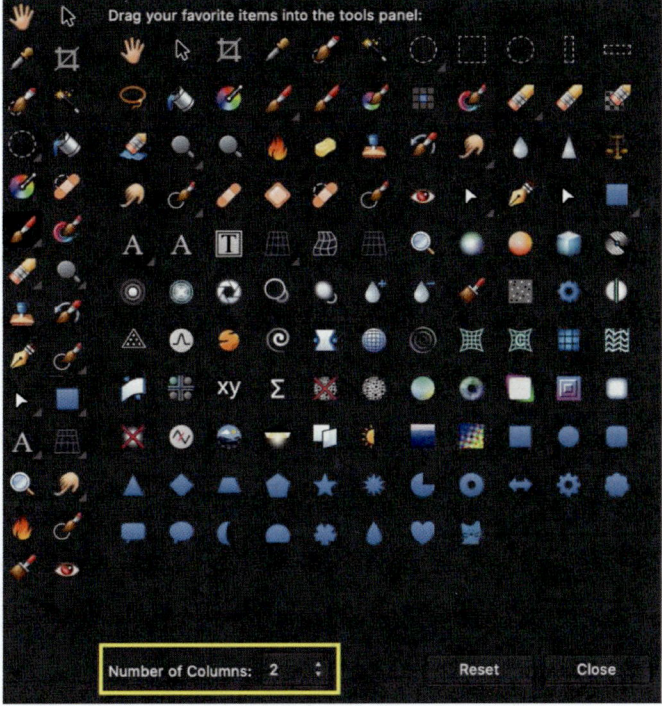

To *reset* the settings of the **Toolbar**, *click* the **Reset** button in the bottom right-hand corner next to Close.

15

The Personas

The different Personas are located on the top left-side of the UI. Each Persona has its own Tools, Studios and/or Panels. As you become more familiar with Affinity Photo the more comfortable you'll be changing Personas to match your job. 95% of the time, you will probably work in the Photo Persona.

Personas = Workspaces

You'll do most of your work using **Photo Persona**.

Here are the five different types:

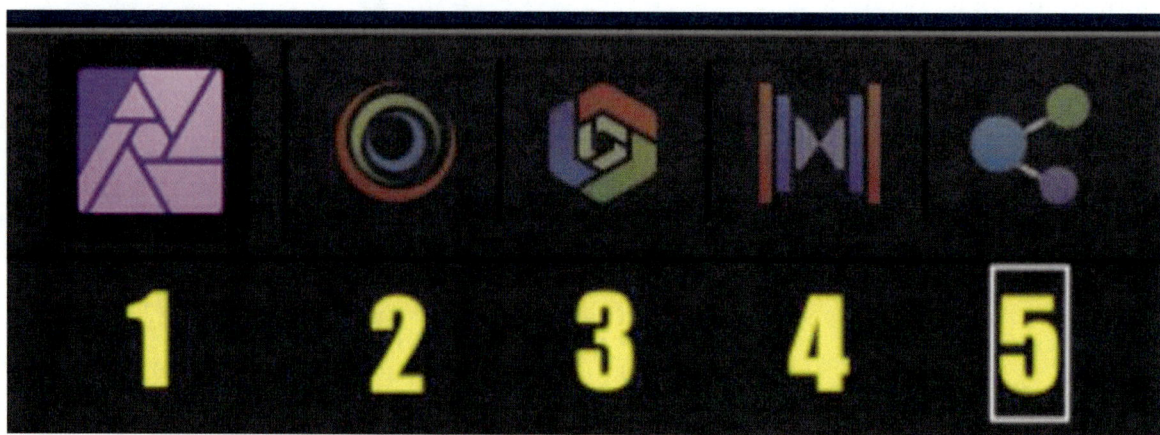

1. **Photo Persona**: This is the persona you will use the most for editing, cropping, making selections, using brushes, retouching, etc.

2. **Liquify Persona**: Used primarily to distort images.

3. **Develop Persona**: Used primarily for RAW images (i.e. when you upload a RAW file, it will automatically be opened into this Persona.

4. **Tone Mapping Persona**: Used for Tone Mapping

5. **Export Persona**: Used to export in different formats.

Finished. This ends this tutorial.

3 – How to Crop Pictures

The 3rd skill to know is to know how to crop pictures.

Here is the webpage for the image we'll be using for this section:

https://www.dropbox.com/s/3l42sx5yzashl2t/Cropping.jpg?dl=0

Ready to start?

With the image open on your screen, let's learn how to crop.

    Select the **Crop Tool** (or *press* **C**).

    Click on the **nodes** located on the image's perimeter & *move* them however you want to create the cropped image you need.

    Press **Apply** when done (you can also simply *press* **Enter** on your keyboard).

Note: After you crop your picture, Affinity Photo keeps the original (see grey area around out cropped portion of the photo). To see where your original image was before you performed the crop, *select* the **Move Tool** (or *press* **V**) and you'll see the original image's perimeter. This image shows the middle-cropped area we selected as well as the part of the original we are excluding.

If you want to recapture some of the original image from the crop:

    Select the **Crop Tool** (or *press* **C**).

    Move the squares to left/right/up/down until you have your original photo back.

    Press **Enter** (or *click* on **Apply**).

Note: Purchase our latest book **The Affinity Photo Manual II** for a more in-depth review of the Crop Tool.

Another great feature of the **Crop Tool** is that it allows you to straighten crooked horizons. To do this:

Select the **Crop Tool** (or *press* **C**).

Press the **Straighten** button in the middle of the Contextual Toolbar.

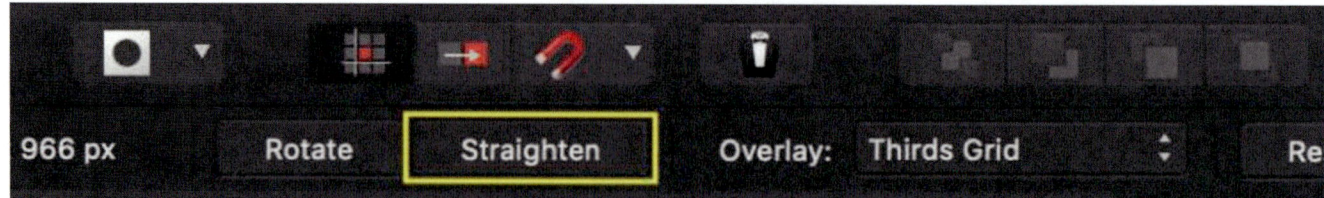

Click & *drag* on the **part of your picture** that you want *straightened*. Look at the left image below where we placed the line on the horizon we want to straighten. As you do this, you will be drawing a white line (see the top of **Before** image).

Release you **mouse button** and the horizon you indicated will be made straight (see **After** image).

Before

After

To *rotate* your **picture** while in Crop mode:

> *Click* with your mouse **someplace outside the image** (creating a 2-arrow cursor). Unfortunately, we are unable to make a screenshot of this 2-arrow cursor to show you).
>
> *Click* & *drag* to **rotate** the photo.
>
> *Press* **Enter** to confirm the rotation.

To remove the transparent area which appeared after straightened the horizon, we need to crop the image again and crop out this transparent area.

This is what our crop looks like now:

Done. This is our final image.

Finished. This ends this tutorial.

4 – How to Remove Imperfections from a Photo

The 4th skill to know is how to remove imperfections from photo.

Here is the webpage to the image we'll be using:

https://www.dropbox.com/s/2u6pw011di5dbyf/How to Remove Imperfections from a Photo - Jumping.jpg?dl=0

In this example, we`re going to remove the poles sticking out of the water.

Before we start, we want to **duplicate** the image by *pressing* **Ctrl/Cmd+J.**

Now we have two copies of the picture. The reason we do this is because we work non-destructively – this will keep the original image safe by working on a copy of it.

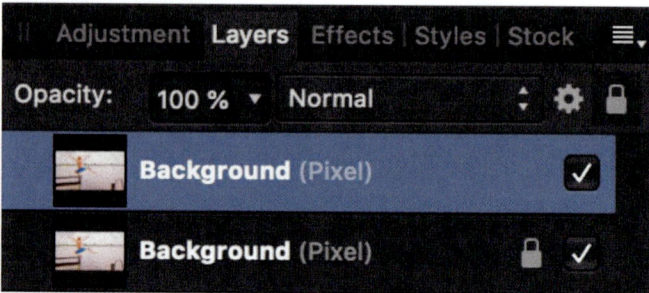

Before we start this tutorial, we want to learn a little about working non-destructively. This is a very important part of photo-editing software that we want to briefly discuss this. We will restart the tutorial on the next page.

If you look at the Layers Panel, you will see that there are two **Background** layers. The layer on the very bottom is the original image. Looking at these layers you might be able to understand how affecting changes on the above **Background** layer doesn't destroy or touch the lowest **Background** image.

You can also tell which is the original image by the **Lock icon** on the right-side of its layer.

Do you understand what it means to work destructively (the opposite of non-destructive)? It means you are working on your original image and making changes to it. When you go to save the image, your original will be lost and, in a sense, "destroyed".

Therefore, whenever you are working with original images that you don't want to be ruined, you should always **duplicate** the original by *pressing* **Ctrl/Cmd+J**. This shortcut will make a **duplicate** copy of your original so that when you add layers (Adjustments, paintings, other images) on top of the duplicated image, your original will not be touched.

This piece of advice is especially important for users who edit RAW images.

This knowledge is very important. We hope you understand its importance. If you need further clarification, we are sure you can do a Google search and read all about "non-destructive image editing".

Now that we have a better understanding of what it means to work non-destructively, let's get back to this important tutorial

After duplicating the image, let's remove the metal poles from the water.

To do this:

> *Select* the **Inpainting Brush Tool** (it looks like a brush with a circle at its tip). Inpainting is smart content removal.

> *Paint o*ver an **imperfection** (the poles in the lower right-hand corner) & Affinity Photo will remove them.

If you want to see before & after, *turn* off the **duplicate** image that you made earlier in this example:

> *Go* to the **Layers Panel**.

> *Check* the **duplicate** picture *off* & *on*.

Note: If you look closely at the two preview thumbnails (the small square images on the left-side of each layer) on both layers, you'll see that the top layer does not have the poles, but the lower layer does. So, when we uncheck (or deactivate) the top layer the poles return. This is because we are only seeing the bottom layer.

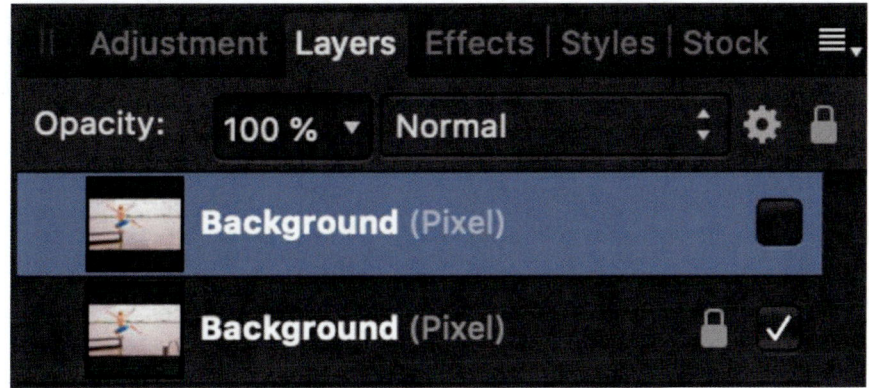

Part 2 of **Removing Imperfections**

For this example, you should be working with the image of a man's face. Ezra is the founder of Affinity Revolution. It is from his lessons that we got our start in Affinity Photo. We recommend his online courses.

Here is the webpage for this image:

> https://affinityrevolution.com/wp-content/uploads/2017/11/Ezra-1.jpg

Here, we are going to use the same tool, the **Inpainting Brush Tool**, but for removing some facial imperfections.

To do this:

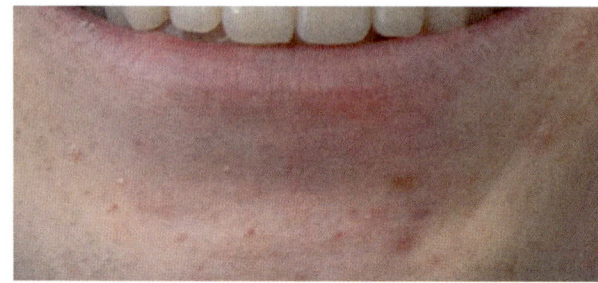

Press **Ctrl/Cmd+J** to *duplicate* the image.

Press **Ctrl/Cmd+** to *zoom in* to the man's face.

Hold-down the **Space bar** and *click* on the **image** & *drag* it **around the canvas** to your perfect position.

Click again on the **Selection Brush Tool** so it's activated.

Go to the **Contextual Toolbar** and *make* these changes to the Brush:

Change the **Hardness** to **100%**.

Change the **Width** to the size of on one of the two front teeth. The Width of the Brush is a personal choice. Personally, when we use the Selection Brush Tool, we try to keep the width of the brush just a little bit bigger than the point on the image we are going to be altering.

In this example, we are working with very small imperfections, so a small brush size should be used.

Note: When *adjusting* the different tool measurements (like Width, Opacity, Flow, Hardness, etc.), there are two ways to increase or decrease their values (or the %).

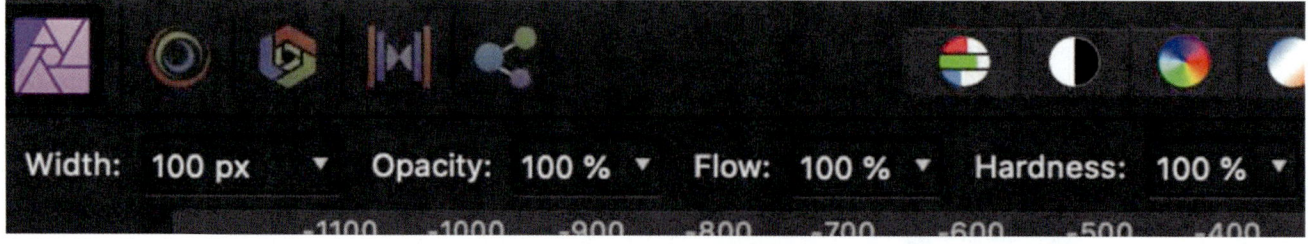

First, *double-click* the window and type in the **#** you want (in this case we typed **100**).

Second, you can *click* on the downward-pointing diamonds located to the right of the % symbol and a slider will appear (see yellow squares). Then you'll *slide* to the left for a smaller amount or to the right for a larger amount.

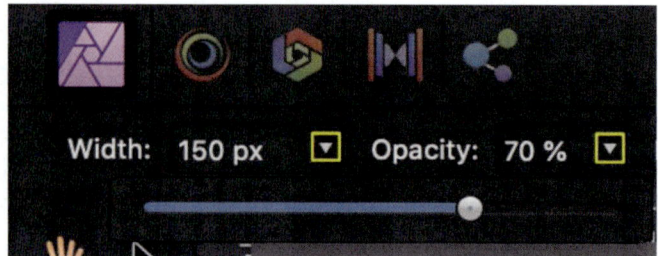

Now we're ready to use our brush to remove the imperfections we find on the man's face.

Click & *drag* the **red-tinted cursor** over the area you want to fix.

Release the **button** & the software will remove the imperfection (just like when we used this tool to remove the poles in the jumping image before.

These are the areas we corrected. For this tutorial, we made the Opacity for these red marks 50% so you could see the underlying acne for reference.

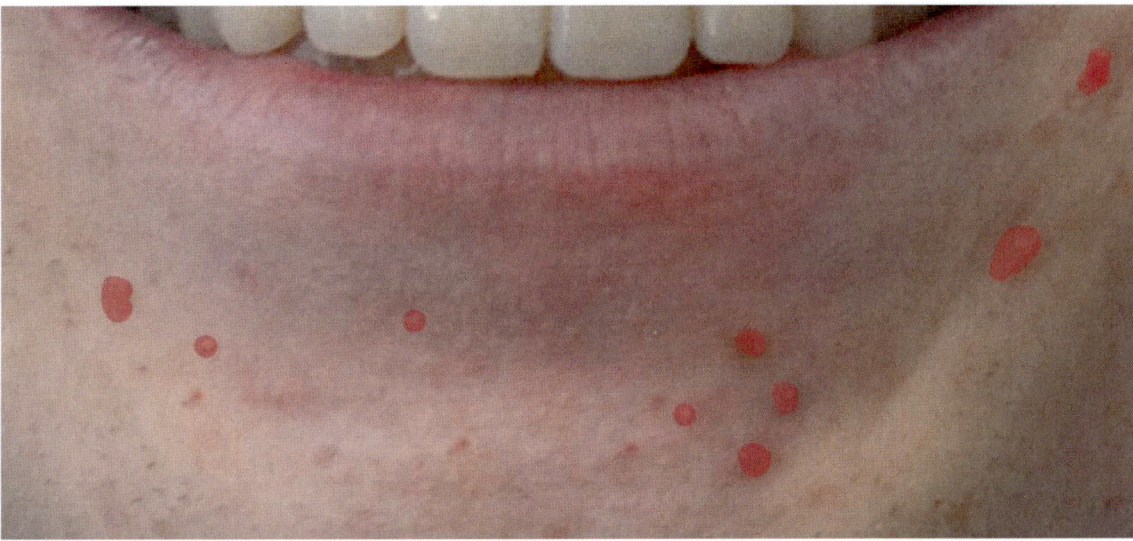

This is image after these edits.

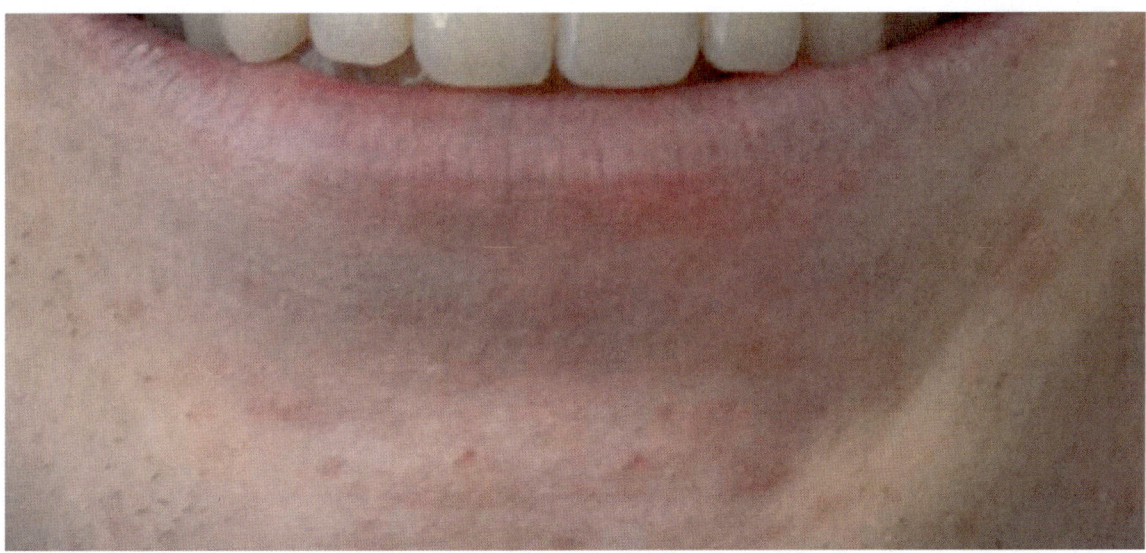

Uncheck the **top layer** in the Layers Panel to see *before* & *after*.

If you are not happy with the result, you can repeat the steps above for removing imperfections until you get the perfect view for your image.

Finished. This ends this tutorial.

5 – How to Use the Adjustments Layer

The 5th skill to know is how to use the Adjustment layers.

Here is the webpage to the single image we will be using in tutorials 5 & 6:

> https://pixabay.com/photos/seashell-shell-shells-sea-ocean-2821388/

In this tutorial, we will be working with the Adjustments and how to use this powerful tool in an interesting way.

Adjustment layers allow non-destructive changes to the colors of your image.

To apply an **Adjustment** layer:

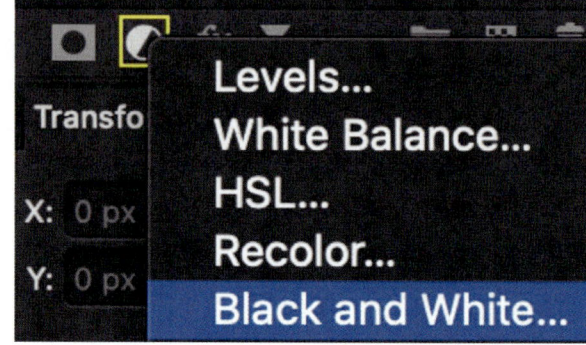

Click on the **Adjustments** icon at the bottom of the **Studios Panel** (see yellow square).

Select **Black and White...** from the drop-down menu.

This will make the picture become **black & white**.

Note: Every adjustment layer works differently. In this case, we can use the sliders in the pop-out window to determine how bright and dark certain colors become in our **black & white** picture.

For example, if we *move* the **Red** slider to the **left**, our **red** colors on the picture will become **darker**.

But, if we move it to **right**, the **reds** will become **lighter**.

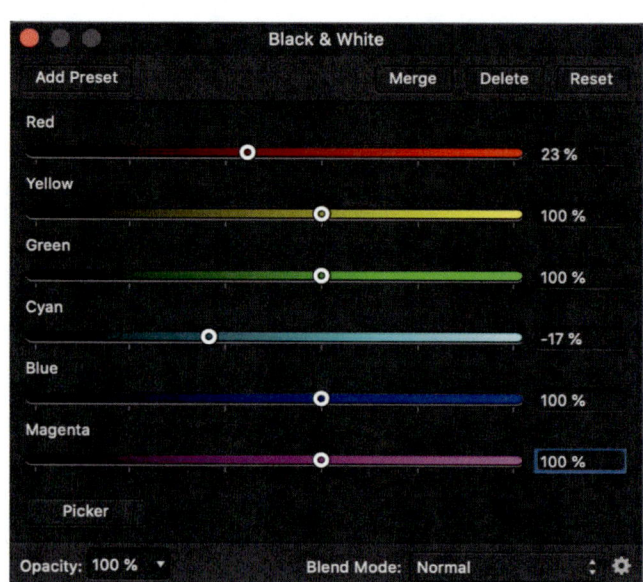

In this example the picture looks better with **darker**, so let`s move it back to the **left**.

Adjust the **Red** slider to **23%**.

Adjust the **Cyan** to **-17%**.

Continue the process with any of the sliders you'd like to change.

Press the **red button** at the top-left of this pop-out window to close.

To see before & after:

>   *Go* to the **Layers Panel** and *uncheck* & *check* the **top layer**. This image shows the top layer is deactivated, thus what you see on your screen is the full-color original image.

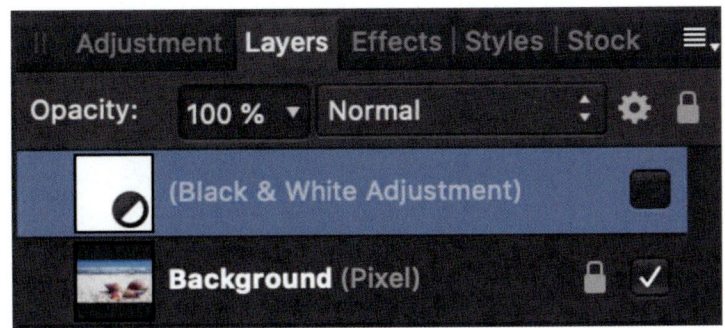

Hint: Active layers are always *highlighted* in **blue**.

If you want to back to an Adjustment layer because you'd like to tweak the values you changed:

>   *Go* back to the **Layers Panel** and simply *double-click* on the **preview thumbnail** for the Adjustment layer you want to go back to. Doing this action is simple because we only have two layers, but for edits that have multiple Adjustment layers, the action is the same.

When you do this, the pop-out window for that specific Adjustment will appear again.

>   *Adjust* the **sliders** however you want.

>   *Close* the Adjustment's **pop-out window** by clicking on the red button.

Another important thing to remember when using the Adjustments effectively is to know each Adjustment layer only affects the layers that are beneath it.

If you look at our Layers Panel, you'll see that the Black and White Adjustment layer is on top of our Background image of the seashells. This means our seashells look black and white because of where it's positioned in the Layers Panel.

Let's change their positions and see if there's any change to our image on the canvas.

To do this:

>   *Click* on the **Background layer** so it's highlighted in blue.

>   *Drag* it to the **top of the Layers Panel** (see the yellow arrow for this action). Notice how when you move this layer, it appears ethereal. This happens so you can see how and where to perfectly place your layer in the Layers Panel.

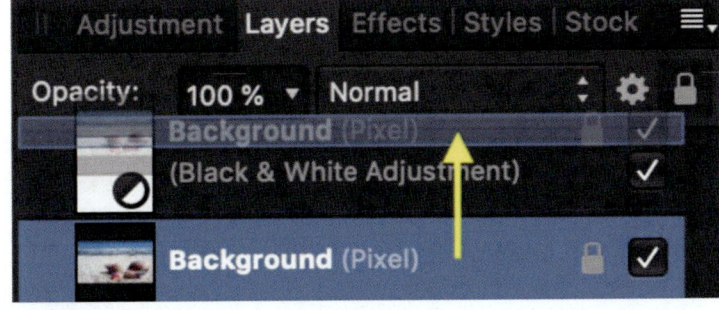

What effect does changing the positions in the Layers Panel have to do with how your image now looks?

Hopefully, you're seeing that your original Background image looks like it did before we worked with the Black and White Adjustment even though both layers are checked on.

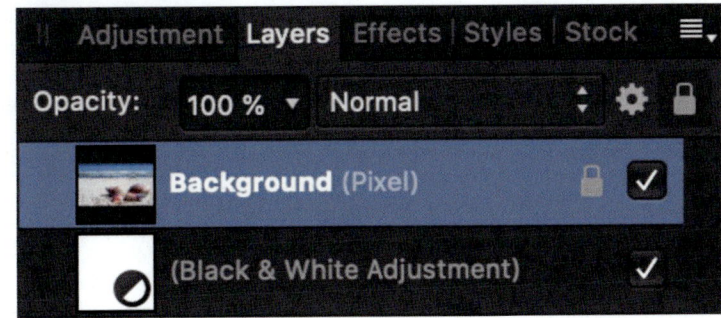

The position is what matters, not whether the layers are checked on or not.

25

If you want the adjustment to affect your picture, you need to be sure the adjustment layer is above your picture.

To do this:

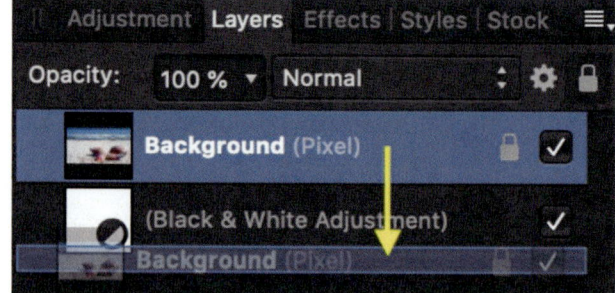

> *Click & drag* the bottom **Background layer** below the Black & White Adjustment layer (see arrow for this action).

We are done using the **Black and White Adjustment** layer. So, we want to **delete** it. Here are three ways we can delete layers we no longer want:

1. *Highlight* the **layer** you want to delete and simply *press* **Delete** key on your keyboard.
2. *Highlight* a **layer** and *click* on the **Trashcan**.
3. *Highlight* a **layer** and *press* **Ctrl/Cmd+X**.

Hint: If you accidently delete a layer, simply *press* **Ctrl/Cmd+Z** to *undo* your last action.

We are going to now use a different Adjustment to continue this lesson.

Ready?

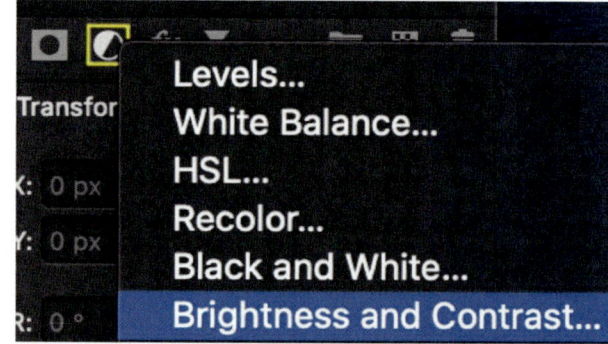

> *Click* on the **Adjustments icon** again & *select* **Brightness and Contrast...**

To increase the **Brightness and Contrast**:

> *Adjust* the **Brightness** slider to **25%**.
>
> *Adjust* the **Contrast** slider to **41%**.
>
> *Press* the **red button** to *close* the window.

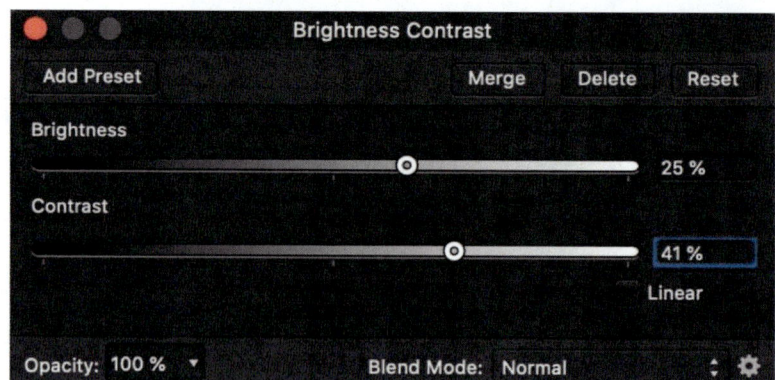

To see **before** & **after**:

> *Go* to the **Layers Panel**.
>
> *Click* the **Brightness/Contrast Adjustment** layer *off/on* (layer is unchecked).

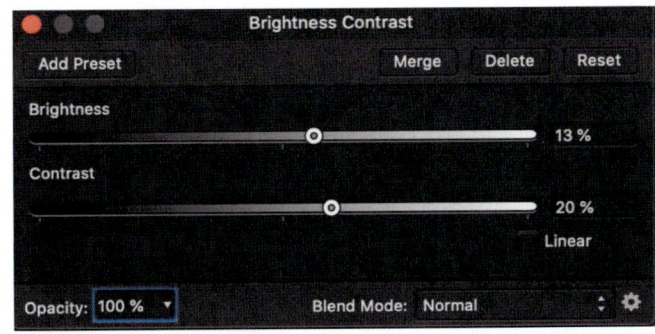

In this example, the **Brightness/Contrast** Adjustment is probably too strong.

To change this:

> *Go* to the **Layers Panel**.
>
> *Double-click* on **Brightness/Contrast Adjustment** square within the *highlighted* layer (see yellow-marked box in above screenshot).

The pop-out window with the sliders will appear again.

> *Move* the **Brightness** to **13%**.
>
> *Move* the **Contrast** to **20%**.
>
> *Press* the **red button** to **close** the window.

To see *before* & *after* (like we did at the top of this page):

> *Go* to the **Layers Panel**.
>
> *Check* the **Brightness/Contrast Adjustment** layer *on/off*.

As a final example of how the **Adjustments** layers work:

> *Click* on to **Adjustments icon**.
>
> *Select* **HSL** to *change* the **saturation** of your picture.
>
> *Move* the **Saturation** slider to **28%**.
>
> *Press* the **red button** to **close** the window.

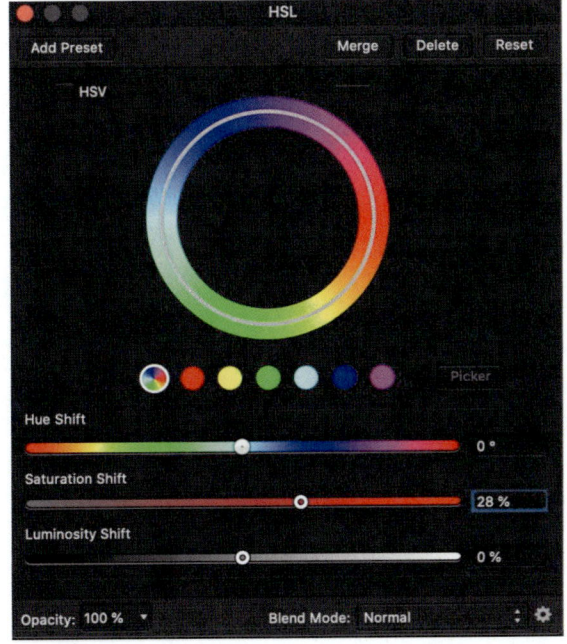

27

To see *before* & *after*.

Go to the **Layers Panel** & c*lick* the **HSL Shift Adjustment** layer *off / on*.

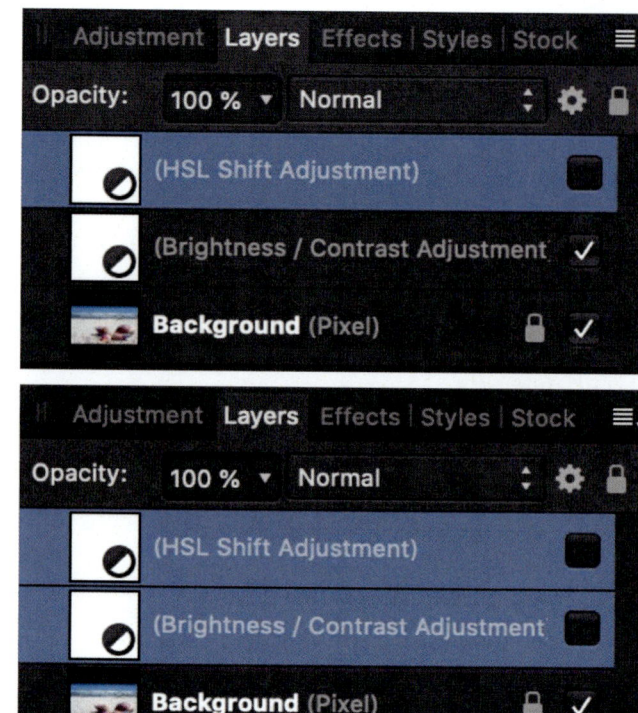

To see both the **HSL** and the **Brightness/Contrast Adjustment** layers *off / on* at the same time, *press* **Shift** and *select* both of the adjustments. Now, when you click on one checked box, both will respond jointly.

Done. This is our final image.

Finished. This ends this tutorial.

Note: We will be using the same image of the seashells for the next tutorial. Please keep this image on your screen. Go ahead and delete the two Adjustment layers.

6 – How to Use Masks

The 6th skill to know is how to use Masks.

Please upload the image of the seashells we used in our last tutorial back onto your Affinity Photo canvas.

Here is the hyperlink again for your convenience (if you aren't continuing from the previous tutorial):

>https://pixabay.com/photos/seashell-shell-shells-sea-ocean-2821388/

Before we get started, let's talk about masks and their functions:

What is the purpose of a mask?

>Masks are used to **hide** or **reveal** parts of the layer.

>Masks allow you to selectively *adjust* the **transparency** of a layer you are working with.

What are the two types of masks? **White** & **Black**.

What is the difference between the two? What are their functions?

>**White** masks make the layer you are working on 100% **visible**.

>**Black** masks make the layer you are working on 100% **invisible** or transparent.

Remember: **White** = visible   **Black** = invisible or transparent

That's the absolute basics of masks. Now, let's work with masks and see practically how they are applied to your work. We hope this tutorial will help you begin to understand how to use this powerful tool.

It's easier to show you than to explain how to use Masks with words.

Let's start:

>*Click* on the **Background** layer so it's *highlighted* in **blue** (or active).

>*Click* on the **Mask icon** (looks like a Japanese flag) at the bottom of the Studio's Panel

You should now see a **white** mask has been applied to this layer. It should look like a **white** box below and a bit to the right of the **Background** layer.

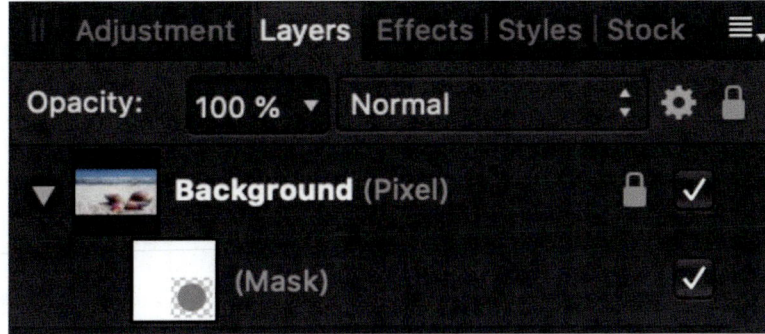

Now, let's have some fun learning about masks:

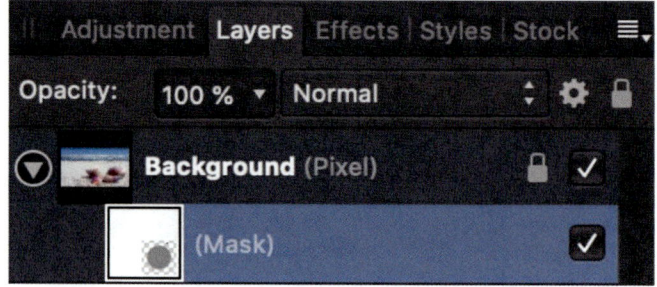

Click on the **preview thumbnail** on the Mask layer so just the bottom Mask layer is active (or highlighted in blue).

Click on the **Paint Brush Tool** (or *press* **B**).

Set the **Foreground color** to **Black**. You can do this by either going to the Colors Studio where the Color Wheel is and *click* on the **black circle** that's interconnected and above a white circle (see yellow square).

You can also, if you set up two columns of Tools, click on the black circle located at the bottom of the Tools panel.

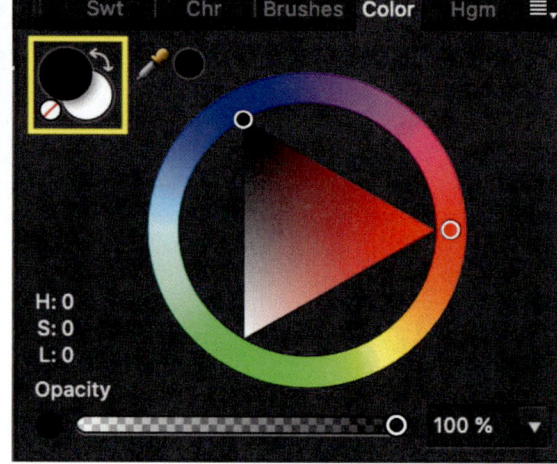

Note: If you wanted White to be the Foreground color, you'd simply click on the White circle and it'd replace itself above the black circle.

Hint: Try pressing the **X** key on your keyboard and watch what happens to the Black & White circles. Do you see how they change position? This is because the **X** key is the shortcut to swap Foreground & Background colors. Do not forget this shortcut. It is one of our favorites.

Now that we have our Foreground set to black, we can continue learning how to use Masks.

So, right now your Paint Brush Tool should be active and its color is black.

Paint (by *clicking* & *dragging*) **over the photograph**. This is what we did below. As you paint in black, on a mask layer, where you paint you will make the area transparent. When you have layers beneath the mask layer, and you paint in black, you will remove the layer you are painting on to reveal the layer beneath your current layer.

30

Let's change the Foreground to White by pressing the **X** key to show you the opposite effect.

Paint in **white** over the areas of the image we painted in black. As you do this, you will see that the seashells image will come back to its original image.

Now, our image has returned back to its original form:

Now that we've working on adding a mask to an image layer, let's now add a mask to an Adjustment layer. We'll start this on the next page.

But, first we need to delete this mask layer. Do you remember the three ways to delete layers?

1. *Highlight* the **layer** you want to delete and simply *press* **Delete** key on your keyboard.
2. *Highlight* a **layer** and *click* on the **Trashcan**.
3. *Highlight* a **layer** and *press* **Ctrl/Cmd+X.**

Ok. Now our Layers Panel should only have the Background image of the shells in it.

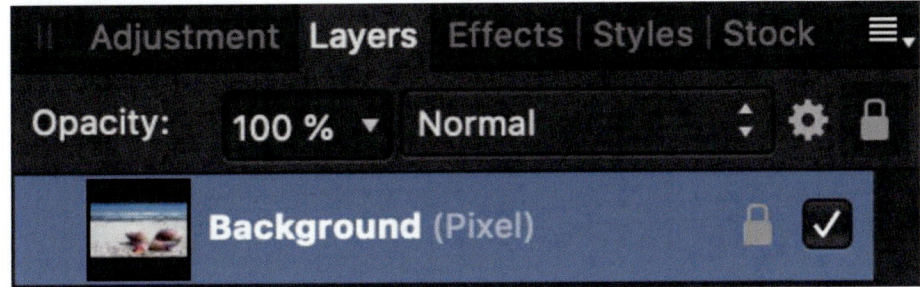

31

This is how you add a mask to an Adjustments layer.

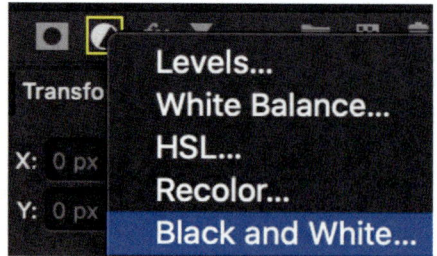

> *Click* on the **Adjustments icon** & *select* **Black and White**...
>
> *Press* the **red button** to *close* out of the pop-out window that will appear. We won't be making any refinements. We chose this Adjustment just to make our image black & white.

Note: It's important to know that every Adjustment layer in Affinity Photo comes with a pre-built mask. What this means is that we can immediately paint in black or white to hide or show its adjustment properties. This is probably a confusing concept, so we'll explain as we go.

We are about to start again. Make sure the Paint Brush Tool is selected and the Foreground color is set to black.

> *Paint* over **the shell in the lower right-hand corner** of the four shells. As you paint in black, you will be removing the Black & White Adjustment from the layer to reveal the color of the shell underneath.

Here is what we did when we painted over this shell. As you can see, painting in black reveals the color image below the top Adjustment layer.

Oops, we accidently painted on part of the shell above the bottom-right shell. Do you know what we can do to fix this?

Answer: If you thought to change the Foreground color to white and paint over the parts of the upper shell we painted in black on, you'd be correct.

> *Press* the **X key** to change the Foreground color to **White**.
>
> *Paint* in **white** over the area on the top shell to hide the color layer beneath and fix the mistake we made.

Review: Paint Brush Adjustments (Opacity, Flow, Hardness)

Opacity is the see-throughness of the color (or layer).

Flow is how much paint comes out of the brush each time you click & drag the brush over the image.

Hardness relates to the sides of the brush stroke. 100% has fine edges. 0% has fuzzy edges.

Finished. This ends this tutorial.

7 - How to Make Selections

The 7th skill to know is how to make selections.

Making selections is one of the most-used skills you'll need. We love working with the **Selection Brush Tool** in Affinity Photo. It's so easy to use and so powerful. This is the tool you will use the most when making one portion of your document stand out or be cut out and placed in another scene. This is why we've added this tutorial to the next Basics tutorial.

Please download these two images to be used in the Basics #7 & #8 lessons.

https://pixabay.com/photos/moon-sky-night-moonlight-nature-2913221/

https://pixabay.com/photos/purple-ship-sailing-ship-3054804/

The image of the moon should be on your canvas.

We are going to make a selection of the moon. Here is how we do this:

Select the **Selection Brush Tool** (looks like a brush with a dotted-circle around its tip)

Go to the **Contextual Toolbar** and look for **Mod**e: Make sure **Add** is *clicked on*.

Note: We use these two buttons (**Add & Subtract**) when we want to make more precise selections and have maybe selected too much or not enough. We will use these two buttons further on.

Go to the **Contextual Toolbar** and *click* on **Width** to *increase* your brush's width to half the size of the moon. While you are on the Contextual Toolbar, look to the right of and...

Check **Snap to edges** *on* (this will make the dancing ants fit the outline of any object you want to select. This is a very important device for all selections.

Click & drag the **Selection Brush Tool** in a small circle inside the moon.

Here is our image. What do you see? You should see that the selection isn't too perfect. The dancing ants appear sometimes inside the edge of the moon and in a few places outside.

To correct this, we can:

Go to the **Contextual Toolbar** and *click* on **Refine**...

Zoom in to the image and *lower* the **Width** of our **Brush** to **1px** or **3 px** and *change* the **Mode** from **Add** to **Subtract** (to remove the selection line outside the perimeter).

What we suggest is that you work on the outline of the selection as best you can before you *click* on the **Refine...** button. It's better to do as much of the work that we can before we turn the refining over to the software.

In this case, we *zoomed in* tight to the **moon** and alternated the **Mode** from **Add** to **Subtract** to get the dancing ants to adhere as closely to the edge of the moon as possible.

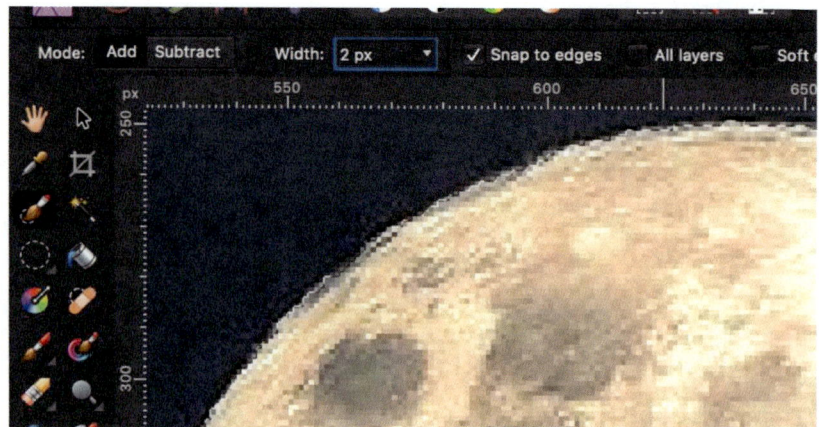

In this image, you can see that we have the **Width** of the **Brush** set at **2 px**.

If we make a mistake while doing this, we'll more often as not *press* **Ctrl/Cmd+Z** to undo what we just did.

Pro Tip: You can also *hold-down* the **Option/Alt key** instead of changing the **Mode**. The **Alt** key will cause the opposite action to happen (e.g. if the **Mode** is set to **Add**, when you *press* the **Option/Alt key** & *click* on the selection, you'll actually **Subtract** the part you *click* on).

Once you've gone around the moon's perimeter and made the selection as good as possible, *click* on the **Refine...** button on the Contextual Toolbar. A pop-out window will open with more information and four sliders.

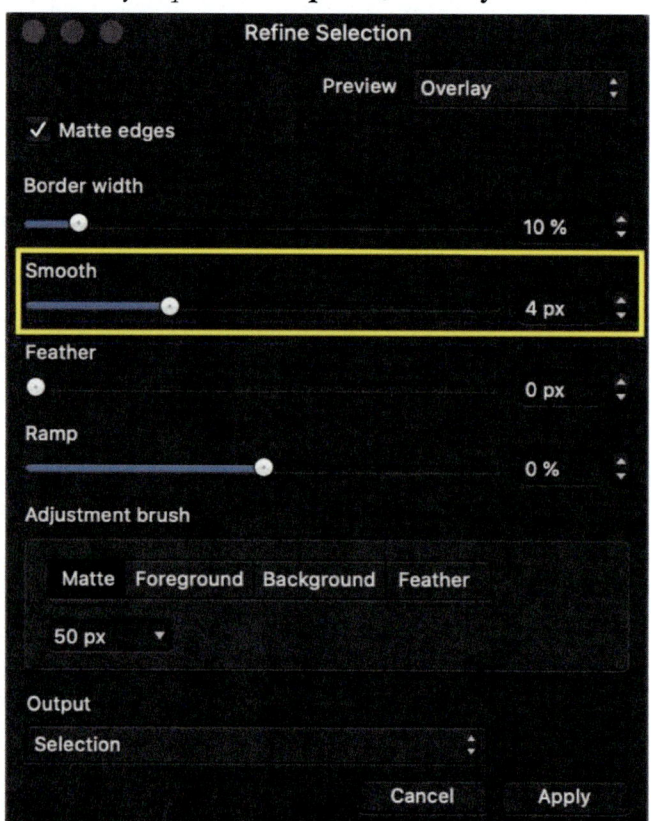

> *Click* on the **Smooth** slider and *increase* its amount to **4 px** (this will remove all of the edges from our selection.
>
> *Press* **Apply** when done.

Now, we are going to duplicate our selected moon and then we'll remove the background. Once the background is removed, we'll add this moon image to another image.

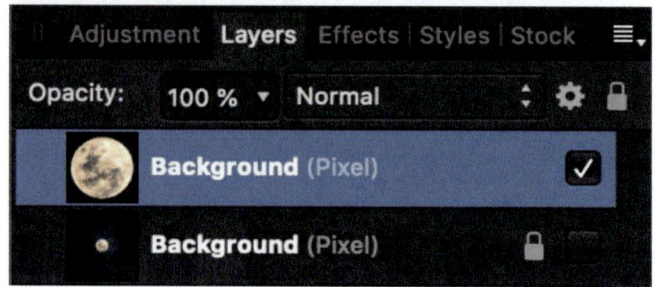

> *Press* **Ctrl/Cmd+J** to *duplicate* the Moon layer.
>
> *Uncheck* the **lower layer**. This will cause the selected moon to be on a now-transparent layer.

34

Press **Ctrl/Cmd+D** to *deselect* the dancing ants.

This ends this first part of How to Make Selections. We will continue working with our currently selected moon image in the next tutorial.

8 – How to Change the Background of a Photo

Whenever you make a selection around an object, that selection gives you many possibilities, like, to change its color, cut it out of its current photo, add it to a new photo, and to make many different adjustments and edits to it that are unique to only the selected item.

In this next part, we'll show you how to take this selected moon and add it to another image. The process of selecting an object(s), persons, or things is the same as we just did above.

Because our moon is now surrounded by a transparent layer, we can now copy this image and place it on top of any other image. The new image will essentially fill the transparent area around the moon giving the appearance that the moon fits to that new image.

Press **Ctrl/Cmd+C** anywhere on our moon image to *copy* it.

Open the **purple sailboat** image.

Press **Ctrl/Cmd+V** to *paste* our moon image onto the sailboat image.

When we do this, our moon will be three things: Too large; in the wrong position; and not the right color to match the scene.

To fix these three issues:

Move the **moon** image to the top-right corner of the image (see yellow arrow for direction).

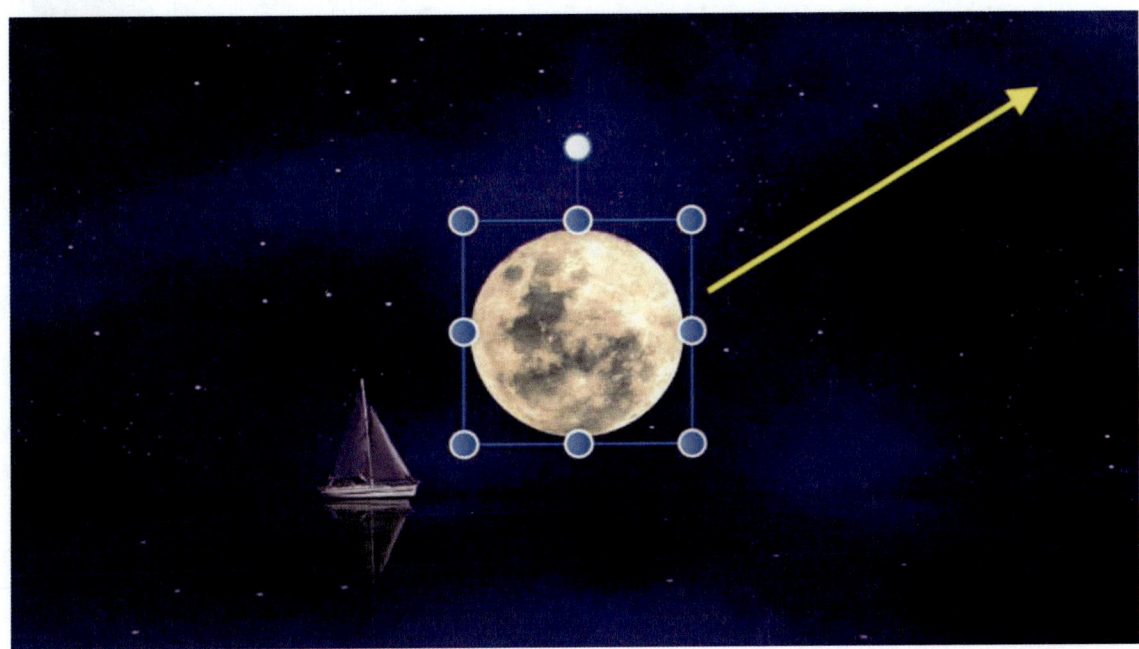

35

Click on one of the **corner blue nodes** and shrink the moon to a little smaller size than the sailboat.

The moon is looking very good, but we can make it match the scene even better by changing its Opacity so its white color isn't so stark and so it blends into the scene much better.

Click on the **top layer** so it's highlighted in blue.

Change its **Opacity** to **50%**. Now, our moon is starting to fit into the image.

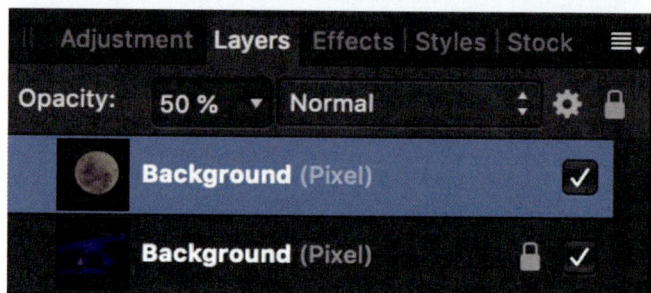

There's just one more thing to do and that's to make it have its own reflecting shadow on the surface of the water. The sailboat has one and so the moon should have one, too. Because the moon layer is already highlighted in blue, this is what we'll do.

Press **Crtl/Cmd+J** to *duplicate* the moon's layer.

Select the **Move Tool** (or *press* **V**) and *click* on the **moon image** & *drag* it **below the surface of the water**.

Change its **Opacity** to **10%** to make it look faded in the water.

Done. This is our final image.

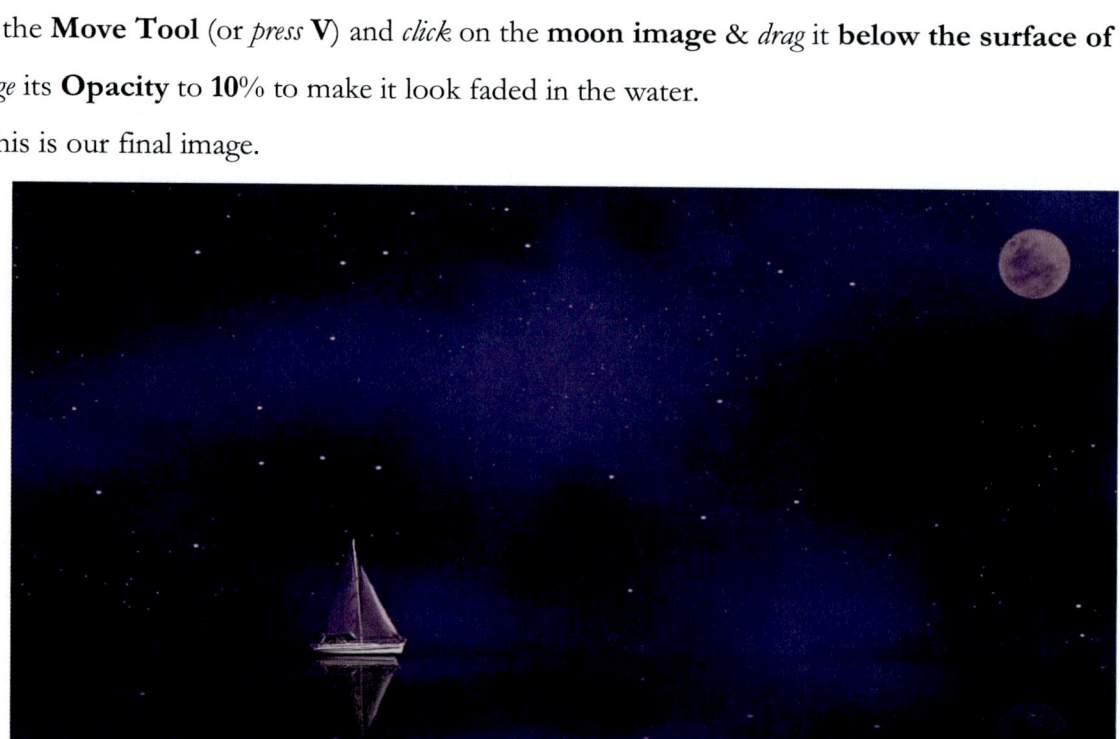

Finished. This ends this tutorial.

Bonus Lesson: How to Make Selections Using the Pen Tool

Here is the webpage to the image we'll be using for this tutorial

https://pixabay.com/photos/present-package-gift-celebration-1893640/

Ok. You should have the image of the two presents on your Affinity Photo screen.

Note: Before we start, we want you to know that using the **Pen Tool** for doing selections should only be done to objects that have definite edges. We use this technique when the background and the object we are selecting blend into each other making using the **Selection Brush Tool** difficult. This image of the present is not one such image we are talking about, but we will use this image because it is a good teaching image to learn how to use the Pen Tool.

Ready? Let's start...

Select the **Pen Tool** (or *press* **P**).

Go to the **Contextual Toolbar** & *click* on the **Pen Mode** button (see yellow rectangle).

Click & *draw* your **outline** around your object.

When you get back around to where you started, make sure you *click* on the first node that you started with.

Hint: Try to draw within your object's perimeter by a pixel and not on the outside of its perimeter. You do not want the background to be a part of the soon-to-be cut-out object.

Note: When you are done, make sure you *press* **ESC** on your keyboard. This tells Affinity Photo that the selection process is over and that when you *click* on the canvas again, a new selection path will start. We can't stress enough that you make sure you've *clicked* on the first node to finish your selection before you *press* **ESC**. This is a learning process, but a frustrating one if you don't do it right.

Let's suppose your job at doing the outline of the perimeter wasn't as perfect as you'd like it to be. Let us show you what you can do to go back and fix any errors.

First, *zoom in* to your object by *pressing* **Ctrl/Cmd +** (see the yellow rectangle to see where we'll be working on).

Select the **Node Tool**.

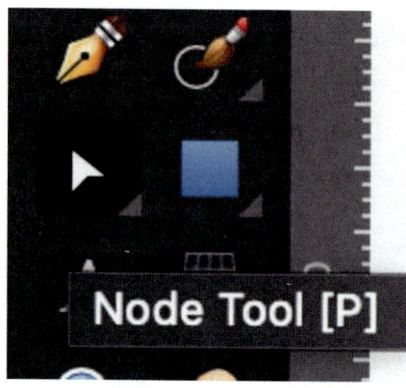
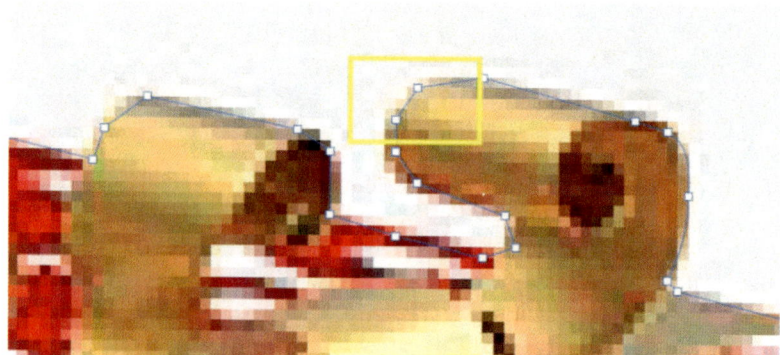

When using the **Node Tool**, hover it on the line between two nodes and a perpendicular small line will appear (see left image below). It is this exact spot on the line that you can bend the line to however you want it (see right image). It takes practice, but we hope you understand.

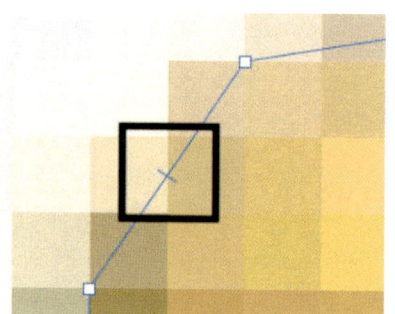
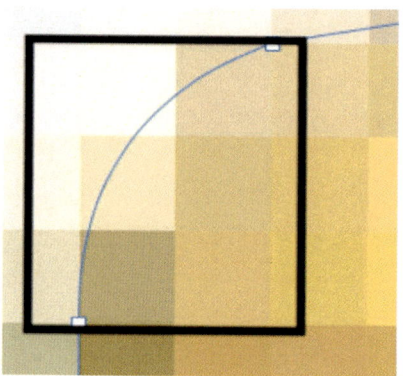

Hint: While practice does makes perfect, when we are making selections with curves while using the **Pen Tool**, we won't worry too much about exact precision. We make the two nodes at the start and the end of the curve and when the whole selection has been made, then we go back and change the curves to our standards.

Let's get back to the tutorial: When you are done changing the nodes into the curves you are satisfied with...

    Go to the **Contextual Toolbar** & *click* on **Selection**. This will create a line of dancing ants where you made your selection.

    Click on the **Mask icon** (looks like a Japanese flag) at the bottom of the Layers Studio. This will cause the background to be immediately removed.

    Press **Ctrl/Cmd+D** to *deselect* the dancing ants.

To change the background to a different color of your choosing...

    Click on **Add Pixel Layer** (next to the **Trashcan**).

This is what our Layers Panel should look like now:

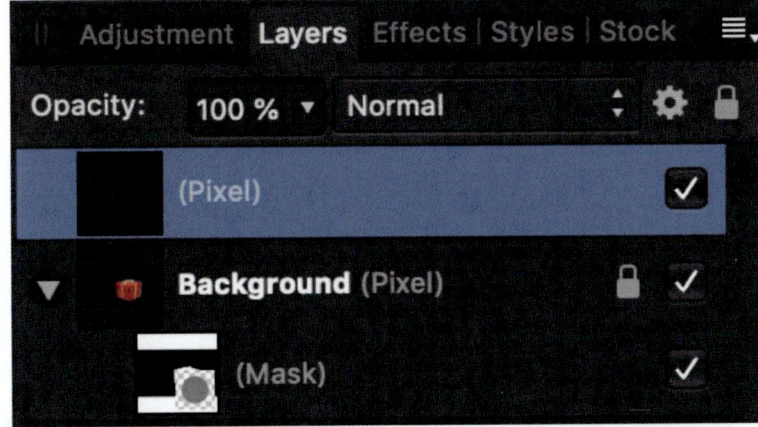

    Go to the **Menu bar** - **Edit** - **Fill**...

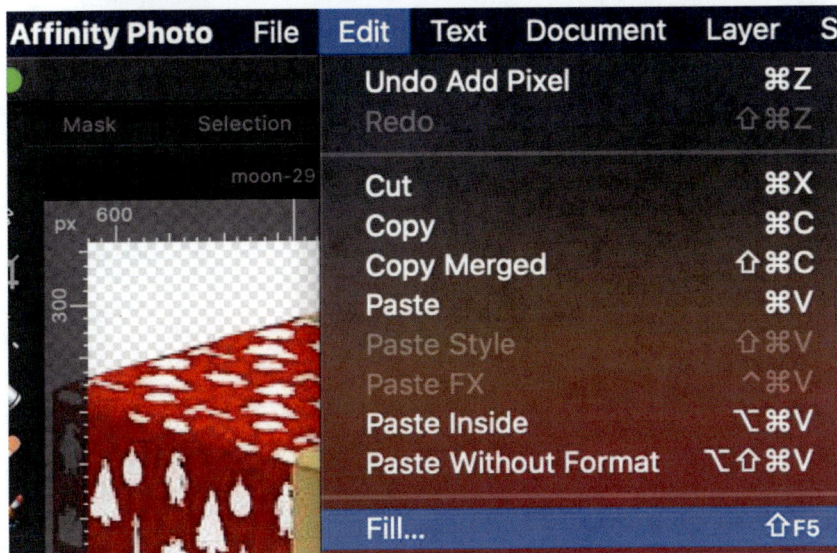

39

A pop-out window will appear that looks like this.

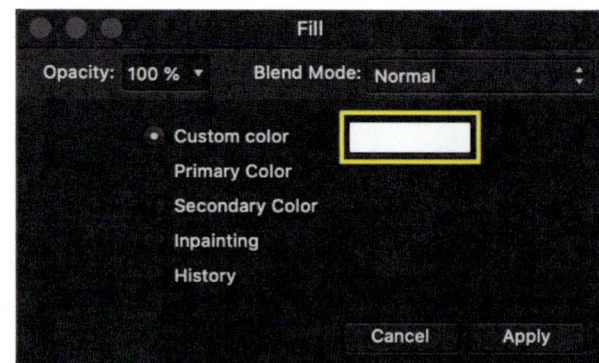

> *Click* on the **white color rectangle** to *change* the color of the fill. When you click on this rectangle, the Color Wheel pop-out window will open.

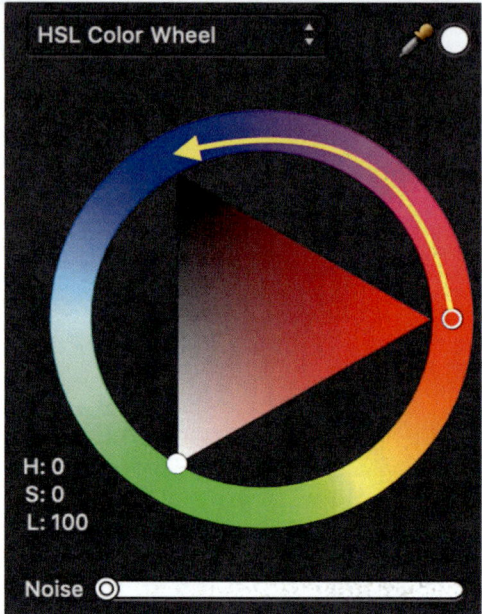

> *Move* the **Hue node** to a deep blue color. The Hue node is the node on outside circle. The node in the inner triangle adjusts the saturation & luminosity of whatever Hue you choose.

> *Click* **Apply** to set the color you want as the fill.

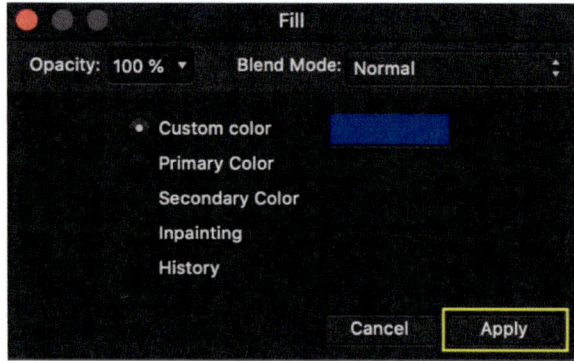

Last step.

> *Go* to the **Layers Panel** and *click* on **top Pixel layer** & *drag* it to the **bottom** of the Layers Stack-

This is what our Layers Panel looks like now:

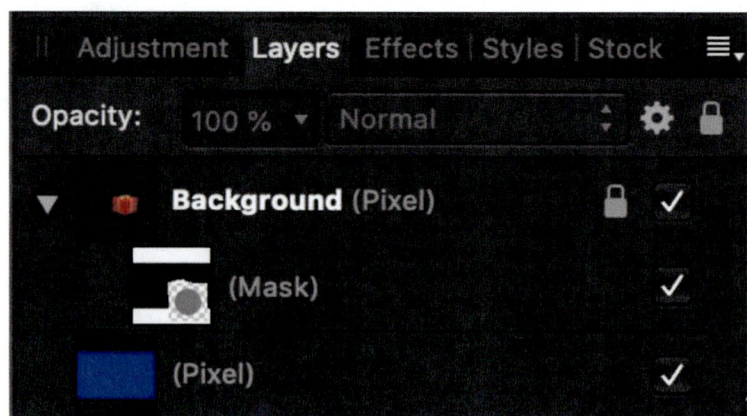

40

Done. This is our final image.

Finished. This ends this bonus tutorial.

Bonus Lesson: How to Very Quickly Remove Backgrounds

If you need to very quickly remove the background from an object that has very clear borders and a uniformly colored background, then this pro tip is for you.

Once you get the hang of this technique, it takes about 10 seconds to execute.

For this lesson, we'll be using an image of a soccer ball. Here is the webpage:

> https://pixabay.com/illustrations/football-ball-3d-raytracing-257489/

Ready?

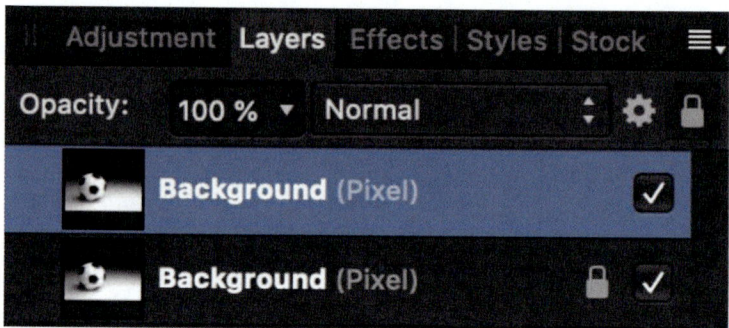

Select the **Selection Brush Tool.**

Paint over the **item** you want to cut out.

Duplicate the **image** by *pressing* **Ctrl/Cmd+J.**

Unclick the **bottom layer** in the Layers Panel.

Done – the background is now gone.

If you want to change the background color from transparent (**gray** and **white** squares), then *press* **Ctrl/Cmd+Shift+I** to *invert* your selection.

Then, on the **Menu bar** *click* **Edit, Fill** (see five pages above to relearn how to use the **Fill**).

A pop-out window will appear.

Custom Color should be the default setting.

Click on the **white** square and immediately a **Color Wheel** will appear and you can now *choose* the background color you want for your cut-out image.

We chose yellow.

Note: This technique is very fast, but not as precise as the 'normal' way of doing a selection. We are only sharing you this expert technique to demonstrate the power of Affinity Photo. It is really an optimal software – much better than the competitors.

Finished. This ends this bonus lesson.

9 – How to Add Text to an Image

Adding text to an image is one of the most basic, but most used skills photo editors use from all things personal and commercial. Thankfully, Affinity Photo makes this a very simple process.

Here is the image we'll be using for this lesson. Have this uploaded to your screen so we can start:

https://cdn.pixabay.com/photo/2014/12/16/22/25/woman-570883_1280.jpg

In this tutorial, we are going to add the text "Each day is a new beginning" to our image.

To add this text:

Select the **Artistic Text Tool** (or *press* **T**).

Click & *drag* on the **picture** to specify how big the text you want to be. Notice how the first letter is created by a click & drag motion. If you don't get the right font size on the first go, it's no problem because Affinity Photo makes resizing text super easy. You can see that our current font size is **188.5 pt** by looking at the text bubble next to our **A**.

Type our **phrase** "Each day is a new beginning." (without the quotation marks). As you can see, our phrase has gone way out to the right-side of our image. All we need to do is to click on one of the right-side top or bottom blue nodes & drag our phrase back into within the borders of our image.

As you can see in this next image, as we moved the text back to within the confines of the image, the font size changed to **114.8 px**.

If you want to change the color of the text, simply click on the Text layer so it's highlighted in blue and then move the Color Wheel to the color of your choice. We'll choose a pink.

Here are those instructions again:

    Click on the **top layer** so it's highlighted in blue.

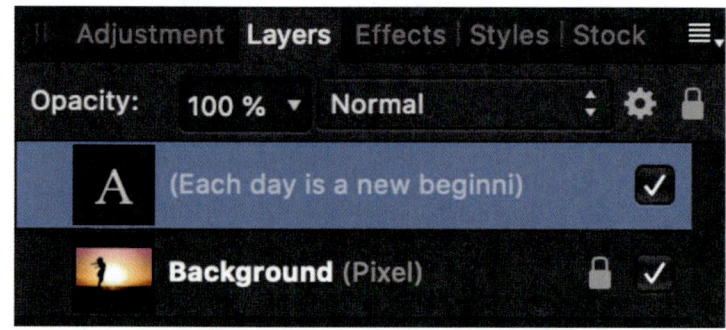

Oops, we misspelt Beginning. To fix this, simply *double-click* on the **layer** again and type the correct spelling.

    Go to the **Color Wheel** & *move* the **outside hue node** to pink.

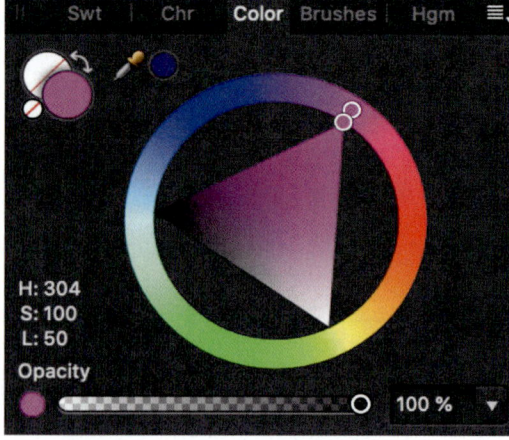

Done. This is our final image.

Finished. This ends this tutorial.

Bonus Tutorial: How to Create a Cool Transparent Text Effect

Here is the webpage for the background image we will be using for this tutorial. Feel free to use any image you want.

https://cdn.pixabay.com/photo/2016/11/29/04/19/beach-1867285_1280.jpg

Before we start, here is what we will create with this effect. We chose this image of the water to signify our beautiful planet Earth and how precious it is for all of us. We hope you like this bonus tutorial.

Here are the steps you need to take to do create this cool effect:

Upload your **image** onto the Affinity Photo canvas.

Select the **Artistic Text Tool** (or use the shortcut **T**).

Change the **Font** to **Impact**.

Click **anywhere** on the image.

Type your all **CAPS word** (**EARTH**).

Change **font size** to **1/3** the vertical size of the image's height.

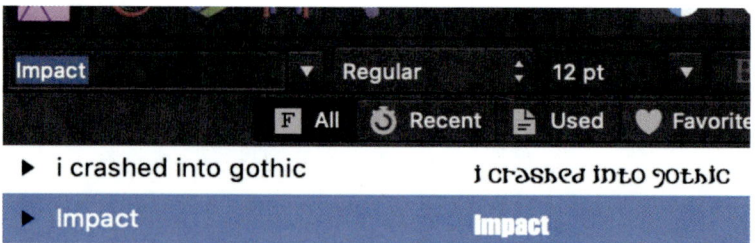

Select the **Move Tool** (or *press* **V**) & *move* the word in the middle of the image as well as use the **blue** dots that surround the text to expand the word to fit both sides of the image.

Note: Play around with the **blue** dots and try to make your text the same size and position as our text.

Once we had our word 1/3 the size of the image, we used the left and right nodes (not the corners) to expand the word to the edges of the photograph.

The next step is to create a colored outline around the text. You need to visualize the individual letters being transparent as in the image on the previous page. We are saying this because if we place a **black** outline on the text, we won't see it. So, for the sake of this tutorial, we'll first create a **white** border and then convert the blackness of the text to a transparent effect and then we'll add the **black** outline.

Ready?

Click on the **tab** labelled **Effects** (see **yellow** rectangle).

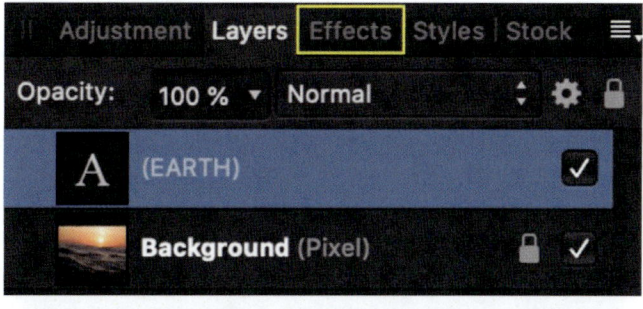

Check the option **Outline**.

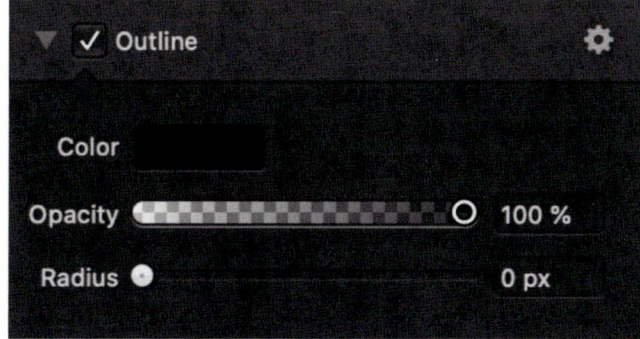

In the pop-out window, there are a couple options:

Color - This is the color of the outline.

Opacity - This is the visibility of the outline color.

Radius - This is the thickness of the outline color.

47

The first thing we want to **adjust** is the color.

> *Click* on the **black rectangle** next to where it says Color and the Color Wheel will pop up (look at the previous image for the black rectangle - in the image to the right it's now white).
>
> *Move* the **inside node** to where the color is **white** (see arrow for this action).
>
> *Close* the **Color Wheel** pop-out by *clicking* on the color square again.

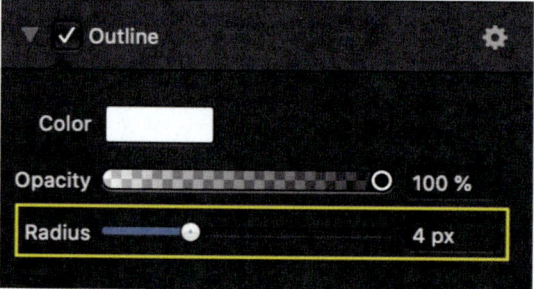

> *Move* the **Radius slider** to **4 px**. This will create the white border around our text we want.

Now, we need to change the **Blend Mode** to create the transparent text effect.

> *Click* on the **Layers tab** (yellow rectangle) so the Layers Panel reappears.
>
> *Change* the **Blend Mode** from **Normal** to **Overlay**. The Blend Modes drop-down menu is immediately to the right of the Opacity value and below the Effects tab.

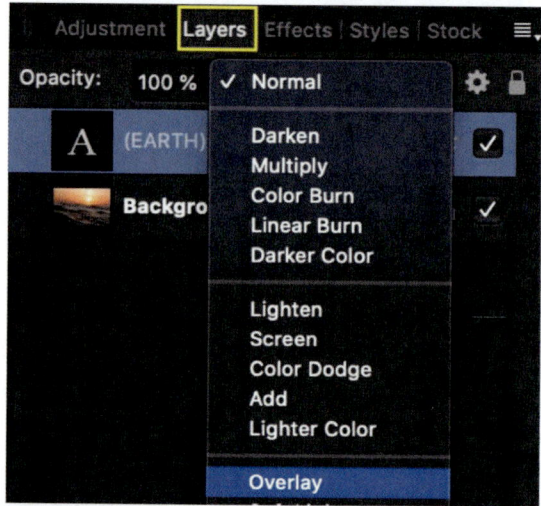

Our effect is almost done. If you like the **white** border on the text, then you're finished. But, if you want to see how to add the black outline, we'll show you on the next page. To quickly open the **Effects** (*fx*) pop-out window on our text layer, all we have to do is to *click* one-time on the symbol (see yellow rectangle).

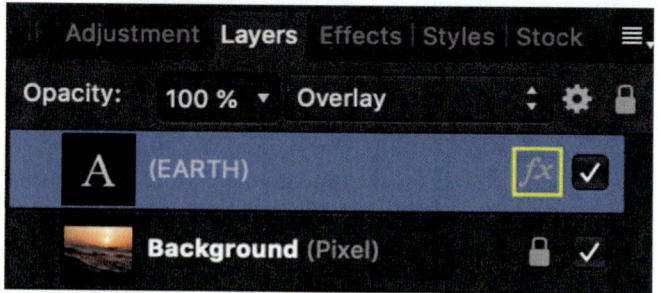

Hint: Knowing how to quickly pull-up previously used pop-out windows is a huge shortcut

48

Whenever you create any kind of adjustment or mask, simply *click* (or *double-click*) on that layer's icon (or preview thumbnail) and the pop-out window for that adjustment (or mask) will pop up.

Here is the **Effects** pop-out window. All you have to do here is to *click* on the Color square and change the color from **white** to **black** (see yellow arrow showing you the action of how to change the color from white to black).

Press **Close** when done.

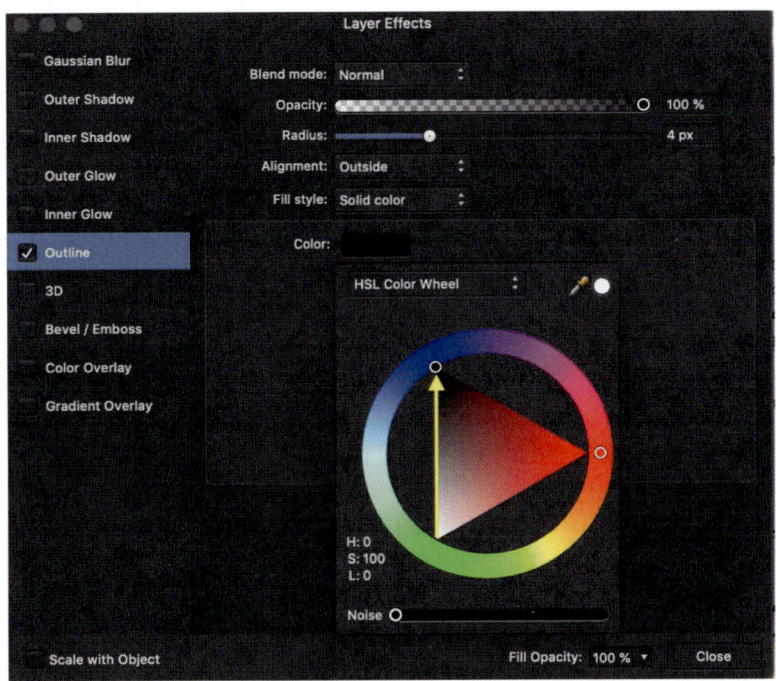

We are almost finished. To move the text around (up or down) on the image, *select* the **Move Tool** (or *press* **V**) to **reposition** your text wherever you want. We raised our text a bit higher than the mid-point.

Note: We will be using this final image in our last basic skill. Please save it as an **.afphoto** file or keep it on your canvas for the next lesson or just turn the page and we'll continue with the basics.

Finished. This ends this bonus tutorial.

10 – How to Save & Export

The 10th skill beginners need to know is how to save & export.

For this tutorial, we are going to use the final image from the previous tutorial. Please have it uploaded to your canvas now. Now, we are going to show you how to save & export this image in the various different file formats. Affinity Photo makes this a very simple process.

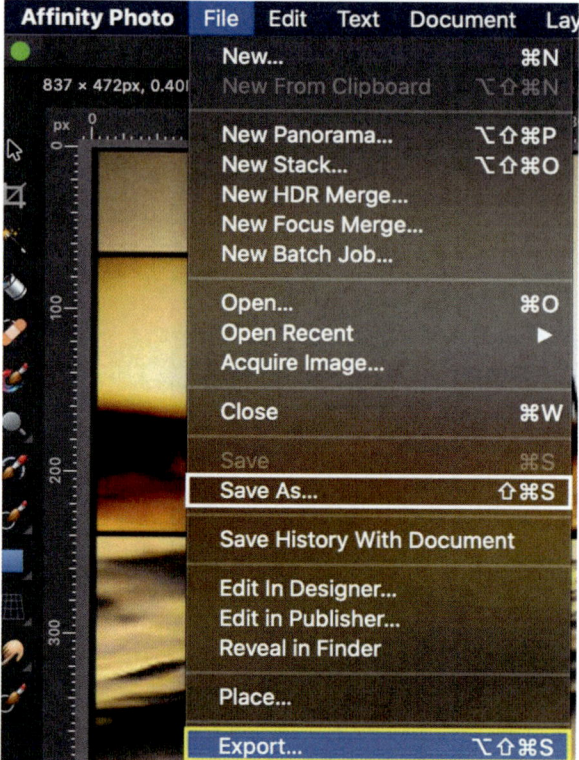

To save the image so you can come back and work on it later in Affinity Photo:

Go to **File**.

Select **Save As** from the drop-down menu. This will save your photo as an **Affinity Photo** file where you can continue working later (see **white** box).

Note: These Affinity Photo files are much larger than .jpeg or .png files, but are necessarily larger because they contain all of different layers and effects you've made to your image.

When you are completely done with your image and want to **export** it in a different file format:

Go to **File** on the **Menu bar**.

Select **Export** from the drop-down menu (see **yellow** box in image).

Before we continue in this tutorial, it's important for you to understand the different file formats you can save your image as.

Affinity Photo has a range of formats that you can use to export. The two most common formats are **PNG** and **JPEG**.

JPEG is useful because it converts your picture into a small size file (i.e. the images typically found in books).

PNG is useful because preserves transparency (in plain English: there will be a white & grey checkered background to an object).

This is what the **Export** window looks like. Here you can see all the different file types you can export your image as. Go ahead and *click* on any file formats you want and you'll see the export options change.

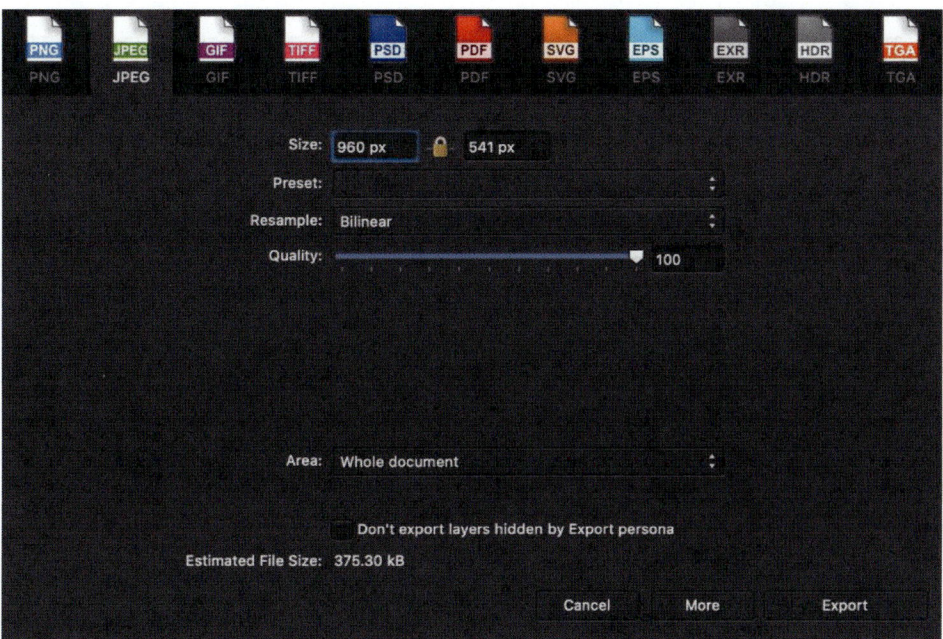

Hint: We recommend you frequent the official Affinity Help website for other search for the meaning of each of these types of files (and any other question you have about Affinity Photo).

https://affinity.help/photo/en-US.lproj/index.html

As a rule of thumb, for us at KuhlmanPublishing, we normally use the .png when we want to keep an image's transparent background and .jpeg when we want the whole image (as opposed to just a selected item in a photo).

Getting back to the image we want to **export**, let's:

Export this **picture** of the water as a **.jpeg** since we will be exporting the whole image and we don't care about transparency.

Since we've selected **JPEG** from the top line of file format choices, the most important part now is the size of our image. Our image is only **375.30 kB** (see bottom left of above image), so it's pretty small.

But, many images you'll work with are huge (**<25 mb**) and in order for you to email them using Affinity Photo, you'll need to first lower their size.

To do this:

Click on the **Preset** window (see **yellow** box). A drop-down menu will appear.

Choose **JPEG (High Quality)**. Immediately, you'll see that the file size has dropped dramatically.

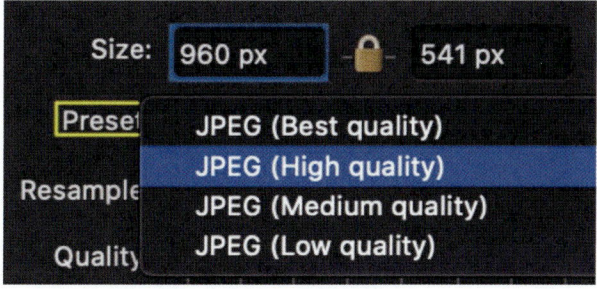

The image size is probably cut down by half or more. Now we have very small file to export.

Click on the **Export** button in the lower right-hand corner of the Export pop-out window.

Type a **name** of your picture in the **Save As** field (ours is "Bonus Text - Final Image").

51

Choose **Where** to *store* your **file**.

Press **Save** to *export* the **file** to your computer.

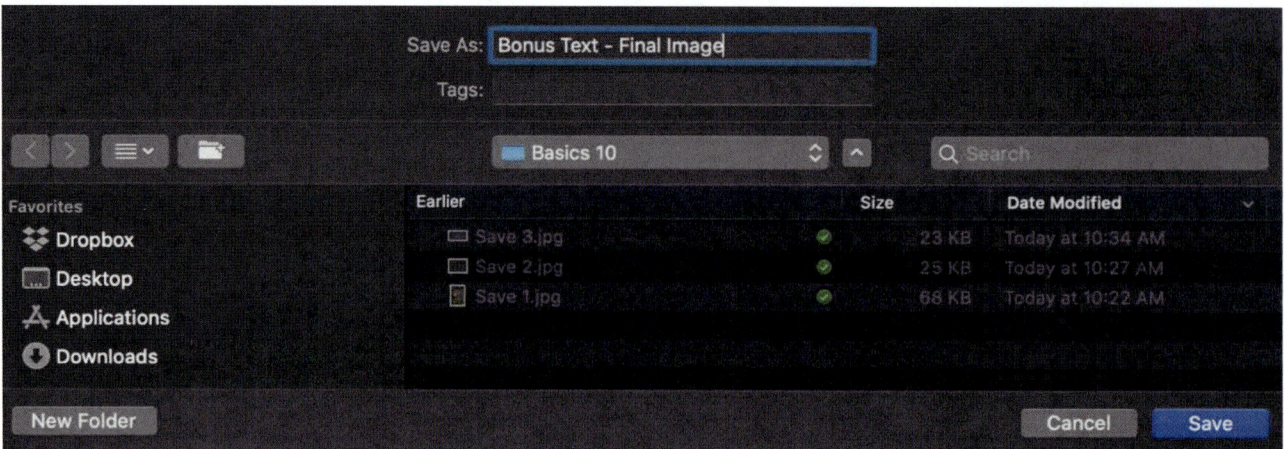

Note: Depending on which type of operating system, your **Save As** and **Export** windows will look a bit different, but the effect is the same.

Special Tutorial: How to Create Specialized Shortcuts

We created this special tutorial because we, too, want shortcuts to increase the Width of our brushes like how the majority of our readers can use the bracket keys. This lesson can be applied to any shortcut key stroke you'd rather have than the ones assigned to you.

We live in Germany, so our keyboard layout doesn't have any bracket keys. Where these keys are, you can find the German Ö and the Ä. Very different-looking letters from our native English language.

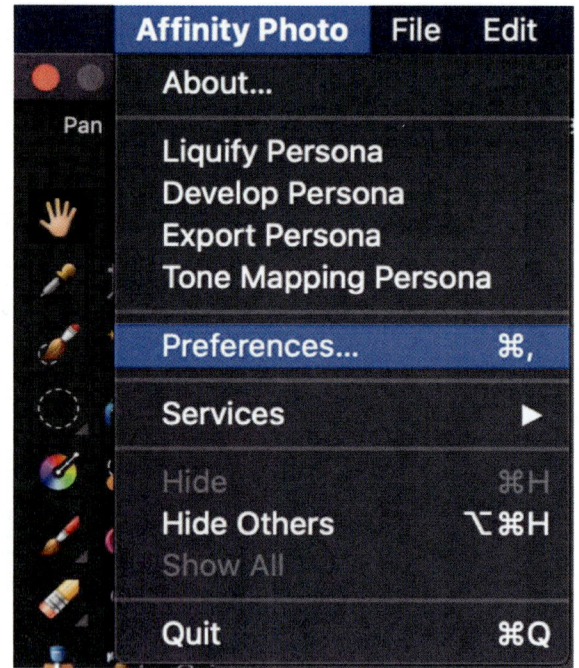

Let's get started.

> *Click* on the **Affinity Photo tab** at the far top left of the screen & *click* on **Preferences.**

52

After opening **Preferences**, there will be another drop-down window where you'll need to *choose* a box labelled **Keyboard Shortcuts**

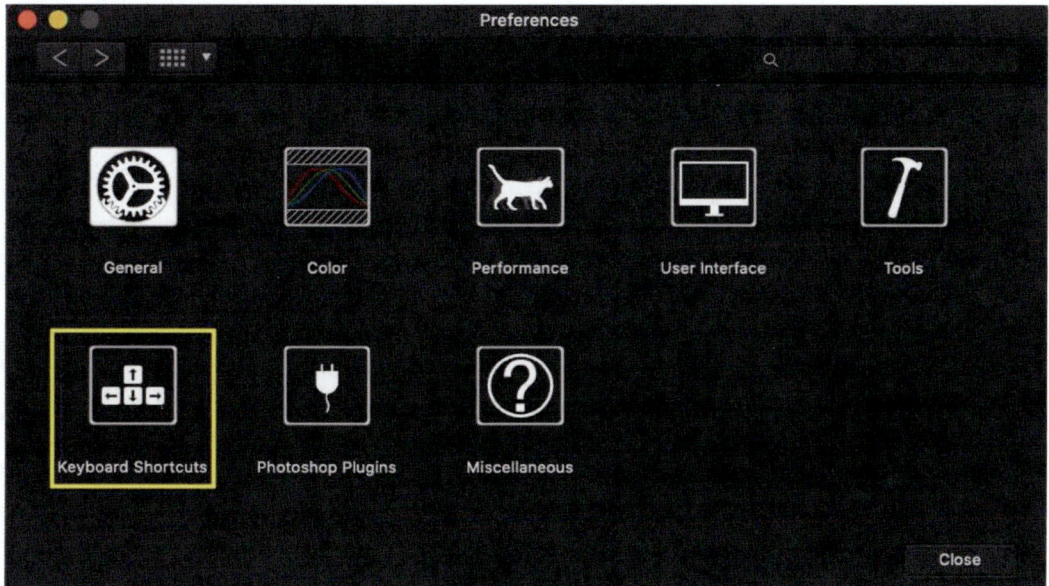

Click on **Keyboard Shortcuts** and then you'll need to *click* on the second drop-down menu in the top left of the new screen (see yellow rectangle in image below).

Choose the **Paint Brush Tool** (highlighted in blue).

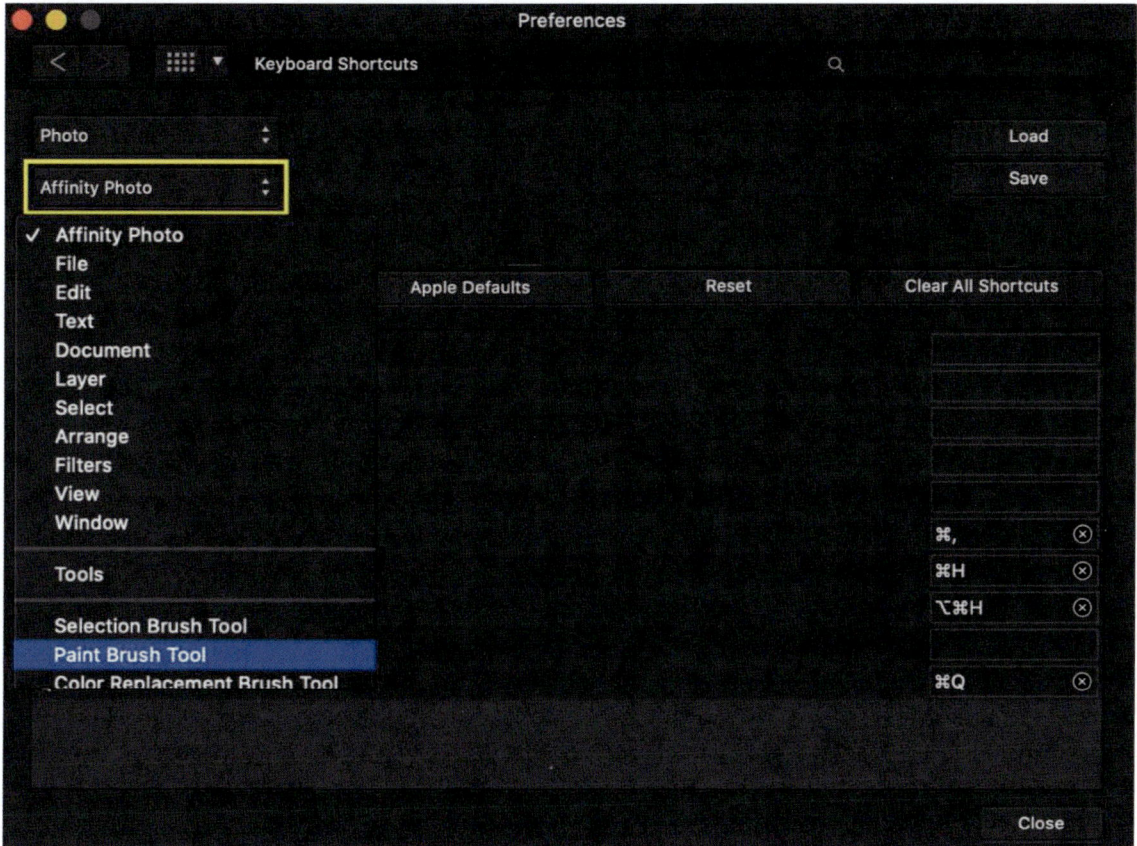

Here you'll have to find buttons on the keyboard that are not being used.

What did we do? We used the German letters **Ö** & **Ä** for our two shortcuts. Yes, we are native English speakers, but we live & work in Germany. German QWERTZ keyboards don't have bracket keys.

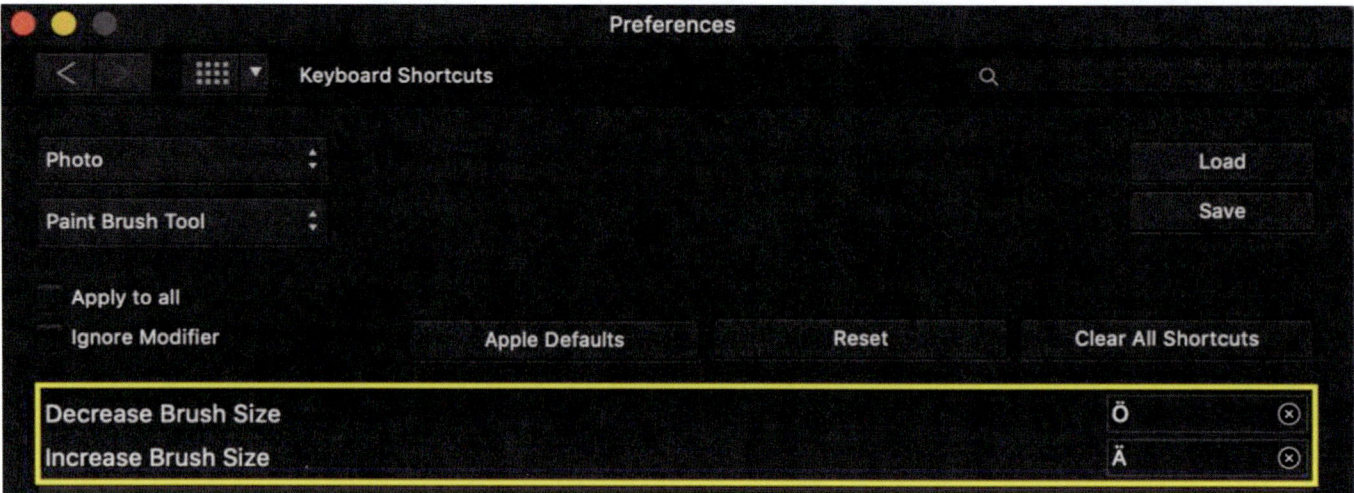

Note: This change of the shortcut letters is the same for all languages and keyboards. Follow these steps and make the changes as you see fit.

Finished. This ends this tutorial & the first section of this book.

Tutorial 1: How to Create a Double Exposure Effect

In this tutorial, we're going to learn how to apply a double exposure effect.

Here are the webpages to the images we'll be using for this tutorial (eagle, mountains):

https://pixabay.com/photos/bald-eagle-raptor-head-close-up-2715461/

https://pixabay.com/photos/zugspitze-alpine-summit-1048995/

Ready?

Ok, let's begin by opening both images onto Affinity Photo. We will be working with the image of the eagle first. Each image will have its own tab at the top of the canvas.

We want the eagle's image to go from left to right and not the way it is.
To change this:

> *Go* to the **Menu bar - Document - Flip Horizontal**.

First, we need to remove the background.

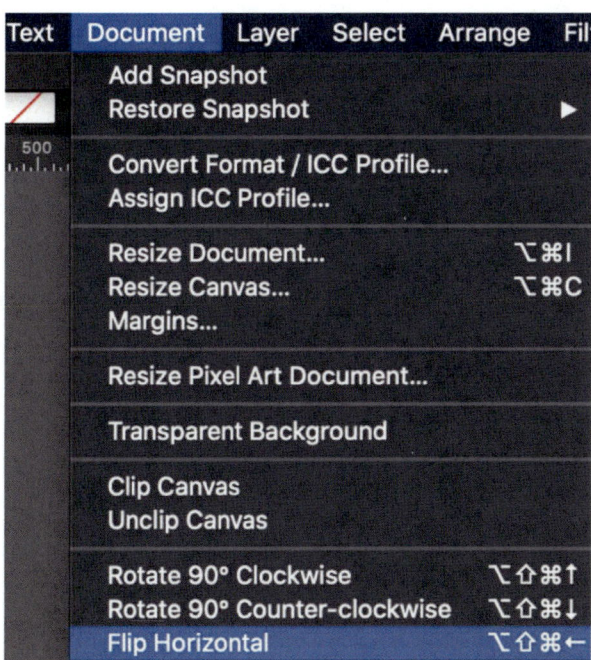

To do this:

> *Select* the **Selection Brush Tool** (make sure **Mode** is set to **Add**). Take your time!
>
> *Paint* over the **eagle** adjusting the width of the brush so you can get to the tip of its beak.
>
> *Go* to the **Contextual Toolbar** and *click* on **Refine...**
>
> *Brush* over the **edges** of the eagle so all feathers and beak are more clearly selected.

This is what our eagle looks like after we used the Refine Selection Brush. The edges should be crisp and clean.

Hint: When using the **Refine** button, make sure the subject you are refining is in color and the background is tinted red.

If your subject is red, then you need to *press* **Cancel** and *invert* your **pixel selection** by *pressing* **Ctrl/Cmd+Shift+I**. Then, when you *press* **Refine**, your subject will be in color and the background in red.

> *Press* **Apply** in the bottom-right corner of the Refine Selection pop-out window when done.

Now, look at the Layers Panel and make sure the single layer is selected and *highlighted* in **blue**.

Click on the **Mask Layer** icon.

Deselect your **selection** (the dancing ants) by *pressing* **Ctrl/Cmd+D**.

This is what our image should look like now:

Click on the **top layer** so it's highlighted in blue. The mask layer will also be highlighted.

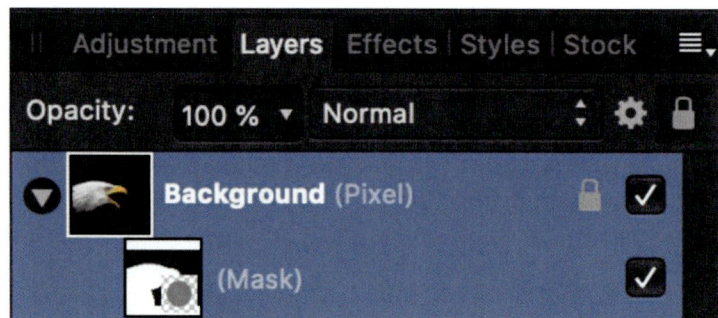

Duplicate this **top layer** by *pressing* **Ctrl/Cmd+J**.

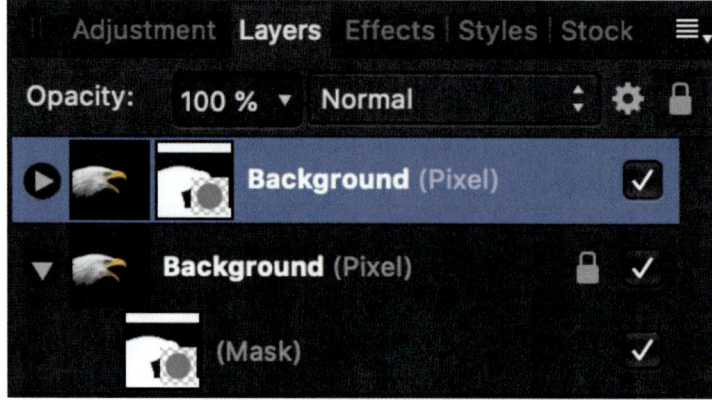

Click on the **Mountains tab** so the image is right in front of you.

Move your **cursor** anywhere on the canvas & *press* **Crtl/Cmd+C** to *copy* this image.

Go back to our **eagle image** & *press* **Ctrl/Cmd+V** to *paste* the mountains image on top of our eagle image.

Go to the **Layers Panel** and *click* & *drag* the **Mountain background layer** underneath-and-to-the-right of the Mask layer. Make sure it is not directly underneath the Mask layer. We want it under the Mask layer and-to-the-right. This special movement of layers creates a child layer. Child layers are layers that only affect the layer it is attached to, its Parent Layer, and not the other layers in the Layers Panel (see yellow arrow for this motion).

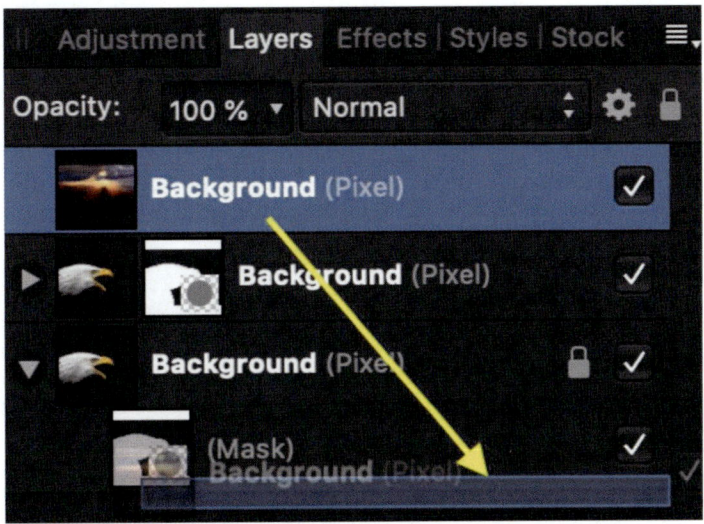

Uncheck the **top layer** and *select* the **Move Tool** (or *press* **V**) to *move* the **Mountain image** around however you want it to be placed underneath your subject. We've added a shot of the Layers Panel so you can see that the top layer is unchecked.

When you're done moving your Mountain image to where you want it, *check* the **top layer** back on and *highlight* it in **blue** as well. This is a very important step!

Change the **Blend Mode** to **Average** by *clicking* on the area we placed the yellow rectangle over and *select* **Average** from the drop-down menu. It's near the bottom of the list. This will blend our eagle image with our mountain image to create the effect we are after.

 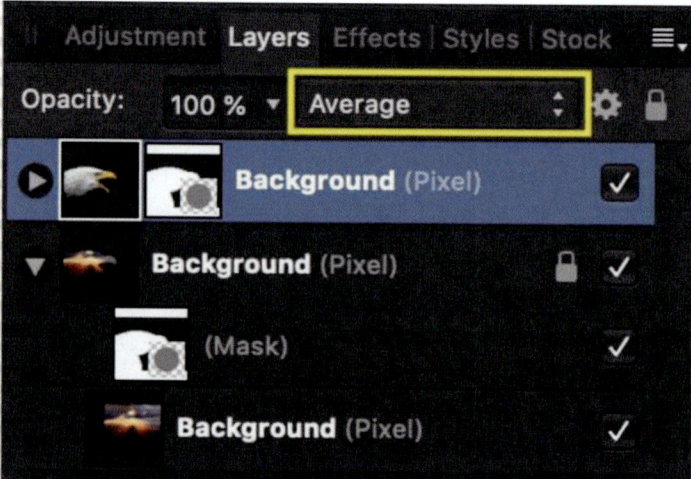

Click on the **Adjustments** icon and *select* **Levels**.

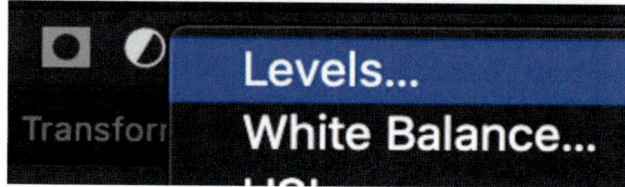

Adjust the **Black Level** to around **15%**.

Adjust the **White Level** to around **85%**.

Click on the **red button** to *close* this window.

These adjustments will increase the detail and the contrast.

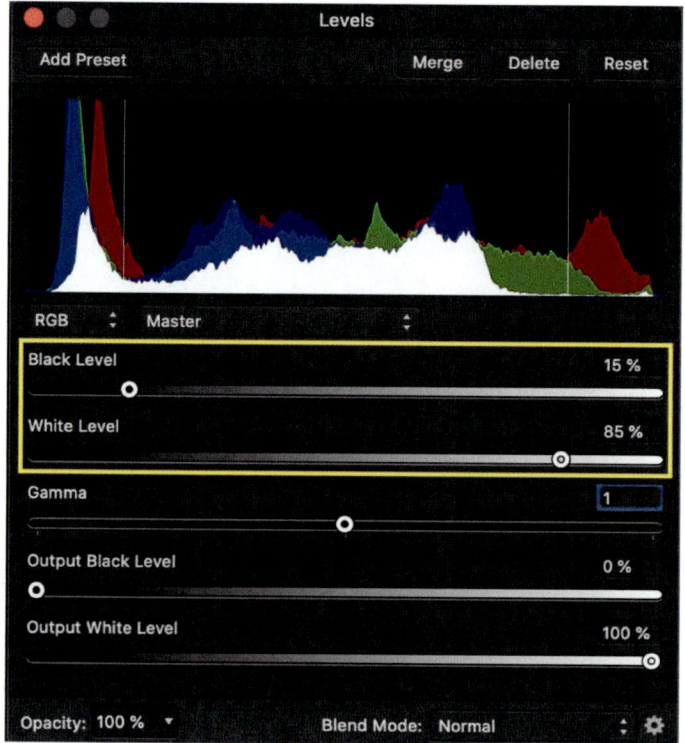

The last step we're going to take is to create a nice black background with a red/black gradient.

Note: Pay attention to how we do this next step. This technique of changing a background's color is one we do very often in Affinity Photo. Once you learn it, it's actually very simple.

Ready to change the background?

Click on the **Rectangle Tool** (or *press* **U**) and *click* & *drag* a **rectangle** over our whole image.

This is what our image looks like now after doing this step:

Go the **Colors Studio** & *move* the **inner color node** straight up vertically so the color of the rectangle changes to black (see white arrow for this action).

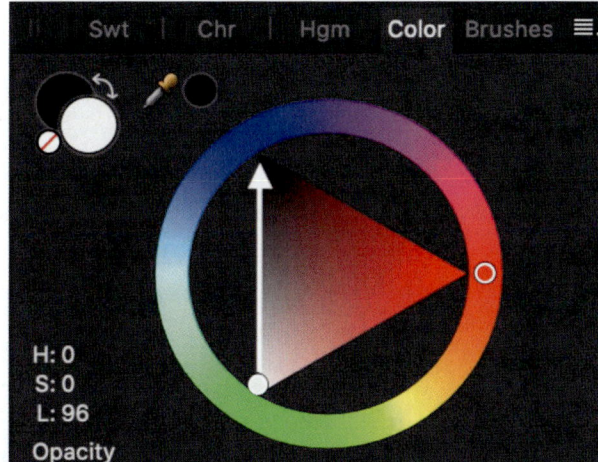

This is what our Layers Panel looks like now. Notice how the preview thumbnail for the Rectangle layer shows the Rectangle is all black. This is what we want.

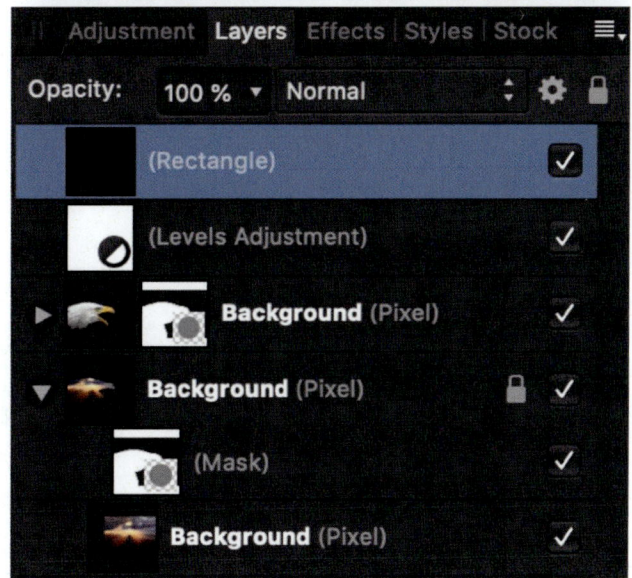

Hint: The image inside each layer's preview thumbnail should be what you see on the canvas.

Ready to continue? We're almost done, just a few more steps.

Click & *drag* the **top Rectangle layer** to the bottom of the Layers Stack. Make sure the left-side of the Rectangle layer is all the way to the left. We want this to be its own independent layer and not a Child.

Click on the **bottom Rectangle layer** so it's highlighted in blue.

Select the **Gradient Tool** from the Tools.

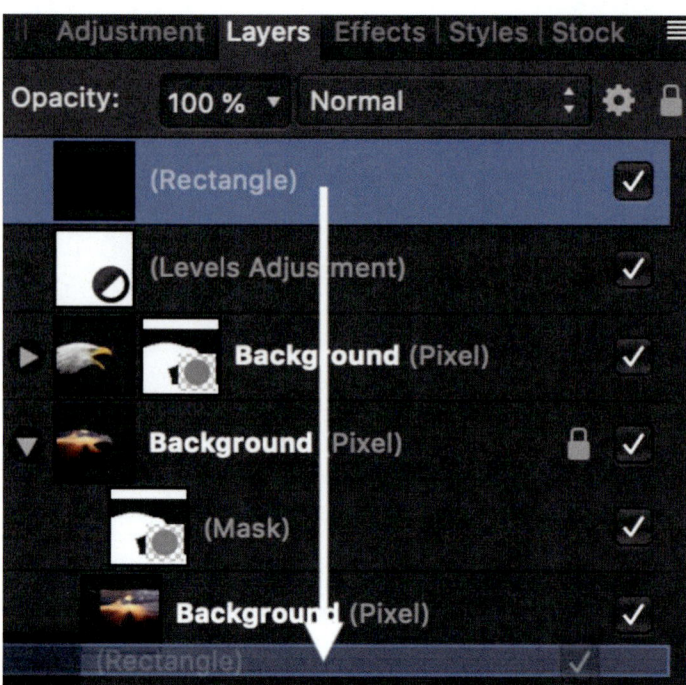

Click once on the **right-side border** of our image & *drag* the **gradient line** across the center of our image stopping on the left-side border. If you *hold down* the **Shift key** when drawing this gradient line, the line will be perfectly flat.

Click on the **left gradient node** that's on the left border and on the eagle's neck so it's bigger than the black node. When you see one gradient node that's bigger than the other(s), then you know that gradient node is selected.

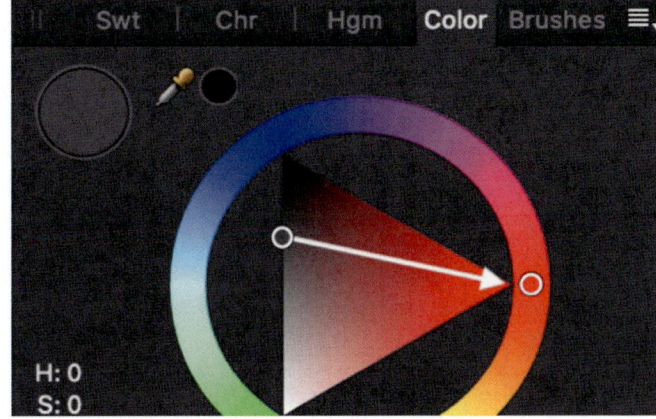

Go to the **Colors Studio** & *move* the **inner color node** to the position nearest the Hue node (see our white arrow for this action). This will cause the selected gradient node to change its color from gray to red.

The red a bit too bright, so let's move the red gradient node further out into the canvas away from our image to decrease the brightness.

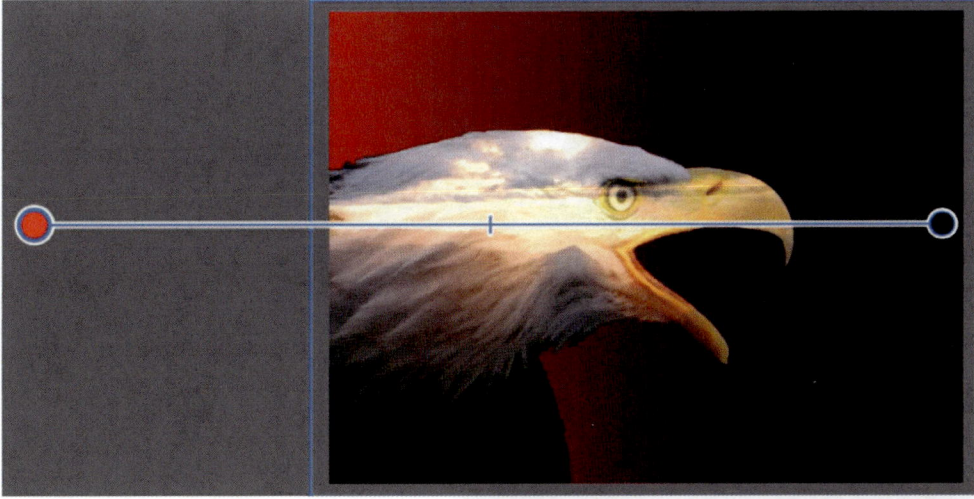

This is what our Layers Panel looks like now:

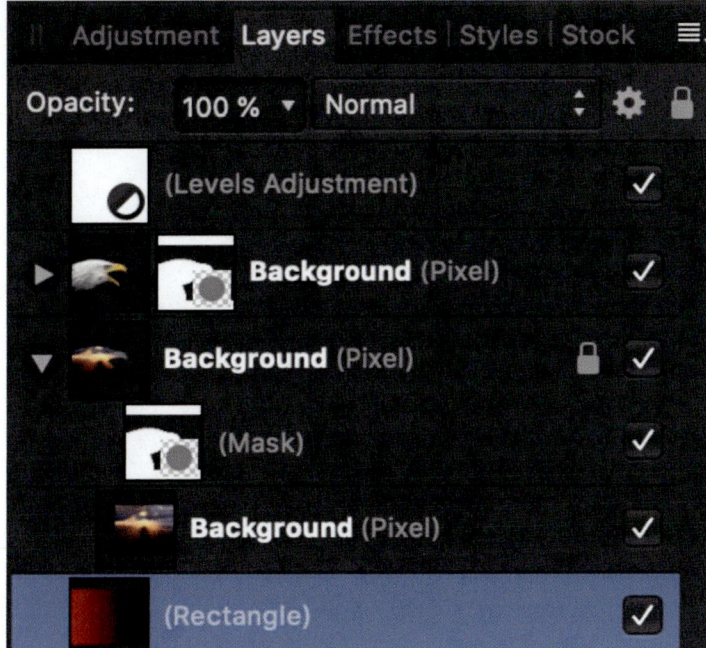

61

Done. This is our final image.

Finished. This ends this tutorial.

Tutorial 2: How to Create a Color Splash Effect

Being able to colorize one object in a **black & white** photo is a very popular technique. This is what we'll learn here. We hope you like this tutorial.

Here is the webpage to the image we'll be using:

> https://pixabay.com/photos/car-racing-motorsport-racing-car-4394450/

Ok. Ready? Please have this image uploaded and on your screen.

Here are the steps to do this very cool technique:

Choose the **object** you want to select. In this image it'll be the front car.

Select the **Pen Tool**.

Click the **outline** of the car. Review **Basics #7** if you need the help.

Click **Selection** on the Contextual Toolbar.

Go to the **Menu bar - Select - Invert Pixel Selection** (or **Ctrl/Cmd+Shift+I**).

Note: *Inverting* the pixel selection will choose everything in the photo except the car you just selected.

Click on the **Adjustments icon** & select **Black and White**...

Click on the **red button** to *close* the pop-out screen. We won't be making any refining adjustments; we only wanted to make our image black & white.

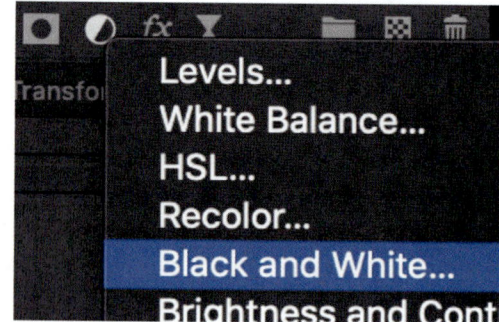

Go to the **Menu bar** - **Select** - **Deselect** (the dancing ants will disappear)

Done. This is our final image. Impressive, isn't it?

Finished. This ends this tutorial.

Tutorial 3: How to Create a Stylish Duotone Effect

In this tutorial we'll going to learn how to create a stylish duotone effect.

Here is the webpage for this tutorial:

https://pixabay.com/photos/guitar-classical-guitar-756326/

Once you have this image uploaded onto your canvas, we'll begin.

Ready? Great. Here's how we create the duotone effect:

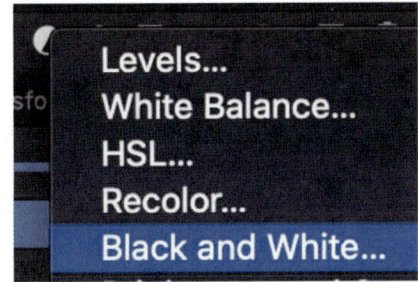

Click on the **Adjustments icon** & *select* **Black and White**...

We aren't going to be making any adjustments from the pop-out window with the sliders. Just *press* on the **X** to get rid of this window. The image is now **Black & White**, which is what we want.

Click again on the **Adjustments icon** and in the drop-down menu *select* **Gradient Map**. This will cause our image to look very strange.

Your image should now look like this:

When you choose **Gradient Map**, its own pop-out window will appear. When you look at this window, there in the top is a color bar with **red** on the left side, **green** in the middle and **blue** on the right side.

Here is what each color stands for:

Red: Shadows   **Green**: Mid-tones   **Blue**: Highlights

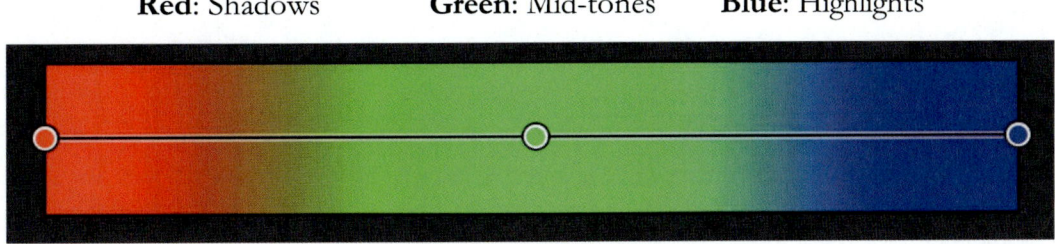

65

For this tutorial, since it's a duotone effect (**duo** meaning **two**), we need to delete one of these Gradient Map nodes. The likely candidate is the middle node.

Click on the **middle green node** (see black square) & *click* on the **Delete button** located in the Gradient Map pop-out window (see yellow rectangle).

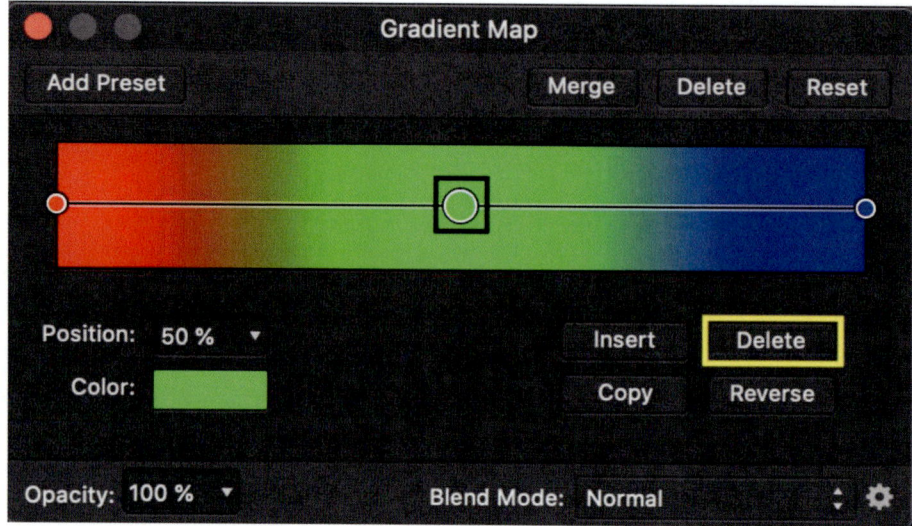

Then *press* on the **Reverse** button located below the Delete button. This will cause the respective colors (red & blue) to reflect different aspects. Reds will now represent the highlights & Blue will represent the shadows.

This is what our image should look like now:

66

We now have a beautiful duotone effect, but let's see if we can make it even better. To do this, we're going to **Merge** all layers into one visible layer.

Here's how:

Right-click on **any layer** and *select* **Merge Visible**.

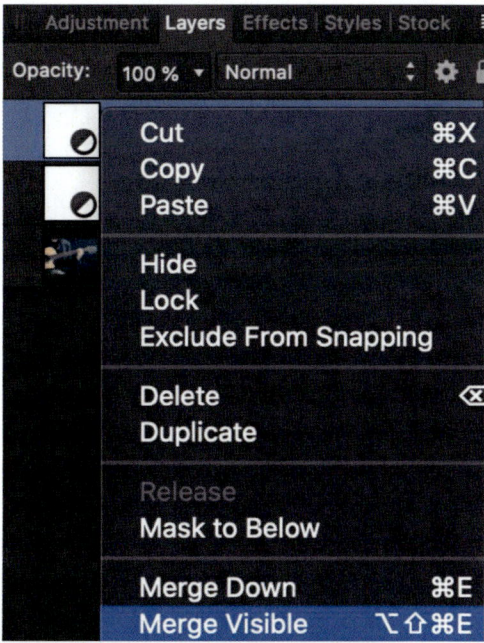

Select the **Selection Brush Tool** and *paint* a **selection** across the man. Make sure you take your time and zoom into the areas around his left hand, the zipper on his sleeve and the tuning knobs on guitar. You'll have to decrease the Width of the Selection Brush's diameter to properly select these minute details.

Pro Tip: Hold-down the Option/Alt key to do the opposite action so when you click to pain the selection, you'll remove parts of the selection instead of adding.

Note: Knowing how to refine selections takes a very long time to master. So, take your time and do as best you can. Over time, you'll get better and better. We are still learning, too. For this lesson, don't worry if your selection isn't perfect.

Go to the **Contextual Toolbar** & *click* on **Refine**... This will allow us to make our selection more precise. But, for this tutorial, total precision isn't necessary since we're only working with two colors.

Paint over the **technical parts** (fingers, zipper, tuning knobs) & then *click* on **Apply**. When you are done, hopefully these more difficult parts will be better selected. One caveat you need to know is that when trying to refine selections where the foreground & background colors are hard to distinguish, the Refine Selection Brush Tool isn't the end all, end all.

Note: You may need, as in this case, go back and again use the Selection Brush Tool and paint in the selection around the areas the Refine Selection Tool missed or improperly marked. Thankfully, for the most of the time the Refine Selection Tool works wonders.

This is our selection:

Make sure the (Pixel) layer is at the top of our Layers Panel before continuing.

Click on the **Mask icon** (looks like a Japanese flag) located to the left of the Adjustments icon.

Press **Ctrl/Cmd+D** to *deselect* the dancing ants.

Note: Make sure the guitar player is still selected (i.e. had dancing ants surrounding him) when you *click* on the **Mask** icon.

This is what our Layers Panel should look like now:

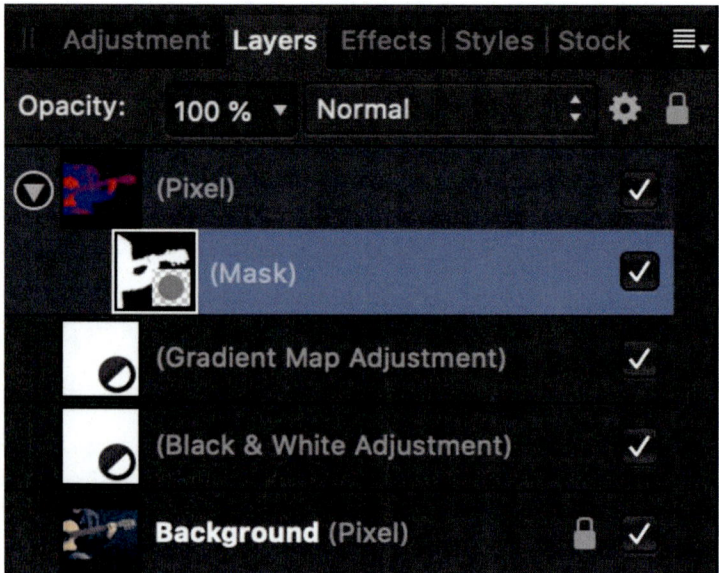

It doesn't look like much has happened but if we *select* the bottom three layers and then *turn them off* you can see that we have just the man with the guitar on the top Layer with a transparent background.

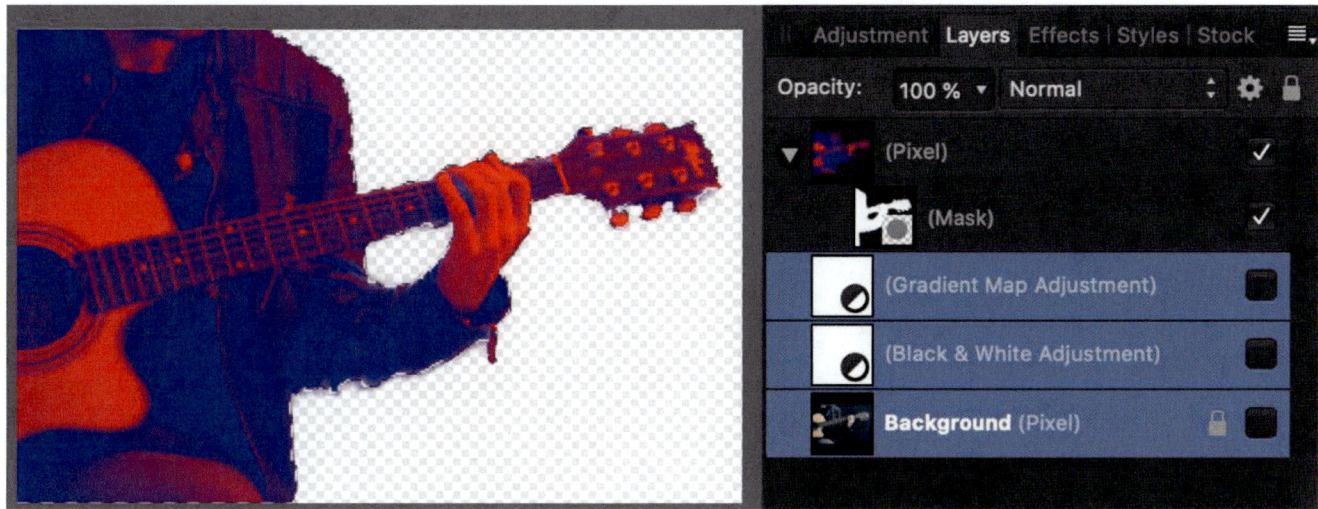

Click these **layers** back on and let's get rid of the dancing ants by *pressing* **Deselect** (**Ctrl/Cmd+D**). You can also ***deselect*** by going to the **Menu bar** -**Select** -**Deselect**.

For this next creative part, make sure the bottom three layers are *selected* in **blue**.

Click on the **small triangle** on the Rectangle Tool's icon (see yellow square) and a drop-down menu will appear.

Select the **Ellipse Tool** (looks like a circle).

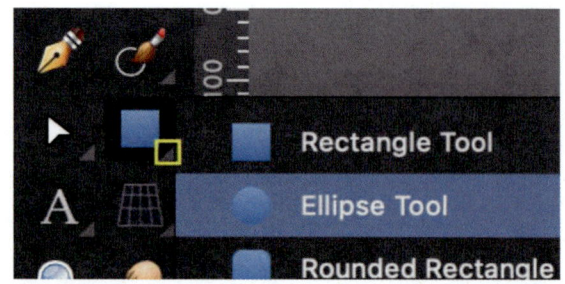

What we are going to do now is add some shapes to the image to make it more interesting. In this case, round balls.

In the right-side of the image, *click* & *drag* a circle about the size of the man's extended hand. This ball will appear behind the man's arm.

With the (Ellipse) layer *highlighted* in **blue**, *press* **Ctrl/Cmd+J** three times to create four of these balls.

Hint: Remember. If you want to *create* perfectly symmetrical shapes, *hold down* the **Shift** button when you *drag* out your shapes.

This is what our Layers Panel looks like now.

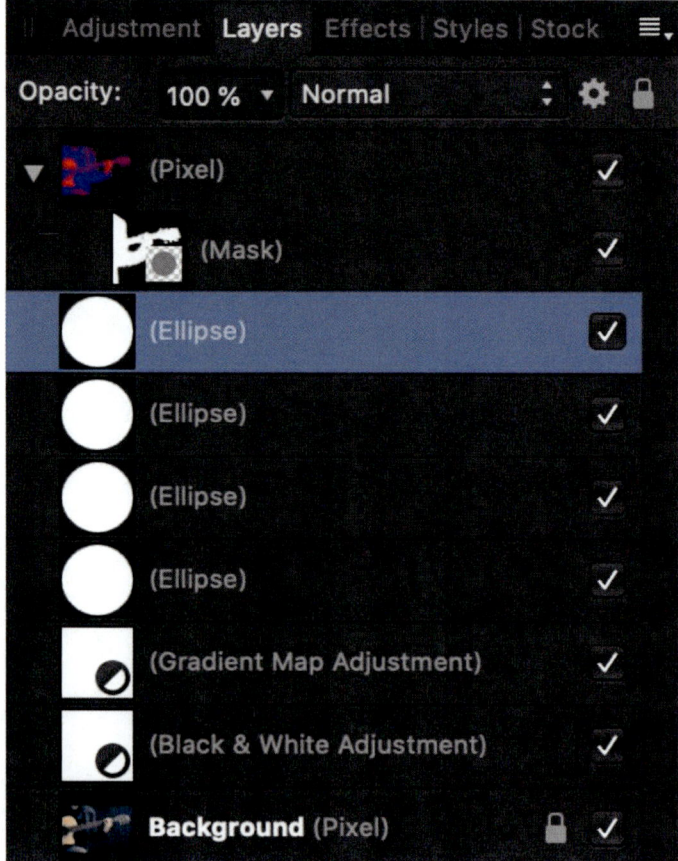

70

These balls (or circles) are looking too stark on our nice duotone image. Let's *highlight* all of the (Ellipse) layers by holding down the **Shift** key and *clicking* on the top and bottom (Ellipse) layer.

With all four layers *highlighted* in **blue**, let's *decrease* their **Opacity** to **30%**.

Hint: There are three ways to adjust Opacity:

1. *Press* the **3** button on the keyboard.

2. *Click* on the **downward-pointing triangle** to the right of the 30% and use the pop-out slider to move the Opacity to the level you want.

3. *Triple-click* **inside the value box** where it now has 30%. This will cause the number to be highlighted in blue. Then you can type the **%** you want.

Next, we want to click on each individual Ellipse layer and using the Color Wheel, change the color of each. We can also change the sizes of any we want using the Move Tool.

Here is a screenshot of our new Layers Panel showing you the four different colors we chose for our circles as well as their different sizes & locations.

71

The last thing we want to do is darken the **Background**.

    Click on the bottom **Background** layer so it's highlighted in blue.

    Click on the **Adjustments icon** & *choose* **Brightness and Contrast**...

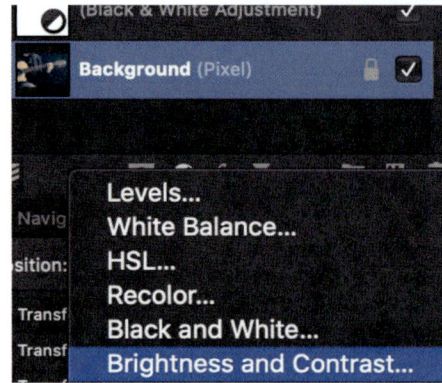

In the **Brightness/Contrast** pop-out window, let's:

    Decrease the **Brightness** to **-40%**

    Increase the **Contrast** to **+40%**.

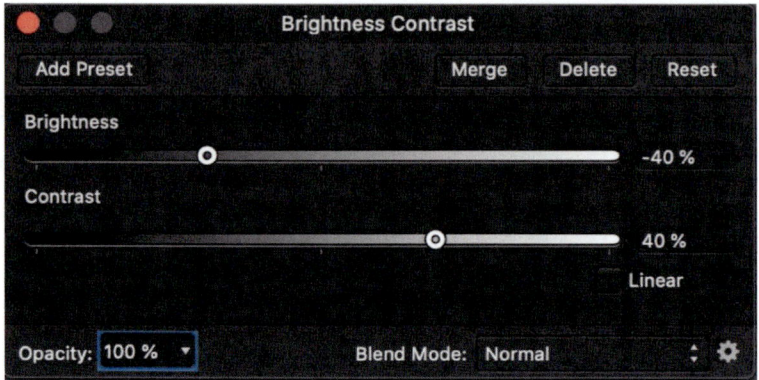

Done. This is our final image.

Finished. This ends this tutorial.

Tutorial 4: How to Create a Matte Image Effect

Every time you go process your photographs, you're given the choice of Glossy or Matte.

The difference everybody knows is that one is shinny and the other, well, not. But, there is an actual difference in the photo processing. Matte images are designed to minimize the reflection of light and it does this by a special coating placed on top of a photograph when processed from digital to print.

Glossy photographs are the polar opposite: They are specifically designed to reflect as much light as possible.

In this lesson, we'll show you how to make any photograph have a Matte look. We've included in this lesson how the matte photograph will look like in black and white, too. We'll also explore the difference between using a simply Black and White adjustment layer with & without tweaking of the different hues in the photo.

Here is the image we'll be using for this lesson:

https://unsplash.com/photos/NOj7slD8qtc

Ready?

Upload the **image**.

Press **Ctrl/Cmd+J** to *duplicate* the image.

Click on the **Adjustments icon** & *select* **Levels...**

Adjust **Black Level** slider to **12%** & **Output Black Level** to **25%**

Uncheck & *recheck* the **layer** to see *before* & *after*.

Done. This is the final image.

Optional Change:

> *Click* on the **Adjustments icon** & *select* **Black and White...**
>
> *Press* the **red button** to *close* out this pop-out window.

How do you think it looks? We think it looks washed out. Lots of the details seem to be blasted away. Let's see if we can have the image be black & white, but in much more detail.

To do this:

> *Press* **Ctrl/Cmd+J** to *duplicate* the top B&W layer. This will create a second Black & White adjustment layer.
>
> *Uncheck* the **top layer** & *click* on the **first B&W layer** so it's highlighted in blue (see this image of our Layers Panel).

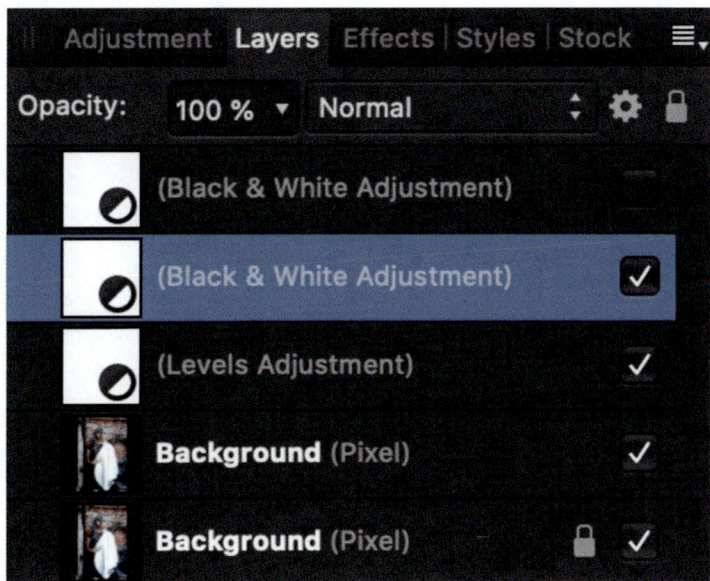

> *Double-click* on this layer's **preview thumbnail** to reveal its pop-out window with its different Hue adjustment sliders.

Now, we will adjust the sliders to reveal the different parts of our model, her clothing, her background and even the shadows.

Adjust the **Red's** to **15%** to accentuate the model's lips.

Adjust the **Yellow's** to **15%** to accentuate the model's skin tone.

Leave the **Green's** alone.

Adjust the **Cyan** to **-45%** to add contrast to her white jacket.

Adjust the **Blues** to **60%** to add reveal the shadows better.

Adjust the **Magenta** to **107%** to even out some skin changes due to the above adjustments.

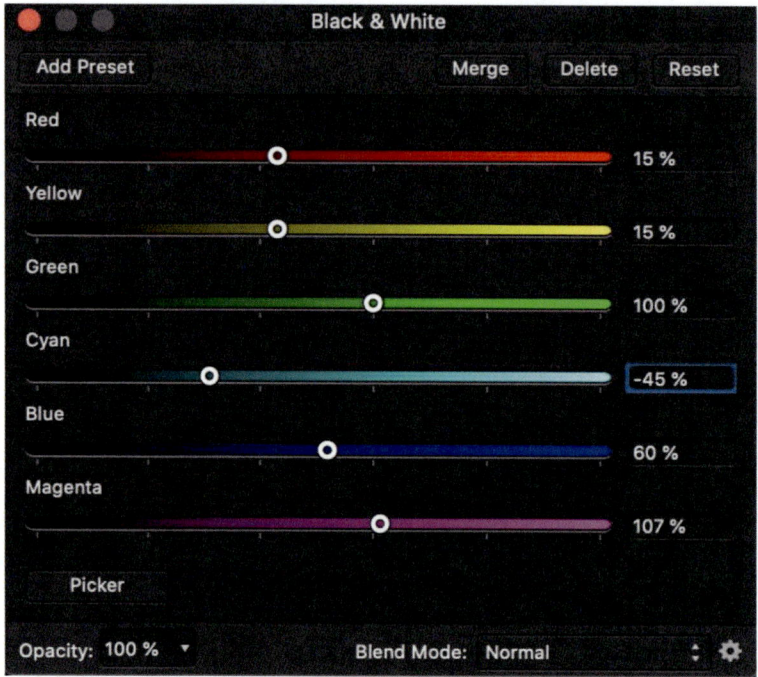

Click on the **red button** at the top-left of this pop-out window to close it.

Check off the **current layer** & *check* on the **top layer** in the Layers Panel. This will show our image with just the B&W adjustment.

Alternate *checking* **on** & **off** the top two Black & White adjustment layers to see the dramatic difference.

This is what our image looks like without the Hue adjustments. Compare this image to the next image where we made the Hue adjustments. Notice how the image looks so washed of contrast.

Note: Please remember these differences when working with your own photos. Making even slight Hue adjustments to B&W images makes a huge difference, as you can see here.

Done.

This is our final image with the Hue adjustments. Which matte image do you like best? Color or Black & White?

Finished. This ends this short, but sweet tutorial.

Tutorial 5: How to do a Sky Replacement

In this tutorial, we are going to learn how do a sky replacement.

Here are the webpages for the image we'll be using for this tutorial:

> https://pixabay.com/photos/mount-rushmore-monument-landmark-902483/

> https://pixabay.com/photos/nature-sky-night-stars-2609647/

With both of these images uploaded to Affinity Photo, we're going to start with the Mt. Rushmore image.

Select the **Selection Brush Tool.**

Select the **sky** by *clicking* on the **left-side of the sky** & *dragging* the **cursor** to the right and off the image's borders.

As you make your selection, you might miss parts of the rock face like we did (see yellow rectangle).

To correct this mistake:

Hold-down the **Option/Alt button** & *paint* over **the rock area** we want to correct from the starting point of underneath the rocks (not from above in the sky area). See this screenshot where we show you the two positions we used our Selections Brush to click one-time in each position to move the selection line (i.e. the dancing ants) up to the border of the rocks & sky.

Hint: Every time you *hold down* the **Option/Alt key** and *use* a **Tool**, the opposite action will occur. This is what professionals use in our workflows. It makes our work incredibly faster.

With the selection now running along the rock face, let's make the selection even better.

Go to the **Toolbar** (horizontal area above the Contextual Toolbar) & *click* on the **Refine...** button.

Paint over the **top of the rockface** and when done, *press* **Apply** to *close* out the Refine Selection pop-out window.

This is where we used the Refine Selection brush (see the matte red brush line over the rock perimeter).

After we *pressed* **Apply**, the selection was much cleaner (notice how the dancing ants fit perfectly).

With the selection done as well as we can, let's continue:

Press **Ctrl/Cmd+J** to *duplicate* our layer.

Press **Ctrl/Cmd+D** to *deselect* out selection (e.g. the dancing ants).

Go to the **second image's tab** & *open* it **onto our canvas**.

Press **Ctrl/Cmd+C** to *copy* this image.

Go back to the **Mount Rushmore image** & *press* **Ctrl/Cmd+V** to *paste* the stars image on top of the Mount Rushmore image.

Let's change the name of the layers in the Layers Panel so we won't be confused as we work on them. Renaming layers is a simple and effect thing to do when working with multiple layers.

Double-click on the **top layer** & *type* in "Sky".

Double-click on the **middle layer** & *type* "MRM 2" for Mount Rushmore 2.

Double-click on the **bottom layer** & *type* "MRM 1" for the original Mount Rushmore image.

When you've done each of these steps, this is what our Layers Panel should now look like:

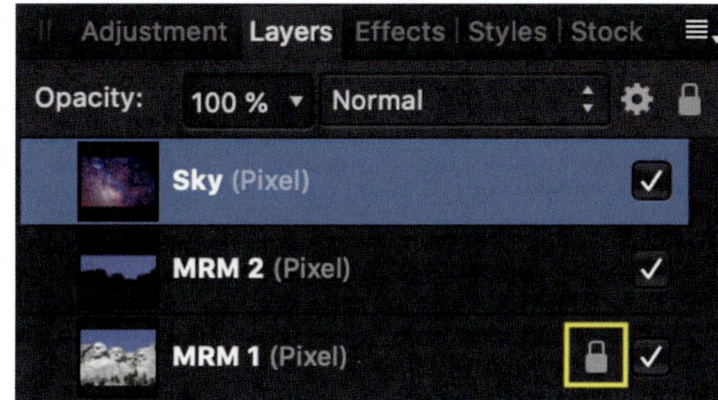

Two things to note about Layers:

One: You can always tell what is the original layer because it'll have a Lock icon on it (see yellow).

Two: Sometimes when you double-click a layer to rename it, the software program won't allow it for one or two tries. We don't know what it happens, but it does sometimes. Just do the operation again until you are able to rename the layer. It's what it is.

With the layers renamed...

Click on the **Sky** layer & *drag* it **underneath-and-to-the-right** of the **MRM 2** layer.

This is a screenshot showing you this action. Notice how the left-side of the Sky layer is not all the way to the left as is being placed underneath the **MRM 2** layer.

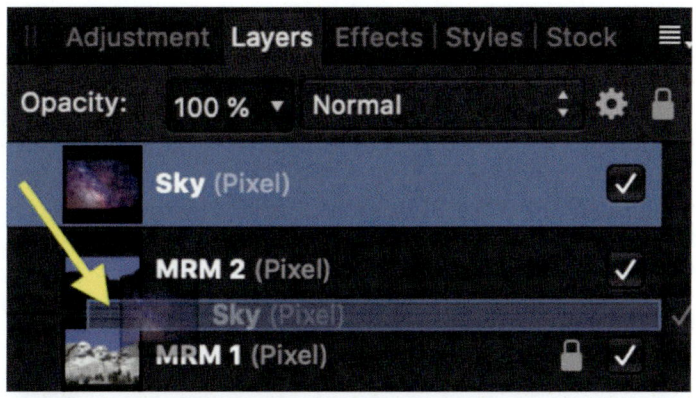

(Optional)

Click on the **Sky layer** & *select* the **Move Tool** and *move* & *rescale* the Sky image wherever you want it.

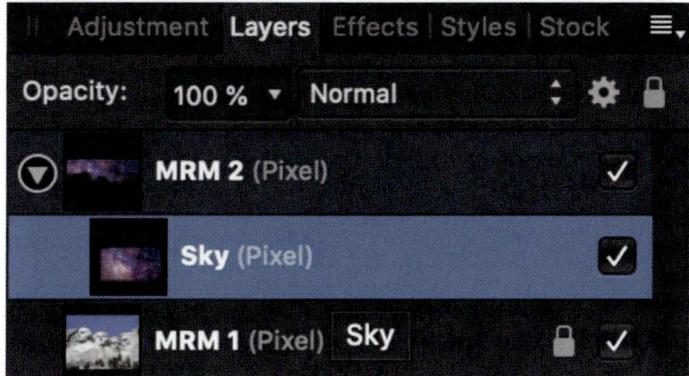

81

We've now done a sky replacement, but there's more to this than just taking one photo and adding to another. We need to now match the colors of both images together. Why? Because we want the composite image to look as natural as possible. Currently, the MRM image is in broad daylight while the Sky image was probably taken at night. So, we've got a bit work to do to blend these together.

Click on the **MRM 1** layer so it's highlighted in blue.

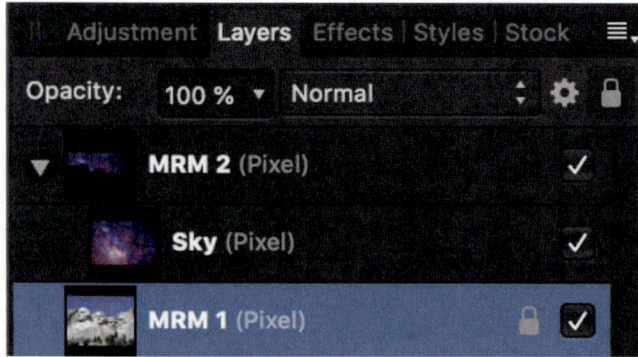

Remember: The most common mistake new users make when using Affinity Photo is that they forget to active the correct layer before continuing on with their work.

Click on the **Adjustments** icon & *select* **Brightness and Contrast...**

A pop-out window will appear.

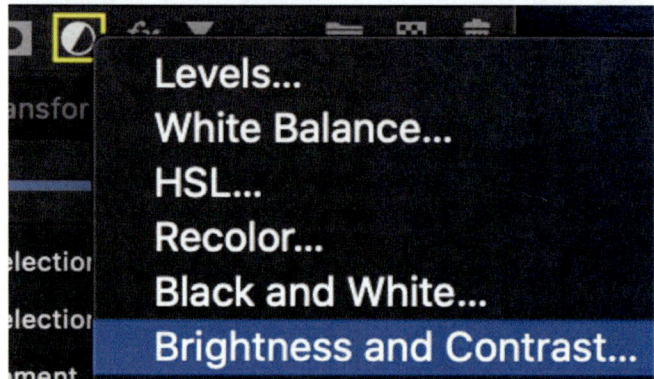

Make the following adjustments:

Brightness to **-30%**

Contrast to **25%**.

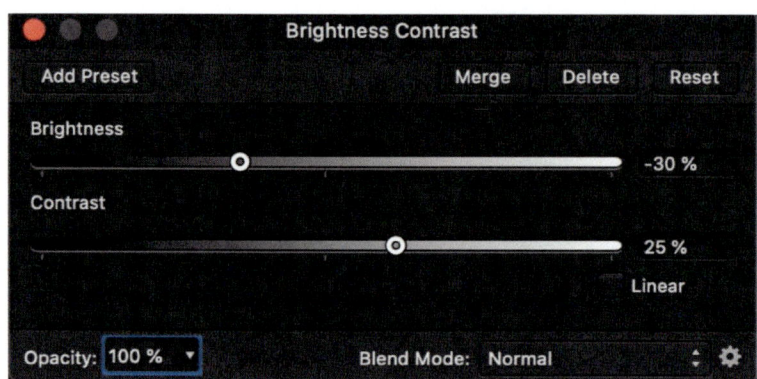

Click **anywhere on the canvas** to make this pop-out window disappear (or *press* the **red** button).

82

The colors aren't yet matched, so we've got one more adjustment to make:

> *Click* on the **Adjustments icon** & *select* **Lens Filter...** from the drop-down menu. It's located near the bottom of the pop-out menu.

This is what our Layers Panel should look like now:

This is what the **Lens Filter** pop-out window looks like. Notice how the default Filter Color is orange (see yellow square).

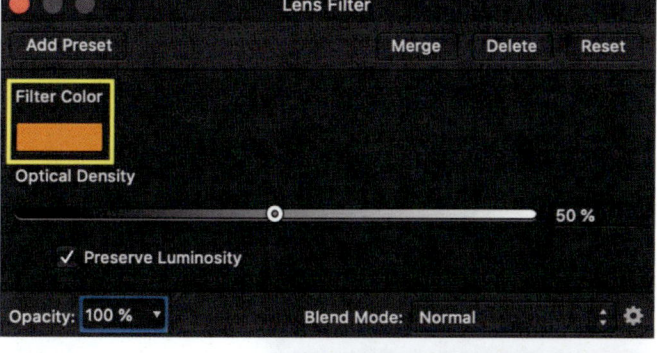

What we need to do is to click on this orange rectangle and when the Color Wheel pops out, we'll change the color to a dark blue. So,...

> *Click* on the **Filter Color rectangle...**

> *Move* the **Hue node** to a dark blue. The Hue node is the small white circle on the outside ring that goes around the middle triangle - both parts make up the Color Wheel.

When you do this, notice how the Filter Color rectangle (yellow rectangle) also changes color to match the color we've chosen with the Color Wheel.

> *Click* on the **Lens Filter pop-out window** and the Color Wheel will disappear.

> *Adjust* the **Optical Density** slider to **65%**.

> *Close* this **window** by either *pressing* the **red button** or *clicking* **anywhere on the canvas**.

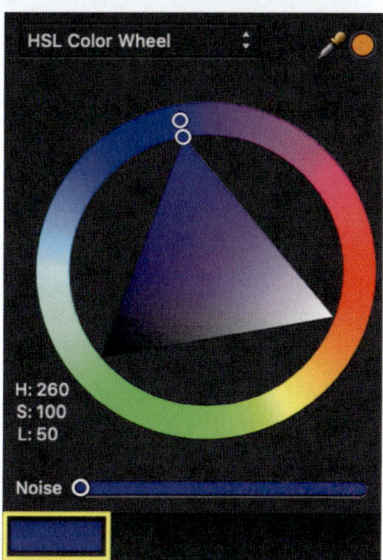

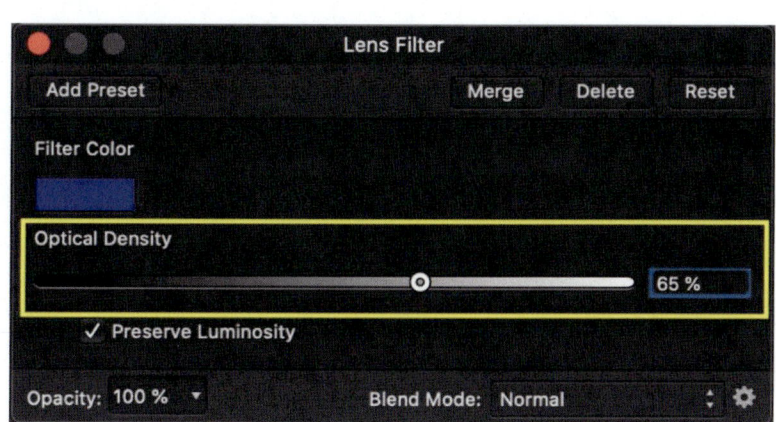

83

This is what our final Layers Panel should look like:

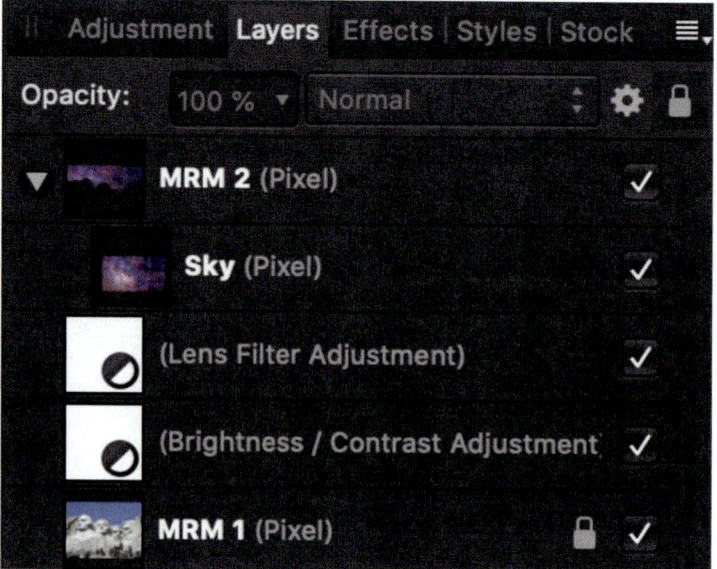

Done. This is our first final image.

84

Before we finish this tutorial, we want to show you another way you can colorize Mount Rushmore other than using the Lens Filter adjustment.

- *Go* to the **Layers Panel** & *uncheck* the **Lens Filter Adjustment layer**. This will deactivate that effect making it like it isn't even there.

- *Click* on the **MRM 1 layer** so it's highlighted in blue.

- *Select* the **Paint Brush Tool** (or *press* **B**).

- *Go* to the **Colors Studio** & *find* the **Color Picker Tool**. It looks like a water dropper.

Note: To use the Color Picker Tool, you need to click on it and while holding-down the left mouse button and then hover the cursor, which will look like a magnifying glass (see image below), over a color on your screen you want to pick (we chose a pink color from the Sky background). When you've found the color you want, release the mouse button. Then, go back to the Color Picker Tool's area & click once on the small circle to the right of the Color Picker Tool (see yellow square in bottom image). This final step will make the color on the Color Wheel the same color you chose using the Color Picker Tool's magnifying cursor. The next steps will tell you what to do.

- *Click* & *hold-down* the **Color Picker Tool** and *bring* it to a **portion of our image** where the color is the same we'd like to paint on top of the MRM image.

- *Release* the **mouse button** when you've found your color.

Go back to **where** the Color Picker Tool is located and *click* one-time on the **small circle** to its right. This will change the Hue color on the Color Wheel to match the color you chose using the Color Picker Tool.

85

Now all we need to do is *paint* over the **MRM 1** layer to make its color the same as the color we chose using the Color Picker Tool. Normally, we need to change the Opacity of this color down to around 20% because the effect will be to drastic. So, let's do that.

Go to the **Contextual Toolbar** & *adjust* the **Opacity** to **20%** and *set* the **Flow** at **50%**.

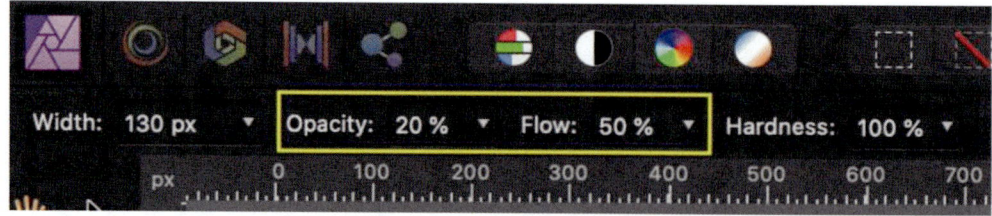

Note: Make sure just the bottom **MRM 1** layer is selected and highlighted in blue before you start painting.

Paint over the **MRM 1** image changing its color to the sky color we chose in the steps above.

Done. This is our second final image.

If you compare this image using this technique with the Paint Brush Tool, you'll see it's a bit more subdued and the image using the Lens Filter adjustment is a bit brighter.

Either way, the image is now finished. You need to decide which method you like best.

Finished. This ends this tutorial.

The Color Wheel

This is a brief overview of the Color Wheel in case you didn't understand how it works. The outside ring represents the different colors (or more formally, Hues). The white node inside the inner triangle allows you to adjust the chosen Hue's Saturation and Luminosity (or Brightness).

So, every time you choose a new Hue, you can also change its appearance with the inner triangle.

In our latest book, The Affinity Photo Manual II, we talk more in-depth about colors. If you want to do some self-learning on colors used in photo editing, we can suggest you do a search for "color theory in photo editing". It's a very involved topic, so be prepared for a steep learning curve.

When we first started using Affinity Photo, we did not know much about the different colors. Now that we do, we highly recommend you do further study on this matter.

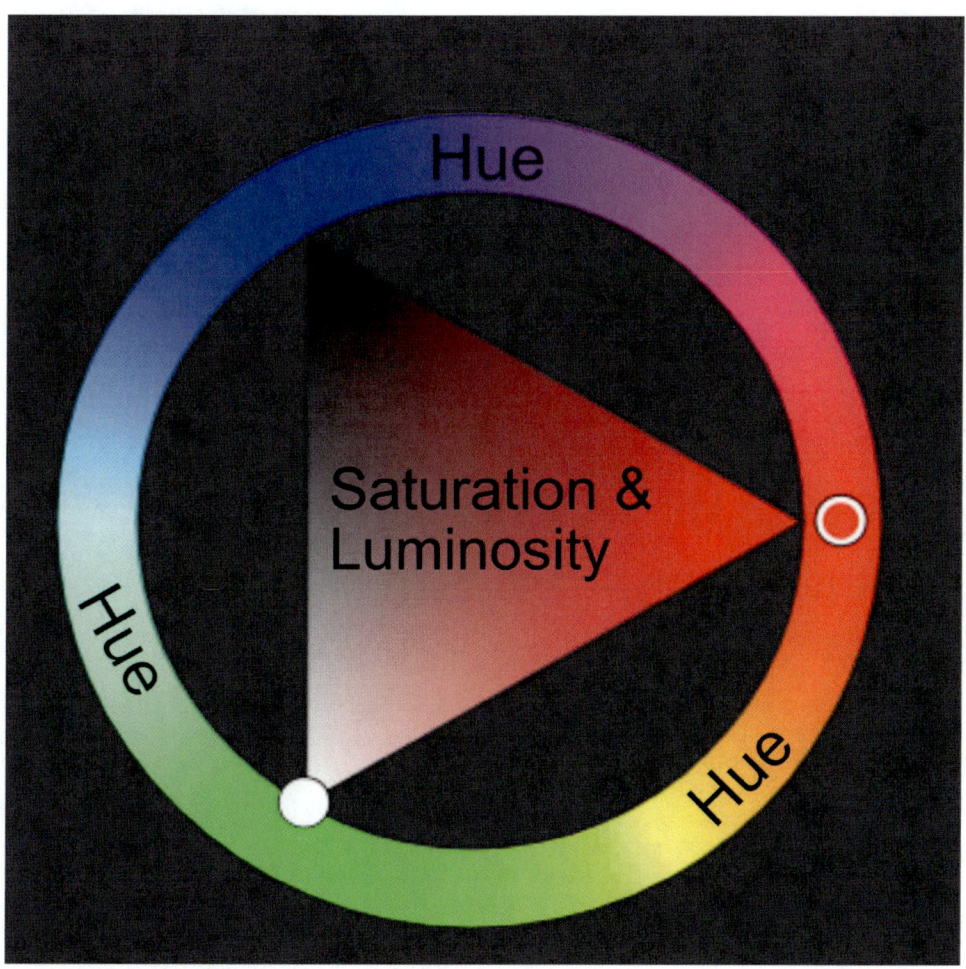

Tutorial 6: How to Create a High-Speed Effect

In this Affinity Photo tutorial, you are going to learn how to make a high-speed effect.

Here is the webpage to the image we'll be using for this tutorial:

https://pixabay.com/photos/architecture-building-infrastructure-2569760/

This tutorial has two parts. The first will show you how to quickly perform this technique, while the second part will show you a second method of creating the same effect, but with more flexibility and control.

Part I

Ready?

Once you have the image uploaded to the canvas, we'll do this:

- *Press* **Ctrl/Cmd+J** to *duplicate* the image.
- *Go* to the **Menu bar** - **Filters** - **Blur** - **Zoom Blur...** A pop-out window will appear.

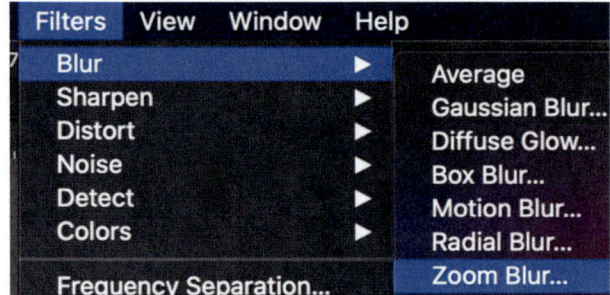

- *Adjust* the **Radius** to **8 px**.
- *Press* **Apply** when done.

The higher the Radius the more blur effect you'll create.

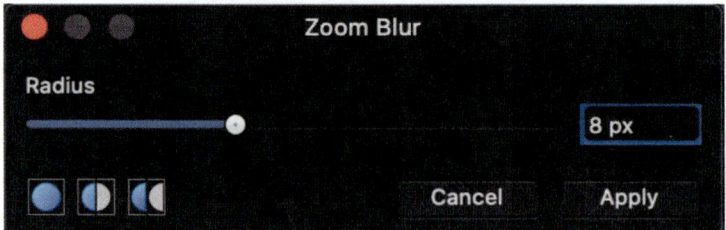

Next, we need to apply a Mask layer to hide part of this layer that has the zoom blur applied.

To do this:

- *Click* on the **top layer** so it's highlighted in blue.
- *Click* on the **Mask icon** (looks like a Japanese flag).

This is what our Layers Panel should look like now:

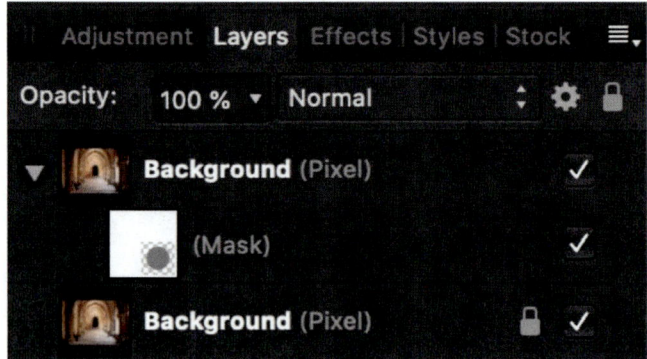

Select the **Paint Brush Tool** (or *press* **B**).

Press **X** if you need to ***change*** the foreground colors. We want **black** (to reveal image below).

Note: When using Masks, like how we talked about in the Basics portion of this book, after you've applied a mask to an image you want to paint on it to reveal the layer(s) beneath, you have to paint in black. To hide the lower layer(s), you have to paint in white. If this is a concept that is hard for you to grasp, just know it was also very hard for us, too. It's just one of those things in life that you have to accept it just the way it is.

Go to the **Contextual Toolbar** & *adjust* these values to our Paint Brush Tool.

    Width (the same size as the rear doorway)

    Opacity: 100%.

    Flow: 100%.

    Hardness: 0%.

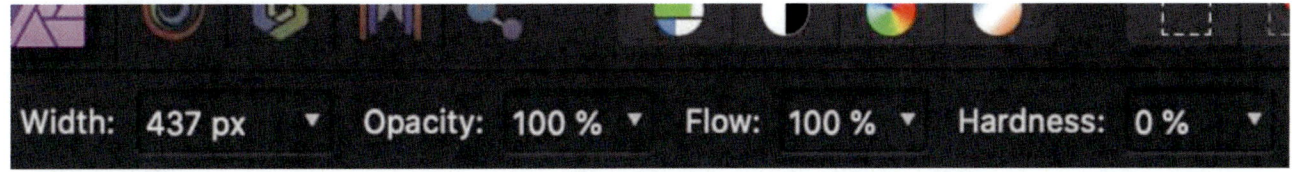

Note: Your Width will most-likely not be the same size as ours. Just make sure the diameter of the Brush's circular cursor is the same height as the doorway and you'll be fine (see bottom image).

Important: Make sure the Mask layer is selected and highlighted in blue before continuing on.

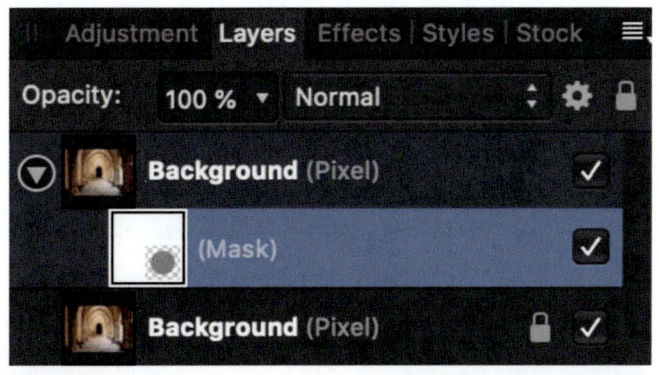

    Position the Paint Brush Tool's **circular cursor** over the doorway & *click* **one-time**. This will remove the effects of the Zoom Blur in that one area of our image.

Here's a screenshot showing you the size of what your Paint Brush Tool's cursor should look like before you click on it.

Done. This is the end picture of Part I. The image looks great and it only took a few steps to create the cool effect. Take a look at back hallway behind the back doorway. It's clear and in focus, whereas the rest of the image has the High-Speed effect added to it.

Do not delete your work. In Part II, we'll be continuing on with our lesson.

Part II

In this second part of this tutorial, we're going to create the same effect, but with the ability to tweak it as we want to. This will be different from the first method because the first method simply adds a one-time paint dot on a mask to remove the blur effect and reveal the original image beneath.

This second method gives us more control over the effect and is a preferred technique.

To keep this as simple as possible, we'll start where we left off, but we'll want to undo the last step we took in Part I, that is, the one-time click in the doorway.

Here are the steps we'll take:

> *Press* **Ctrl/Cmd+Z** one-time to **undo** the last move where we *painted* in **black** to reveal the layer beneath. This will allow us to continue with the same Layers Panel as in Part I.
>
> *Click* on the **preview thumbnail** (the white box on the Mask layer) to make the Mask layer highlighted in blue (we've added a red square around the preview thumbnail. You need to remember what this is for future tutorials).
>
> *Go* to the **Tools** & *select* the **Gradient Tool**.

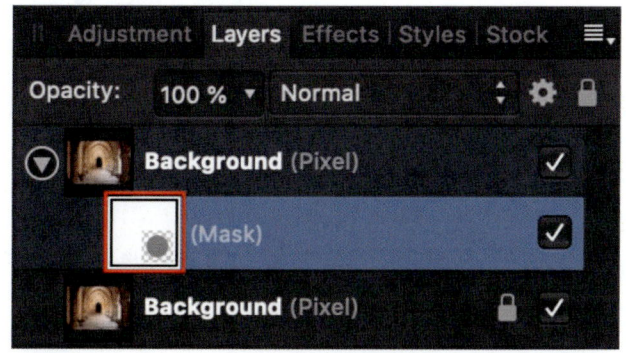

> *Click* & *drag* a **gradient line** starting in the middle of the doorway extending out into the hallway (see our image for reference).

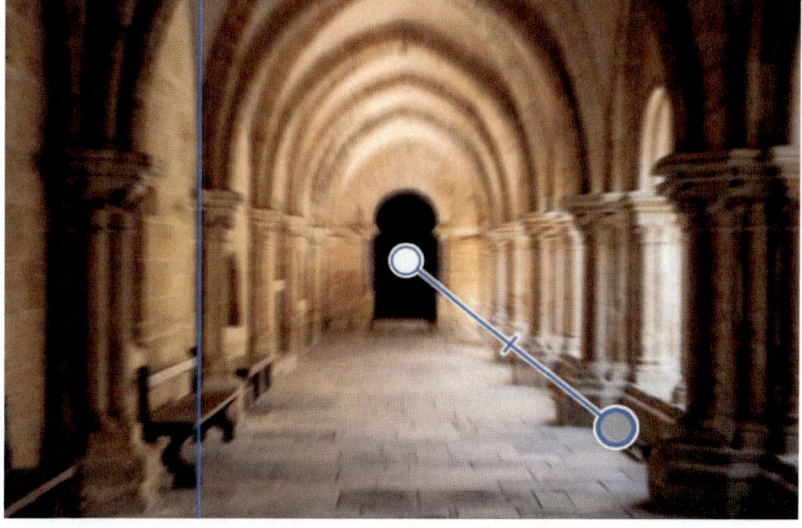

Right now, our gradient line is going from white to gray. The white node acts the same ways as if we were painting on a mask with white. It means the blurred effect is fully visible in the doorway. Likewise, the gray node (the middle color between white & black) affects the blurred effect only partially (or 50%).

What we are going to do now is that we want to make the white node black (to remove the blurred effect) and make the gray node white (to retain the blurred effect). We can do this by simply clicking on each node and by using the Color Wheel, change each node's color to the color we want.

Ready to get started changing the colors (with their effects) of the two nodes?

The gray node is bigger than the white node, which means it's selected, so we'll start with it.

Go to the **Colors Studio** & *double-click* on the **gray circle** (see yellow square). This will open a pop-out window called Color Chooser.

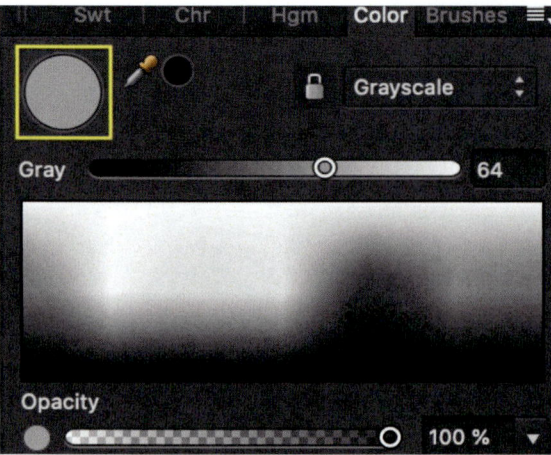

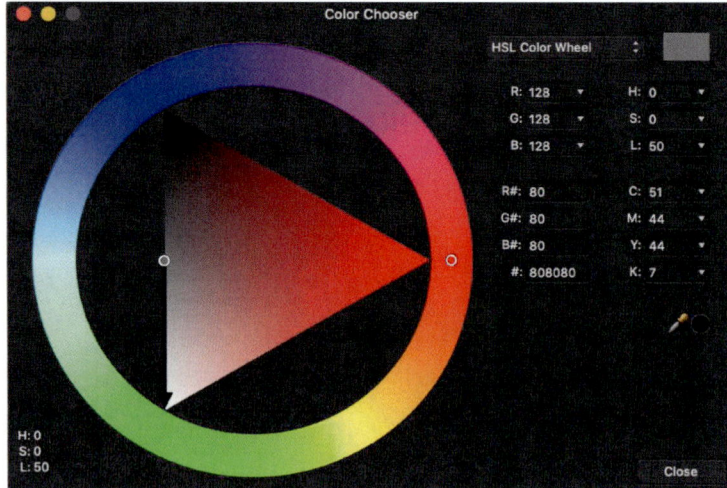

Move the **inner node** straight down to the white area of the inner triangle. This will change the gray node to white (see black arrow in the above image for this action).

Press **Close** when done.

Let's do the same thing for the white node in the middle of the doorway.

Click on the **white gradient node** so it appears bigger.

Go to the **Colors Studio** & *double-click* on the **white circle** (see yellow square).

Move the **inner node** straight up to the black area of the inner triangle. This will change the white node to black (see white arrow for this action).

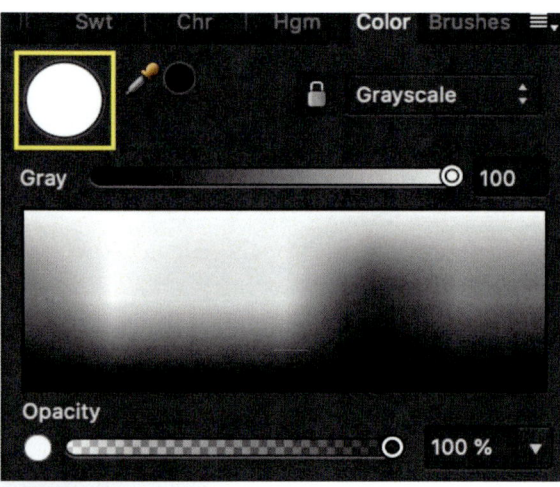

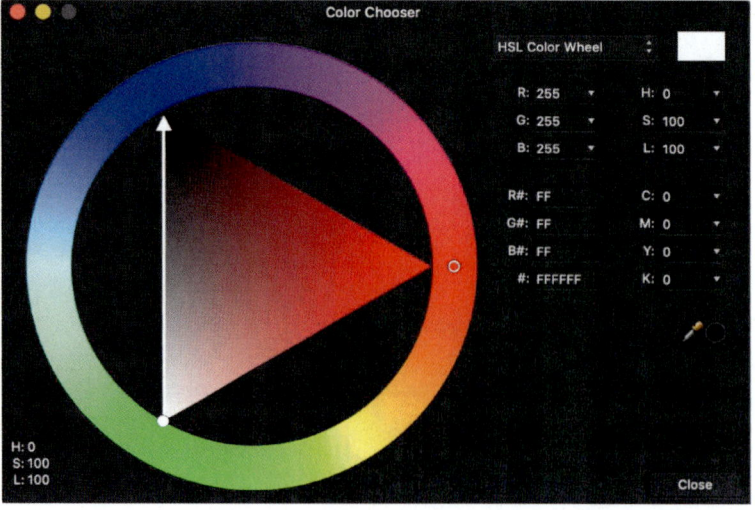

92

This is what our image looks like now. Notice how the blurred effect is gone in the middle and still visible where the gradient node is white.

The next step is to change the type of Gradient. This will give us the look we want.

Go to the **Contextual Toolbar** & *click* on the drop-down menu for **Type:** (see yellow rectangle).

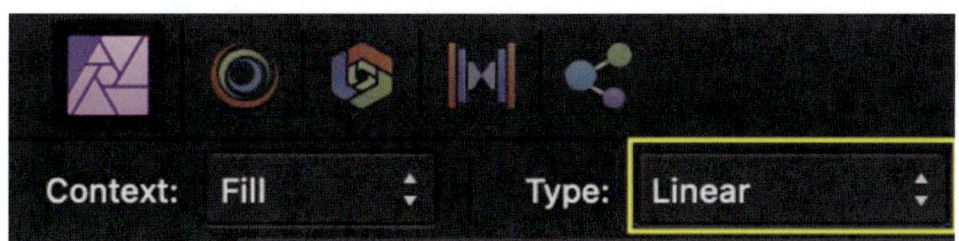 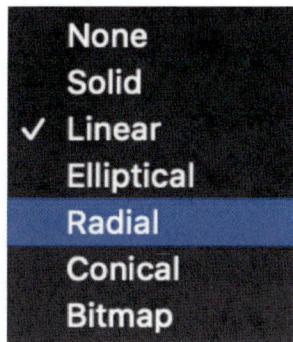

By changing the type of gradient to Radial, we now have total control over the strength of our blur effect.

Let's show you instead of trying to explain what we mean. First, we'll show you how you can make the blur effect less strong. These will be our two final images.

> *Click* on the **white gradient node** & *move* it **towards the black node**. You'll see that the blurred effect gets stronger.

Now, let's do the opposite:

> *Click* again on the **white gradient node** & *move* it **off the edge of the image**. Now the blurred effect has been greatly reduced.

Finished. This ends this tutorial.

Review of Masks

In our professional opinion, learning how to use masks is a vital part of learning Affinity Photo. If you are an experienced editor, please feel free to skip this quick review.

We know that when you learn a new skill, a lot of the time the new information comes at you so quickly that it's hard to really let the info sink in. To help you as much as we can, we want to review briefly the previous tutorial from a different perspective.

At top of the last page there is an image of the hallway and the gradient nodes.

Let's discuss what's going on in this image and break down its different parts.

- In the 1st step of the tutorial, we uploaded the image of the hallway, which was all "in focus".
- In the 2nd step, we added a Motion Blur layer, which covered the entire image with a blurriness.
- In the 3rd step, we added a Mask to the Motion Blur layer.
- In the 4th step, we selected the Paint Brush Tool and started painting in black to remove the blur.
- In Part II, we changed the Gradient nodes to black & white (which has the same effect as changing the Paint Brush black & white).

What happens to the layer we are currently on when we not only apply a mask to it, but also paint in black?

Answer: We are effectively deleting the current layer we are on to reveal the layer (see Layers Panel) below.

That answer is for Part I. In Part II, we are affecting the current layer (the Motion Blur layer with its mask) by using the Gradient nodes. The black node in the middle reveals the "in focus" layer below it, while the white node retains the blurriness of the current layer.

A) So, what happens if the white node is kept closer to the black node? _____

B) What happens if the white node is moved further away from the black node? _____

                Answers:

                A) The strength of the Motion Blur is greater.

                B) The strength of the Motion Blur is lessened.

Author's Note: When we first started learning Affinity Photo, it took us a better part of a year to understand what a mask was. It seemed the different online instructors always assumed we newbies instinctively knew what masks could do. Sorry for the redundancy on masks in this book, but, if we had to redo our training, learning what masks are and how to use them would be the first skill we'd teach ourselves. We hope we've done an adequate job in preparing you as you make your start with this amazing software.

Tutorial 7: How to Create a Dispersion Effect

Here is the webpage for the image we'll be using in this tutorial:

https://www.pexels.com/photo/selective-focus-photography-of-monk-during-meditation-2421467/

Make a **selection** of the monk.

Click on the **layer** & *press* **Ctrl/Cmd+J** two times so the layer is duplicated twice. We should now have three layers in the Layers Panel.

Click on the **original layer** (it has a lock icon) & *move* it to the **Trashcan** (see our image for this action).

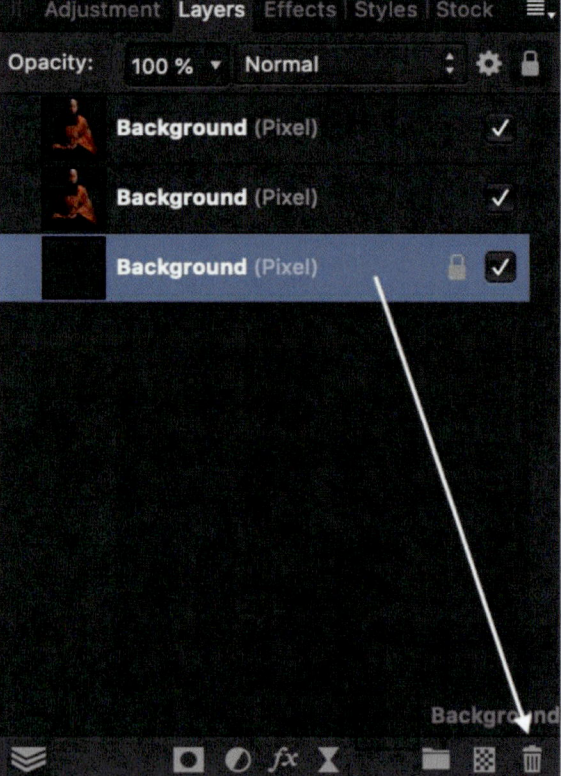

Press **Ctrl/Cmd+D** to *deselect* the dancing ants

Click on the **top layer** so it's highlighted in blue.

Click on the **Liquify Persona**.

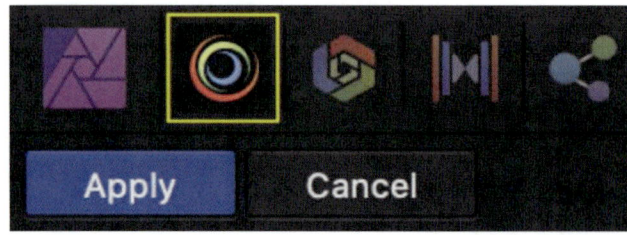

96

Click & *drag* the **Monk's image to the right**. It will look weird (see our image).

Focus primarily on the right-side.

Press **Apply** when done.

Note: When using the Liquify Persona, any adjustments you make the image takes time to master. For this lesson, plan on clicking & dragging 20 times to the right. If you feel you've made a mistake, simply press Ctrl/Cmd+Z to undo what you've done.

Like everything, practice makes perfect.

Go to the **Layers Panel** & *click* on the **top layer** so it's highlighted in blue (it should already be highlighted, but it's better to make sure).

Click on the **Mask icon** (looks like a Japanese flag).

Click on the Mask's **preview thumbnail** so just the Mask layer is highlighted in blue.

Press **Ctrl/Cmd+I** to *invert* the new Mask layer. You will see its preview thumbnail is now covered with a thick black line. The image will have returned back to its original image.

We've placed a yellow square around the preview thumbnail. Notice how there is a thick vertical black line covering the image of the monk.

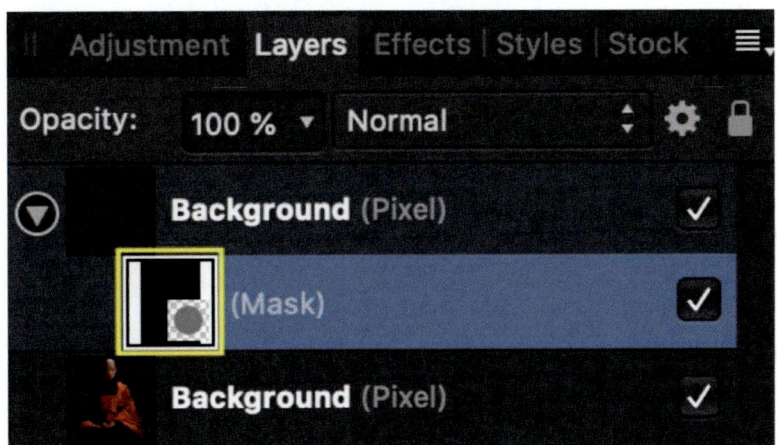

This preview thumbnail will look different from the mask we'll apply to the bottom layer. That mask will be white.

97

Click on the **bottom layer** so it's highlighted in blue.

Click on the **Mask icon** to create a new Mask layer. We will not invert this mask.

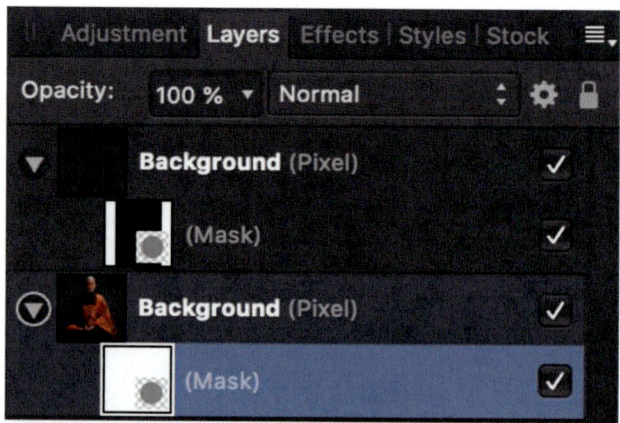

Click again on the **bottom Mask's preview thumbnail** so it's highlighted in blue (see image).

Select the **Paint Brush Tool**.

Go to the **Color Panel** & *click* on the **Brushes Tab**.

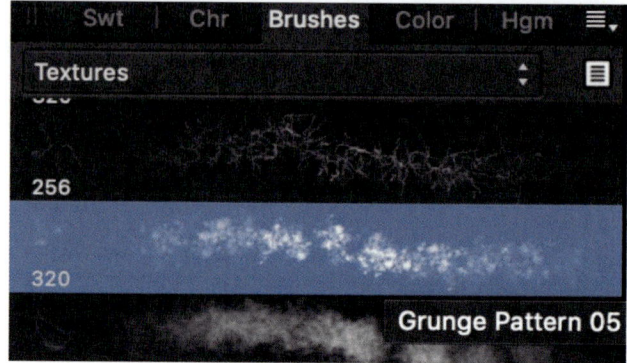

Scroll down to **Textures** & *select* **Grunge Pattern 05**.

Click on the **Color Tab** & *set* the **Foreground** to *black*.

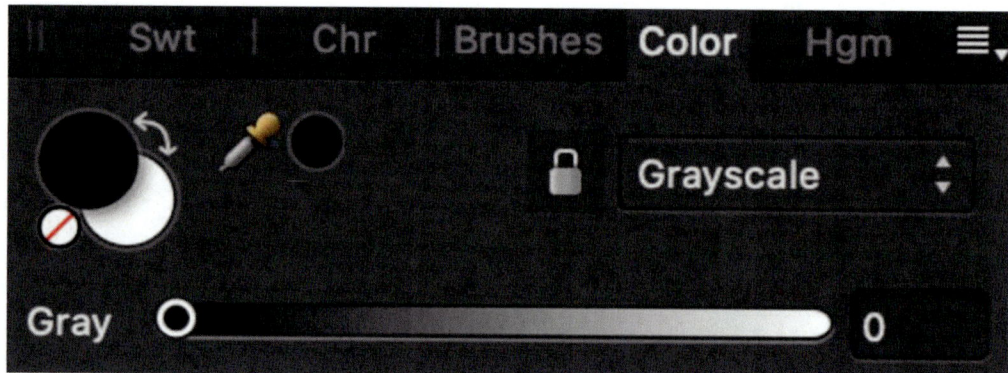

Note: When you paint in black, you will make the look like it's disintegrating a bit. The black paint on the mask removes the parts of the image you paint on revealing a transparent background.

Paint over the **right-side** of our monk. Feel free get as creative as you want.

Go to the **Contextual Toolbar** and *vary* the **size** of your Paint Brush's **Width**. The different sizes of disintegration paint strokes will make the effect look better.

This is what we've done to our image:

Now, we want to bring back some of the monk we removed. To do this, we'll click on the top layer's mask preview thumbnail and paint in white.

Click on the **top layer's mask preview thumbnail**.

Change the **Foreground** color to **white** (or simply *press* **X**).

Paint over the **areas of the monk we've painted over** to remove parts of the monk, as well as paint to the right of the monk to create the right-going disintegration effect.

Go to the **Contextual Toolbar** and *change* the **Width** of your Paint Brush. The different sizes of disintegration paint strokes will make the effect look better.

This our disintegration effect.

Note: When you paint, don't click & drag the paint brush cursor. Instead make single mouse-clicks to bring back a portion of the disintegrated monk we use the Liquify Persona for.

Once you are done creating your dispersion effect using the paint brush strokes, we'll want to add a background to our photo. You are free to choose the color of your choosing. We will make our background color gray.

To do this:

Click on the **Rectangle Tool** and *click* & *drag* a **rectangle over the entire image**.

Click on the **top Rectangle layer** & *move* it to the **bottom** of the Layers Panel (see the image for this action).

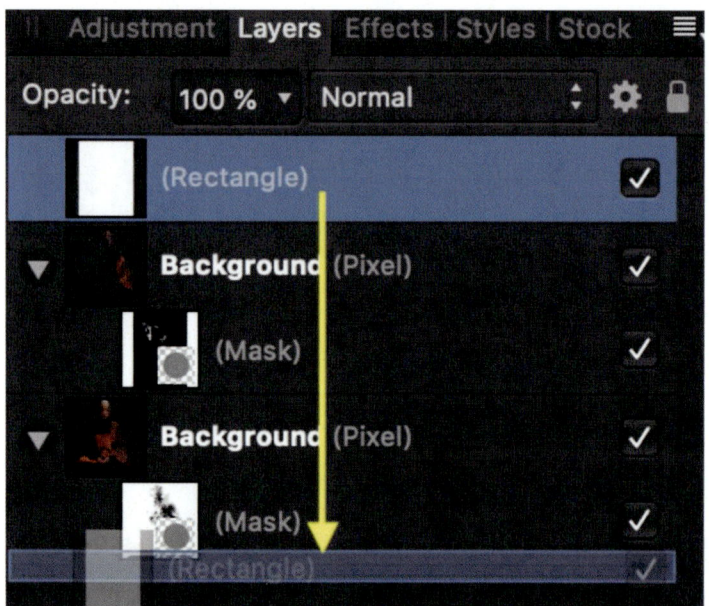

Click on the **bottom rectangle layer** so it's highlighted in blue.

Go to the **Color Studio** & *move* the **inner Saturation/Luminosity node** halfway up to make its color gray (see yellow arrow for this action).

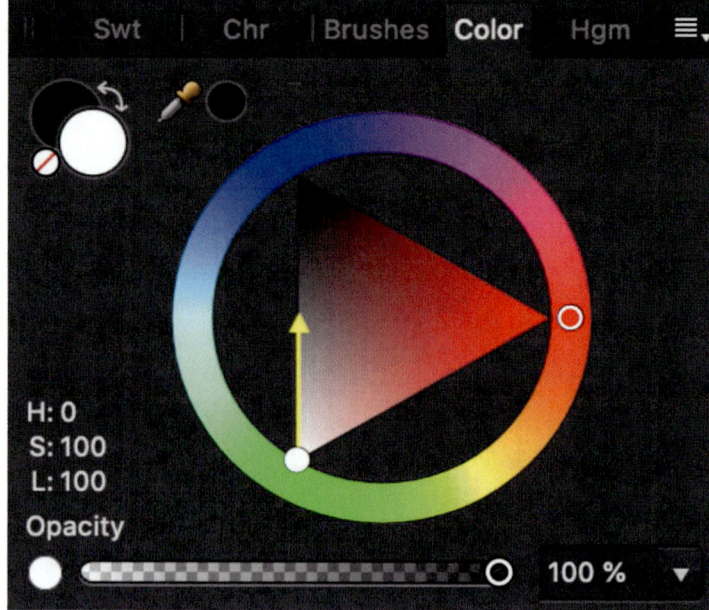

Done. This is our final image.

Finished. This ends this tutorial.

To you the reader: Please send us your creations. If you follow the steps we've provided, you can change your image, use different brushes and patterns, and probably do a better job than we can. Please email us and let us share with you your new skill.

Tutorial 8: How to Create a Face Warp

In this tutorial, we are going to learn how to create a funny face warp (or a Caricature).

Here is the webpage to the image we'll be using for this tutorial:

https://pixabay.com/photos/model-female-girl-beautiful-woman-429733/

Ready?

Open the **image** onto the canvas.

Press **Ctrl/Cmd+J** to *duplicate* our image.

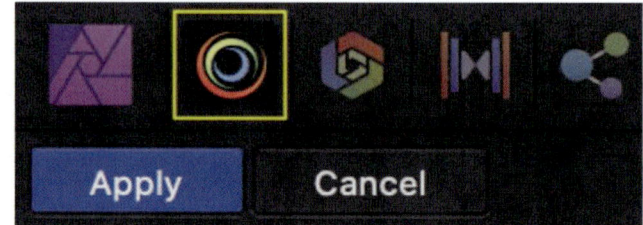

Click on the **Liquify Persona**, like we did in the tutorial above.

Look to the right of the User Interface (UI) and see the three vertical panels.

These are **Mesh/Histogram**, **Brush/Navigator**, and **Mask**.

In the Mesh/Histogram panel:

Uncheck the **Show Mesh button**. We don't need to see this to do our technique.

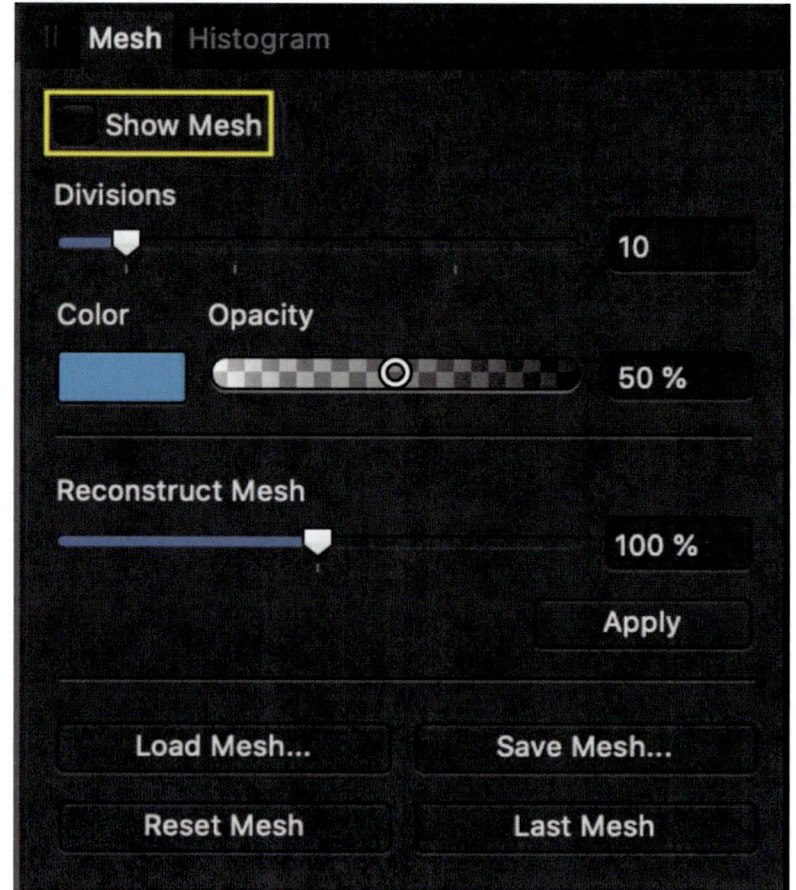

102

In the Brush/Navigator panel:

Press **Ctrl/Cmd+0** (zero) to *fit* our image into the screen. For this step, make sure your Affinity Photo screen is maximized on your computer's screen.

Move the **Size** to **350 px**.

Move the **Hardness slider** all the way to the left so its value is **0%**.

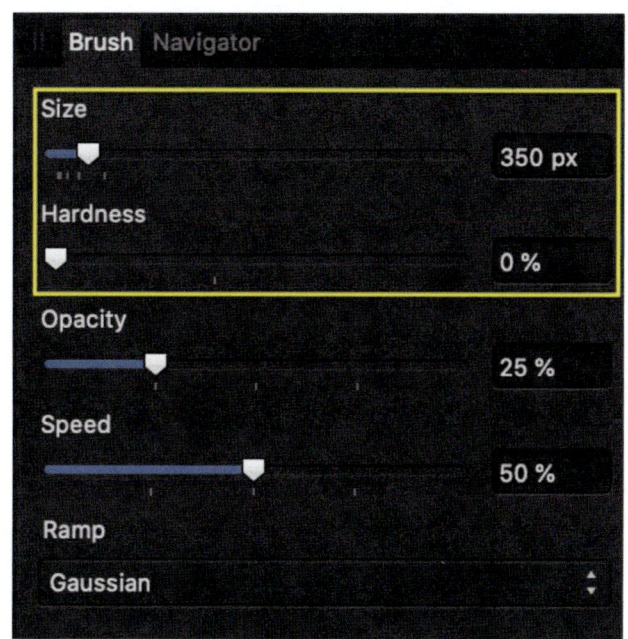

Now, we can begin warping her face.

Click on her **hair over her left eye** (our right side) & *move* **it to the right away from her eye**.

Note: This action of warping this image is exactly the same mouse cursor movements as the previous tutorial. Take your time and click on the hair and move it just a bit to the right.

This is what we've done:

Click on the **Liquify Pinch Tool**. This will allow us to make things bigger just by *clicking* & *holding* the **mouse button**.

103

Move the **Speed slider** from **50%** to **100%**. Otherwise, using this tool takes way too much time.

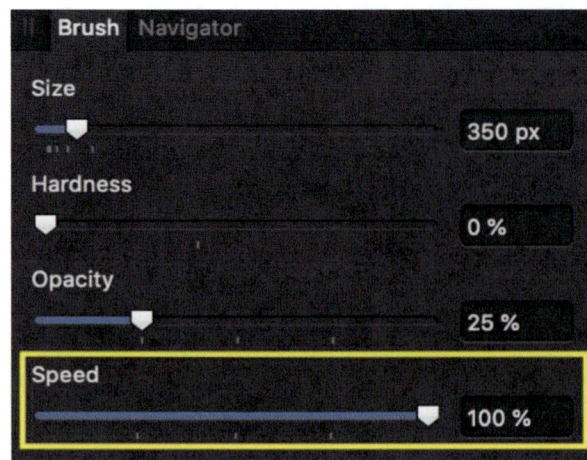

This is a really funny tool. We clicked on both eyes and I swear she looks like a human-bug hybrid. Her eye on our right side got a bit distorted, so we released the mouse button, pressed the Option/Alt button and clicked & held our mouse button again. This time, because we were also holding the Option/Alt button, her eye got smaller.

Click & *hold* the **mouse button** over the mouth and the nose to your liking. At this point, this technique is totally personalized. It doesn't matter how your image looks in comparison to ours.

Done. This is our final image. The bug woman, herself.

Finished. This ends this funny tutorial.

Tutorial 9: How to Create a Beautiful Pop Art Effect

In this lesson, we`re going to learn how to make a beautiful pop art effect.

Here are the webpages for the images we'll be using for this image (a woman and a granite background):

      https://pixabay.com/photos/woman-model-young-model-fashion-2381628/

      https://pixabay.com/photos/kennedy-stone-background-ground-3740228/

Ready?

Ok, let's begin by opening the images we are going to use for this tutorial onto the Affinity Photo canvas. We'll start with the image of the woman. Have that in front of you so we can begin.

    Click on the **Adjustments icon** & *select* **Threshold**.

    Adjust the **Threshold** slider to **40%.**

    Exit out of the **pop-out window** by *pressing* the **red X**.

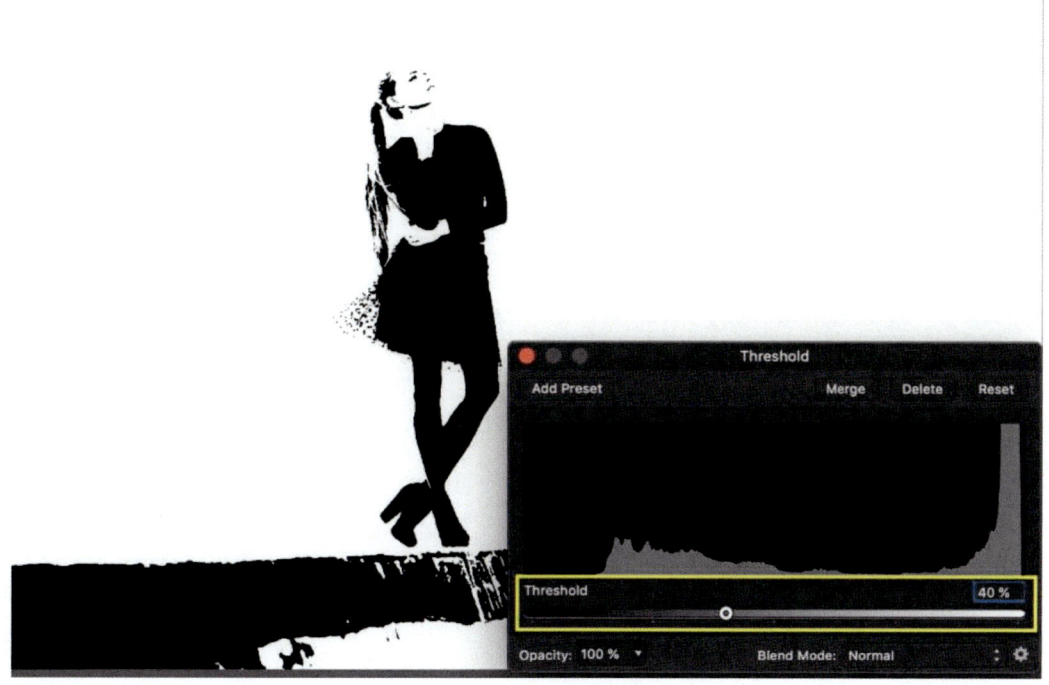

Note: Using the **Threshold** adjustment makes the image **black & white**. Moving the slider to the right & left changes the image.

    0% makes the image entirely **white.**   **100%** makes the image entirely **black**.

For this effect, we want to make it so the woman is the only thing that's **black** in this entire picture, and everything else is **white**.

That means, everything surrounding her needs to be *painted* white.

To do this:

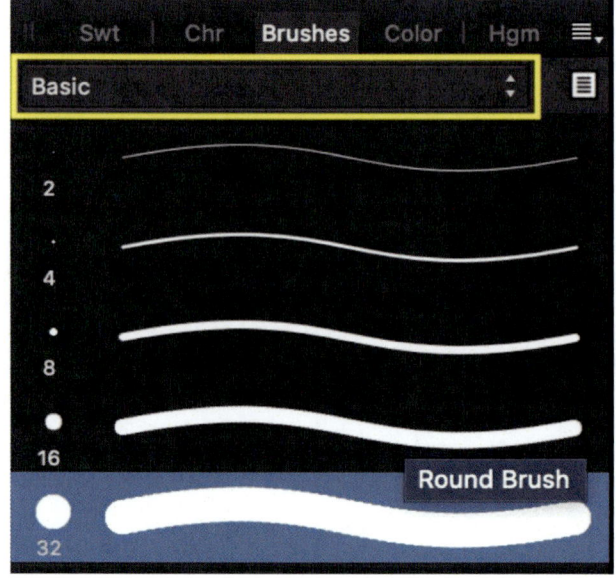

Select the **top layer** so that it's *highlighted* in **blue**.

Click on **Add Pixel Layer** (located next to the **Trashcan**).

Select the **Paint Brush Tool** (or *press* **B**). Make sure you've changed the Paint Brush back to a Basic brush. If not, go to the Brushes Tab in the Colors Studio and click on the types of brushes drop-down menu (see yellow rectangle) and select Basic.

Press **X** to *change* the foreground color to **white** (see Color Panel to check if the **white** circle is on top of the **black** circle - **X** is the keyboard shortcut to switch these two foreground & background colors).

Go to the **Contextual Toolbar** and *set* the **Hardness** to **100%**.

Adjust the **Width** of the brush to about the 1/3 the height of the woman.

Paint in **white** to cover the lower object she is standing on. Take your time and do a good job. If you make any mistakes, simply *press* **Ctrl/Cmd+Z** to *undo* your error.

Press **Ctrl/Cmd + 0** (zero) when you're done to see the entire picture on your canvas.

We are half way done. Next, we want to add some color to the image.

To do this, we'll be adding a Gradient Map.

Ready?

> *Click* on the **Adjustments icon** & *select* **Gradient Map**...

In the pop-out window you will see the color bar colored **Red** - **Green** - **Blue** (with different shades in-between).

Here, you need to look at the line going through the colors and the three circles on it. We want to delete the **green** circle. To do this, *click* on the **green** circle (see the **black** square) and *press* the **Delete** button that's inside the pop-out window (white square).

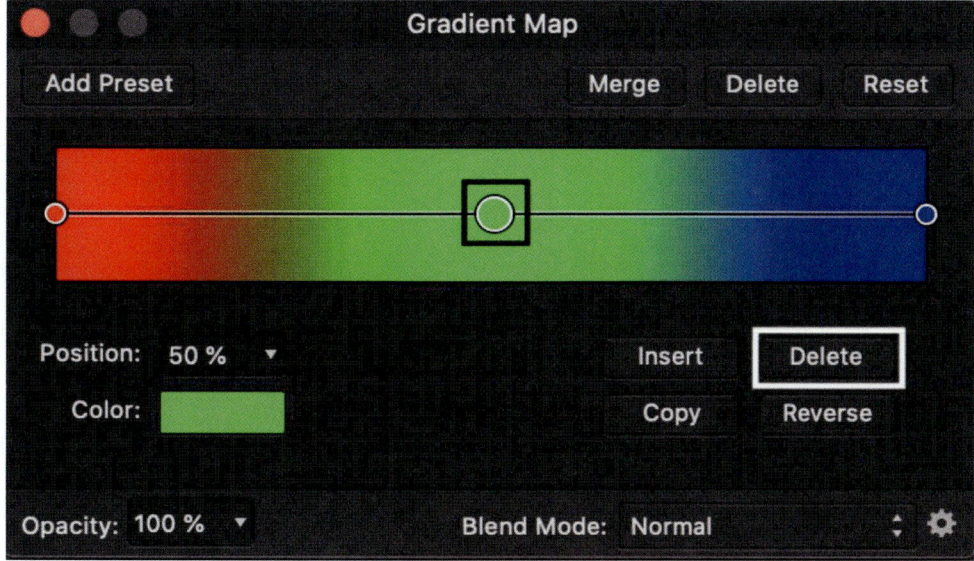

Now, we want to **Reverse** the Gradient. *Press* the **Reverse** button underneath the **Delete** button (see image above). This will change the places of the **reds** & **blues** in the image (see image here).

Note: To save space, our images are not the entire image as we have it on our canvas.

The **Gradient Map** has made it so everything that was **black** in our picture has now become **blue**, and everything that was **white** has become **red**. If we want to, we can change these colors. We personally like the red/blue look, but for practice we'll change the red to a hot pink and the blue to black.

Double-click on **preview thumbnail** on the top Gradient Map layer and the pop-out window will reappear.

Click on the **right red node** (white square) so it's larger than the blue node.

Click on the **Color Box** (green rectangle) and the Color Wheel will pop-out.

Move the **Hue node** to the hot pink color (see yellow arrow for this action).

Let's *change* the **blue** color to a black.

Click on the **left blue node** (white square) so it's larger than the pink node.

Click on the **Color Box** (green rectangle) and the Color Wheel will pop-out.

Move the Color Wheel's **inside node** straight down to make to black (yellow arrow).

Press the **red X** to *close* these windows.

108

Our pop art effect is just about done. As a finishing touch though, let's add a little bit of texture to our picture

Click on the **tab** for the second image for this tutorial.

With the Granite image in front of you...

Press **Ctrl/Cmd + C** to *copy* it.

Click again on the **image** of the woman.

Press **Ctrl/Cmd + V** to *paste* the granite image on top of it.

Select the **Move Tool** (or *press* **V**) and *resize* the **granite image** so that it's covering the entire picture.

Then we're going to change this granite's **Opacity** from **100%** to **10%**. You will see the woman under the granite layer. This has now added a nice little bit of texture to our image.

Hint: To change the Opacity of a layer, simply have that layer selected and press 1 for 10%, 5 for 50% and 0 for 100% Opacity.

This is what our image looks like now:

Finally, let's **Crop** the girl so we have less pink background.

Select the **Crop** Tool (or *press* **C**).

Move the **Crop's Thirds Grid** and line up the woman on one of the vertical lines like how we have it.

Press **Apply** when satisfied.

Done. This is the final image.

Finished. This ends this tutorial.

Tutorial 10: How to Create a Pop Out or 3D Effect

Creating 3D effects that make it look like different cool objects are literally coming out of computer and smartphones is a favorite edit of most photo editors. The limits of creativity are limitless.

In this fun tutorial, we'll be making a horse jump out of a laptop's screen (see our image on this page).

Here are the hyperlinks to the images we'll be using in this tutorial. Have them downloaded before we start.

https://pixabay.com/photos/horse-horseback-riding-721136/
https://pixabay.com/photos/footpath-pathway-rural-green-road-691021/
https://pixabay.com/photos/home-office-workstation-office-336373/

This is the final image we'll be creating. We think it looks impressive.

This tutorial has four parts:

Part I: Make the screen of the laptop transparent.

Part II: Make a selection of the top part of horse that is clearing the hurdle.

Part III: Import the footpath image onto the laptop's image.

Part IV: Import the selected horse image and place it in the computer screen to finish the effect.

Part I: Make the screen of the laptop transparent.

Please have the image of the laptop in front of you.

> *Click* on the **Pen Tool** and *go* to the **Contextual Toolbar** and make sure the **Mode** is clicked to **Pen Mode**. It's the first button.

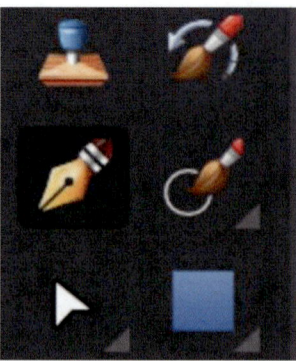

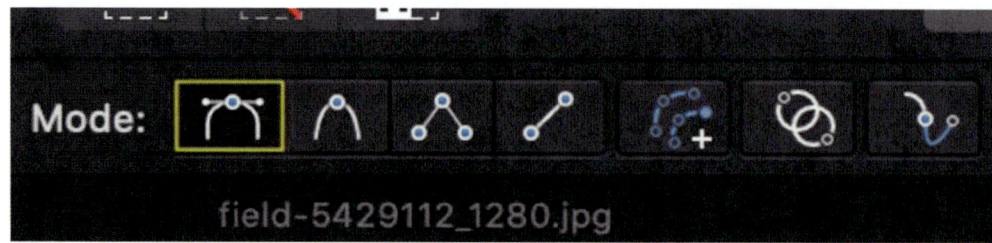

For this part of this lesson, what we need to do is to use the Pen Tool and create four nodes at the four corners of the screen just outside the screen itself. We don't want our lines created by the four nodes to come too close to the screen, nor do we want to have the lines inside the screen. This is because after we have used the Pen Tool to make this selection, we will cut out the screen area and make it transparent. We make it transparent so we can add any picture inside of it that we want to.

Take a look at this image. Think to yourself which lines (or nodes) are done correctly, and which are not.

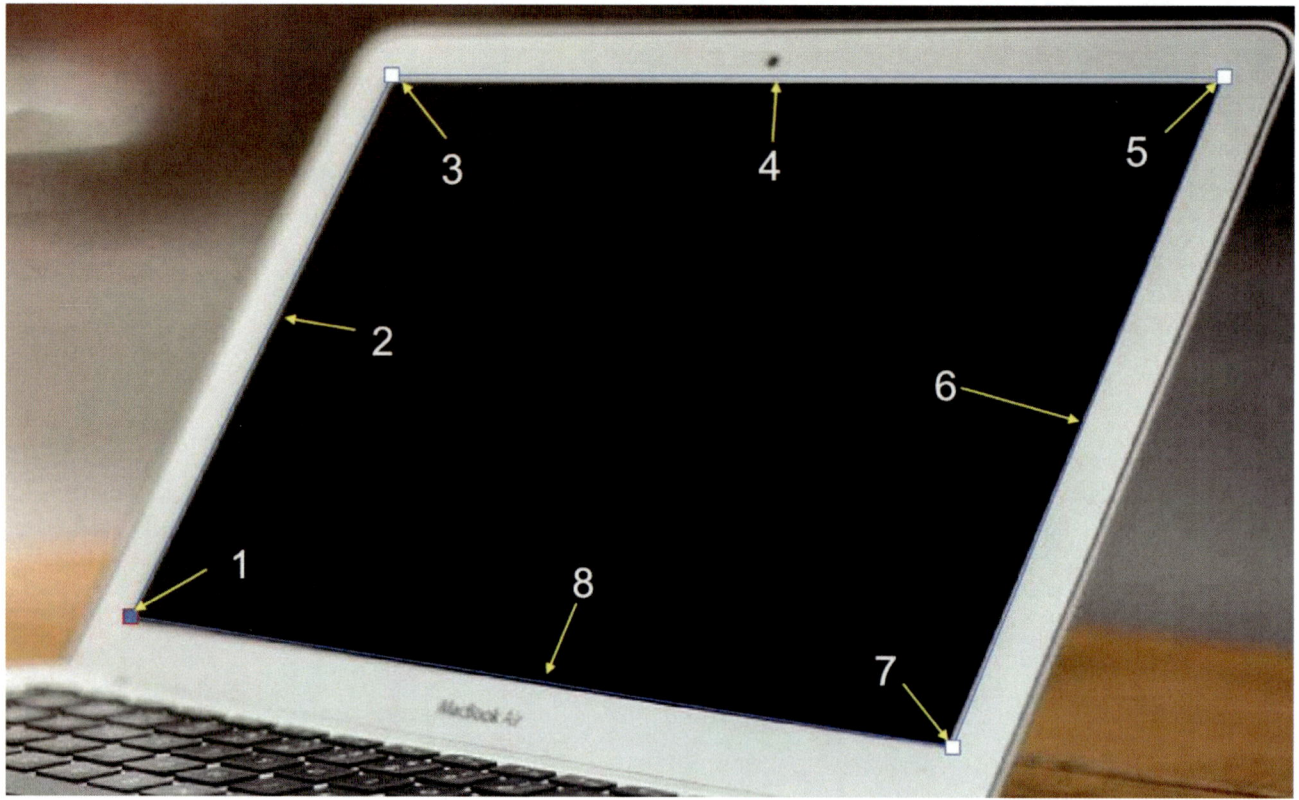

Answer: **Node 1** is too close to the screen, which makes its line (8) it shares with **Node 7** go over the screen area.

To fix this:

Click on the **Node Tool** and *click* & *drag* **nodes 1 & 7** a bit further away from the screen's corners. Make sure line 8 is outside the screen area like lines 2, 4, 6 already are.

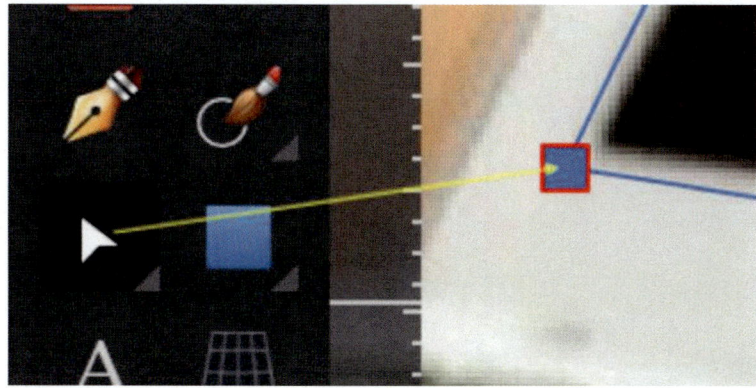

Is there any other part of our screen image that could be worked on?

Maybe line 4 is a bit too high off the screen. To fix this, again use the Node Tool and lower the Nodes 3 & 5 just a bit. But, for this lesson, Line 4 is ok where it is.

With the lines completed, all we need to do is *go* to the **Contextual Toolbar** & *click* on **Selection**. This will create a selection of the screen we just used the Pen Tool with.

Note: If you skip this step, the technique will not work. Whenever you "make a selection" you will see the typical 'dancing ants' move around the selection. Make sure you see these 'ants' after you've pressed **Selection**.

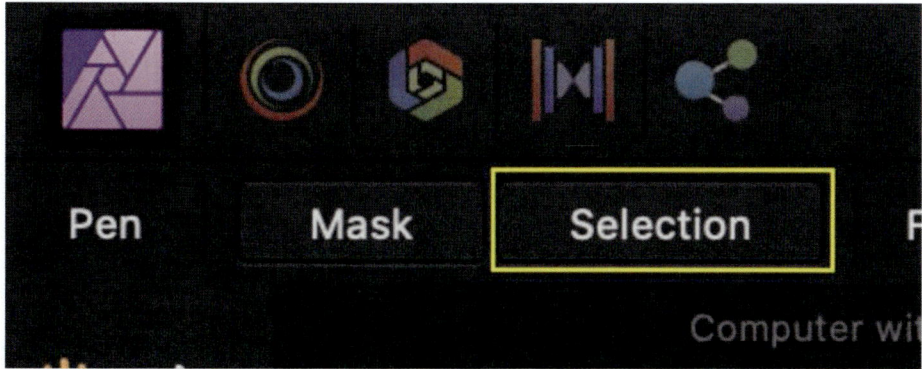

Because the selection we made is directly in the middle of our image, we need to invert our pixel selection so it differentiates itself from the whole of the image.

Go to the **Menu bar** - **Select** - **Invert Pixel Selection**.

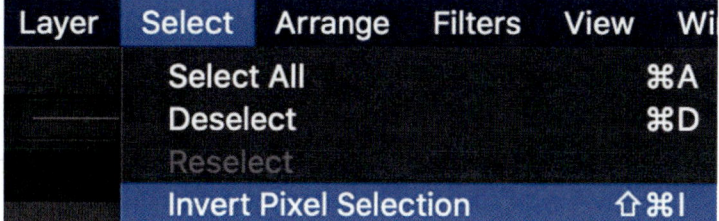

113

Note: When you invert the pixel selection, you will see that the dancing ants have attached themselves to at least one of the four borders of the image. Most of the time, these adhere to only one side, but in this tutorial, the dancing ants decided to adhere to three of the four sides.

Click on the **Mask icon** and this will *remove* the **screen area** and make it **transparent**.

Press **Crtl/Cmd+D** to *deselect* the dancing ants.

This is what our image looks like now:

We are finished with Part I. Please click on the tab for the horse image.

Part II: Make a selection of the top part of horse that is clearing the hurdle.

Click on the **Selection Brush Tool** & *adjust* its **Width** to about the size of the horse's left foot.

Check the box to activate the **Snap to edges** option on the Contextual Toolbar.

Set the **Mode** to **Add** (see left part of this image and how Add is depressed).

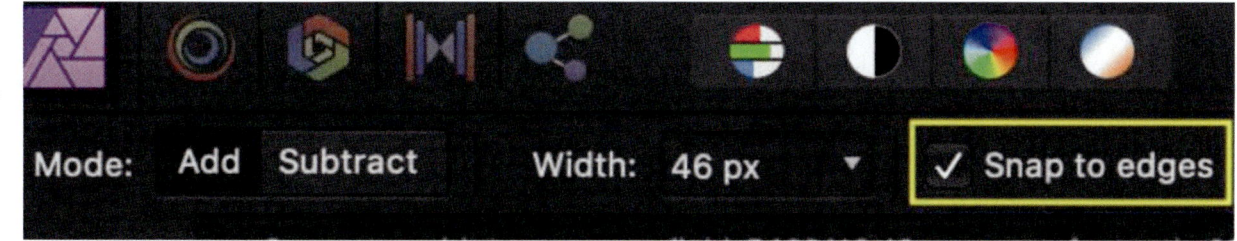

Click & *drag* a **selection** over the horse and woman for the parts that are above the hurdle.

Note: The yellow arrows represent areas of the horse image that the Selection Brush missed. Because of this, we'll need to use the Refine Selection Tool located on the Contextual Toolbar. Do you see any other areas of the horse we missed?

Answer: If you noticed the shadowed area directly underneath the horse's left hoof, you'd be correct. We'll address this area soon.

 Go to the Contextual Toolbar & *click* on **Refine...** to *refine* the missed areas our Selection Brush missed.

Here is a screenshot of where we painted over our image. You should do the same. It isn't important to paint over the entire horse with one click & drag like we did. We only did it this way to be able to show you where we used the Refine Selection Brush in one image. Normally, we will paint over small sections of our subject.

After we *pressed* **Apply** in the pop-out window for the Refine Selection Brush, we were shown what our image looked like afterwards.

If you look closely at your image after you've pressed Apply, you will notice that there are some dancing ants inside your woman's & horse's bodies. To remove these glitches, simply hover your cursor over these spots and click once with you mouse. This will remove these leftover 'ants'.

To illustrate what we mean, we've added white circles to the image to mimic the Selection Brush Tool that is already activated. These are the areas on our woman/horse that have these leftover 'ants'. By clicking one-time in the areas of our white circles, these 'ants' will disappear.

Note: When using the one-click method near the border of the image (see woman's helmet and lower back), make sure the inside of the brush's cursor not touching the dancing ants. This will cause the selection to be skewed.

Yellow Circle Note: After you've used the Refine Selection tool and have one-clicked away the annoying leftover ants, to remove portions of the selections all you need to do is hold-down the Option/Alt button and click one-time where the yellow circle is (again, it represents the Width of your Selection Brush Tool). When you hold down the Option/Alt button and click, you're telling Affinity Photo that you want to do the opposite of what your chosen tool normally does.

Pro Tip: Using the Option/Alt button while working on photos greatly increases your workflow speed.

This is what our selection looks like now after these tweaks we did on the previous page. Much cleaner!

Now, we want to remove the background from our image so everything will be transparent. With that image, we can simply copy & past it onto our laptop image and fit it inside the screen.

We'll remove the background in a similar fashion we used for the laptop image.

Click on the **Mask icon** and everything will disappear.

Press **Ctrl/Cmd+D** to *deselect* the dancing ants.

This is the image you should have on our screen:

That's the end of Part II. This is the image we'll be placing inside the laptop screen to finish out 3D effect.

Part III: Import the footpath image onto the laptop's image.

This step is simple.

Click on the **footpath image's** tab so the image is in front of you.

Press **Ctrl/Cmd+C** anywhere on the canvas to *copy* this image.

Go to the **laptop image's** (or the home-office) **tab** and *press* **Ctrl/Cmd+V** to *paste* the footpath's image on top of the laptop image.

When we copy & pasted our footpath image on top of our laptop image, the field image covered 95% of the image of the laptop. So, we clicked & dragged the blue nodes of the footpath image so it covers the entire laptop image.

We moved and shrank our image(s) so they fit next to our Layers Panel and we could take one screenshot to show you what our image & Layers panel looks like.

Look at the Layers Panel. Do you see the bottom layer? It has two preview thumbnails on one layer. This is because it is a grouped layer. If you click on the circled-triangle on the left-side of its layer, it will open up and show its two layers. Here is a screenshot of what this looks like. Notice how in the image below the circled triangle is a bit different looking than in the image above.

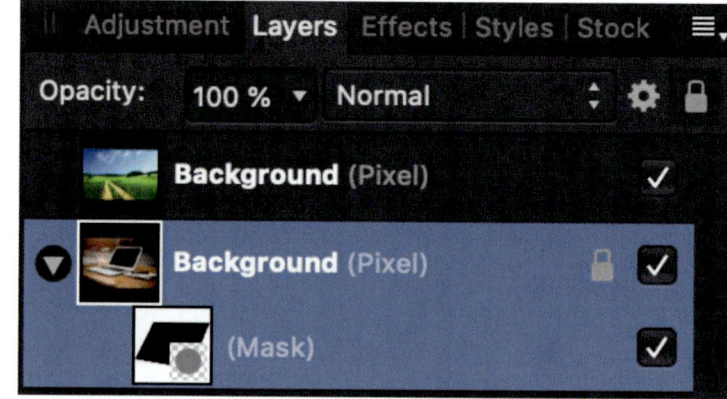

To get the top layer, the footpath image inside of the laptop's screen, all you need to do is...

Click on the **top footpath layer** & *drag* it **below the grouped layer**.

This is what you Layers Panel should look like now:

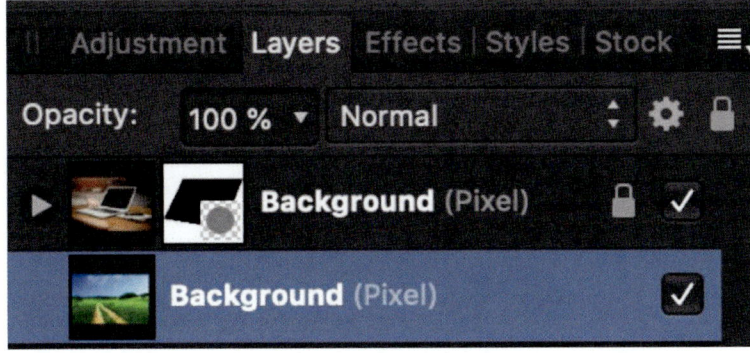

Note: When you click on the bottom footpath layer, you can use the blue nodes that surround its image to resize & reposition the image however you want it.

This is an image of the blue nodes you can use to resize & reposition your image:

We are done with Part III.

Part IV: Import the selected horse image and place it in the computer screen to finish the effect.

This last part is very similar to Part III. Ready?

Click on the **horse image's tab** with its transparent background.

Click on the **top layer** in the Layers Panel so it's highlighted in blue. This is a very important step!

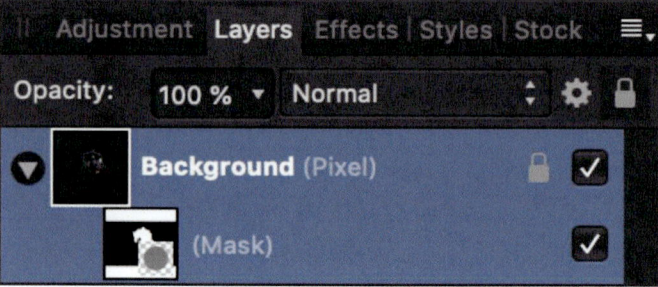

Press **Ctrl/Cmd+C** to *copy* it.

Go to the **laptop image's tab** & *press* **Ctrl/Cmd+V** to *paste* the horse's image on top of the other images.

Move the **horse's layer** to the top of the Layers stack.

This is what our Layers Panel should look like now:

The tutorial is almost completed: All we need to do now is adjust the positioning of the field and the horse.

We'll start with the horse.

Click on the **Move Tool** (or *press* **V**) to *resize* & *reposition* the image of the horse.

This is where we've moved ours. Try to match what we have.

122

Now, we need to remove the parts of the horse that's covering the outside of the laptop. To do this, we'll use the Erase Brush Tool.

Note: When using any brush in Affinity Photo you can paint precise straight lines by clicking one-time in one position and then holding-down the Shift key press the mouse button one-time and the brush will affect the area between you two mouse clicks in a perfectly straight line. We will use this brush technique now.

Click on the **Erase Brush Tool** & *click* **one-time** right below the left-bottom corner of the laptop's screen. Now, as you move the cursor to the right where the horse's legs are covering the laptop, the Erase Brush Tool will reveal what's hidden by the horse.

While this method is one of our favorites, there's a more precise way to remove the horse's image from the laptop. Make sure the top horse layer is highlighted in blue before you do this next step.

Click on the **Opacity slider** & *reduce* the **Opacity** of the horse's layer to **50%**. This will allow us to use Erase Brush Tool with greater precision (the lower image shows this change in Opacity).

We've marked out image with a yellow rectangle to show you the precision we could have in using the shift-erase-in-a-straight-line technique.

Now, with the edge of the horse/screen done, we can use freehand to use the Erase Brush Tool to remove the rest of the horse from in front of the laptop.

When you are done painting away the horse, don't forget to click make the Opacity 100% when done.

Note: When Opacity is selected, if you press 0 (zero), the Opacity will change to 100% and if you press 5, the Opacity will change to 50%.

This is final Layers Panel (notice how the Opacity is back to 100%).

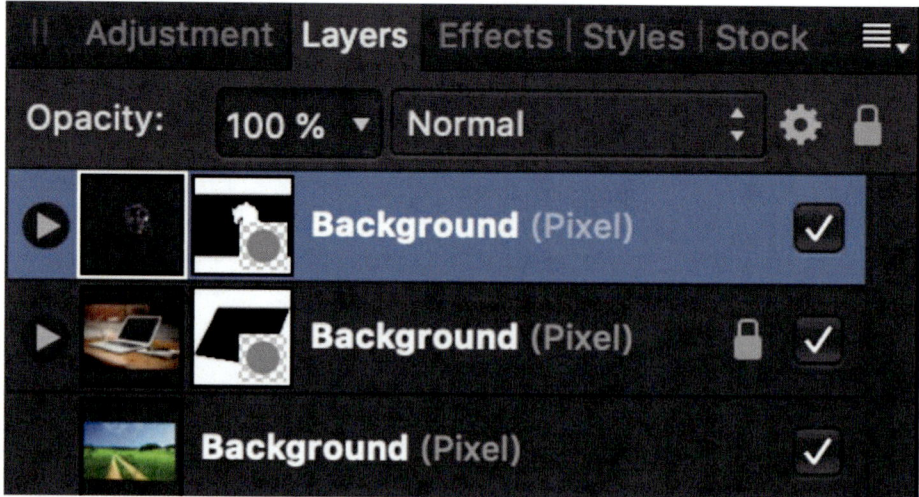

As a final touch, we clicked on our footpath/field layer to resize & reposition it to fit what we personally prefer. Feel free to manipulate yours however you want.

Done. This is our final image.

Finished. This ends this tutorial.

Tutorial 11: How to Create a Water Flame Candle

In this tutorial, we're going to learn how to create a water flame candle.

Here are the webpages to the images we'll be using for this tutorial:

https://affinityrevolution.com/candle/2590837/

https://pixabay.com/illustrations/water-splash-png-2748695/

Ok. Ready?

Upload these images to Affinity Photo and let's start.

Click on the **Water Splash** image and *press* **Ctrl/Cmd+C** (to *copy*).

Click on the **Candle** image and *press* **Ctrl/Cmd+V** (to *paste* it on top of the Candle image).

Select the **Move Tool** (or *press* **V**) to *resize* & *move* the splash on top of the candle (left image).

Click on the **top white node** & *turn* the **splash image** 90° counter-clockwise (right image).

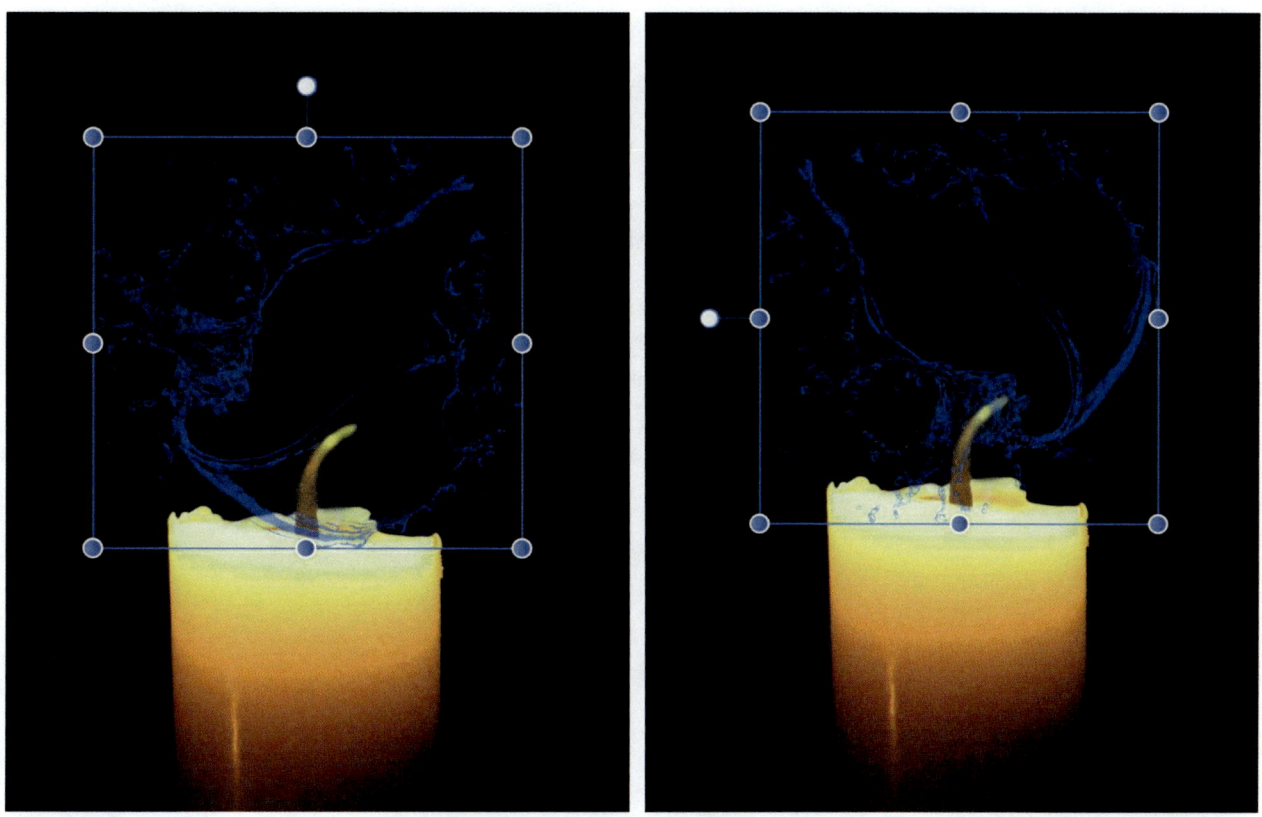

125

Now, we want to *flip* the Splash so it'll look better as a water flame.

Using the **Move Tool**, *click* on the water flame image and *right-click* your mouse.

Choose **Transform - Flip Horizontal**.

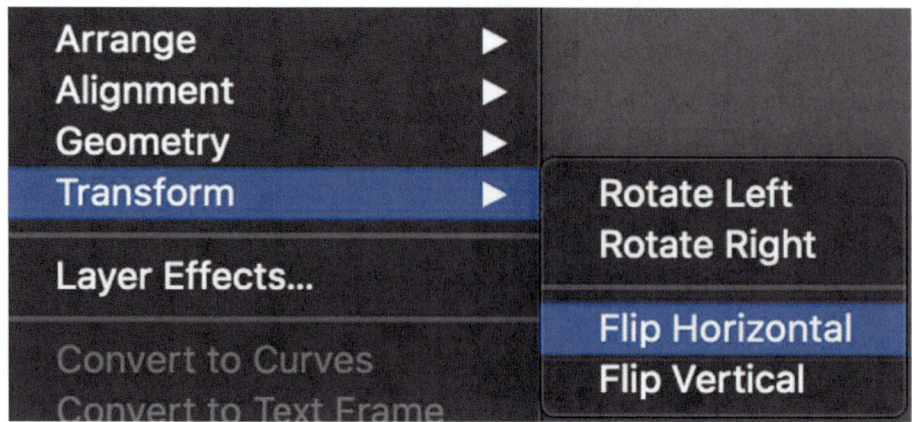

To make the flame look even more realistic, we need to remove some of the excess water we don't need. To do this:

Click on the **top layer** so that the **Splash Background** is *highlighted* in **blue**.

Click on the **Mask Layer** icon (looks like a Japanese Flag).

Click on the **preview thumbnail** on the Mask layer so the Mask layer is *highlighted* in **blue**.

Select the **Paint Brush Tool** (or *press* **B**).

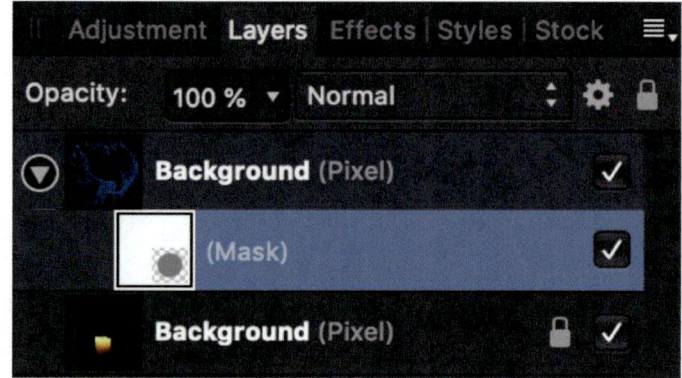

Set the **Foreground** color to **black** (use the shortcut X to alternate between the white & black foreground positions).

Go to the **Contextual Toolbar** and *set* the **Hardness** to **0%**.

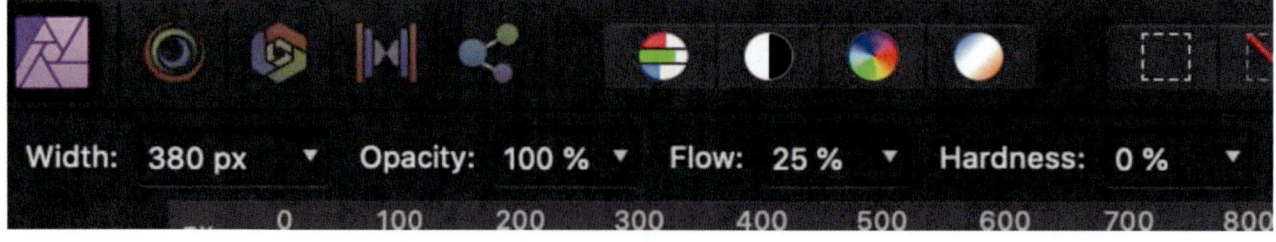

126

With the **Mask layer** *selected*, the **foreground** set to **black** and the **Hardness** set to **0%**, *paint* over the left side of the water splash so only the big flat section remains.

This is what your water splash should look like:

With the wick going to the right and the water splash going in the opposite direction, maybe we should switch the splash again.

>   *Click* on the **top layer** so it and the Mask layer are highlighted in blue.
>
>   *Click* on the **Move Tool** (or *press* **V**).

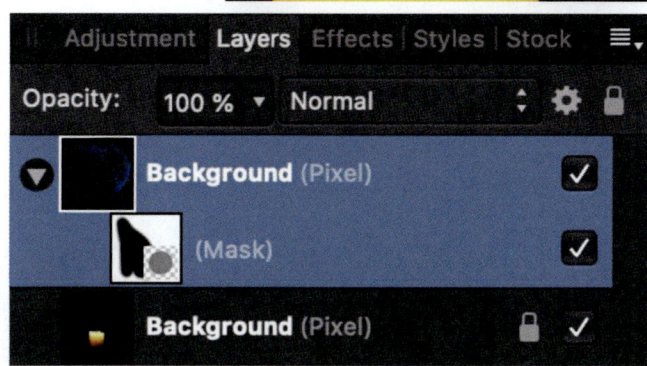

>   *Click* on the **Splash image**, which is over the candle. Immediately, the Move Tool nodes will surround the splash image.
>
>   *Right-click* on the splash and choose **Transform - Flip Horizontal**.

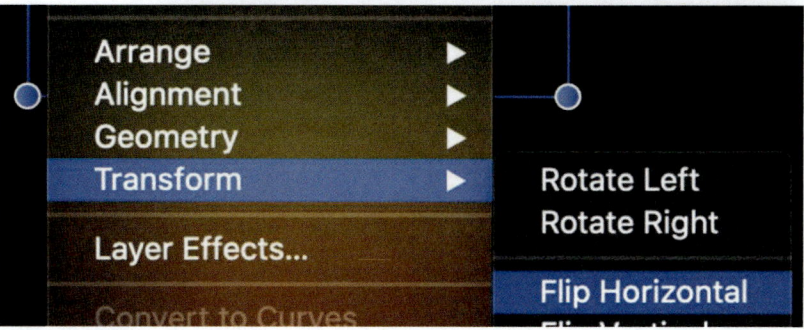

Now, we're just going to paint away some of the water splash we don't need for the image we want to create and to make it look as realistic as we can make it.

To do this:

>   *Click* on the **preview thumbnail** on the Mask layer so only the Mask layer is highlighted in blue. We do not want both top layers selected. Only the Mask's layer.
>
>   *Press* **B** for the **Paint Brush Tool**.

Set the **Foreground** color to **black**.

Go to the **Contextual Toolbar** & *adjust* **Flow** to **15%**.

P*aint* carefully over **some of the bottom of the water** to make it look like the water flame starts someplace in the air (like a real flame would).

Select the **Move Tool** & *reposition* the newly changed water splash over the candle's wick.

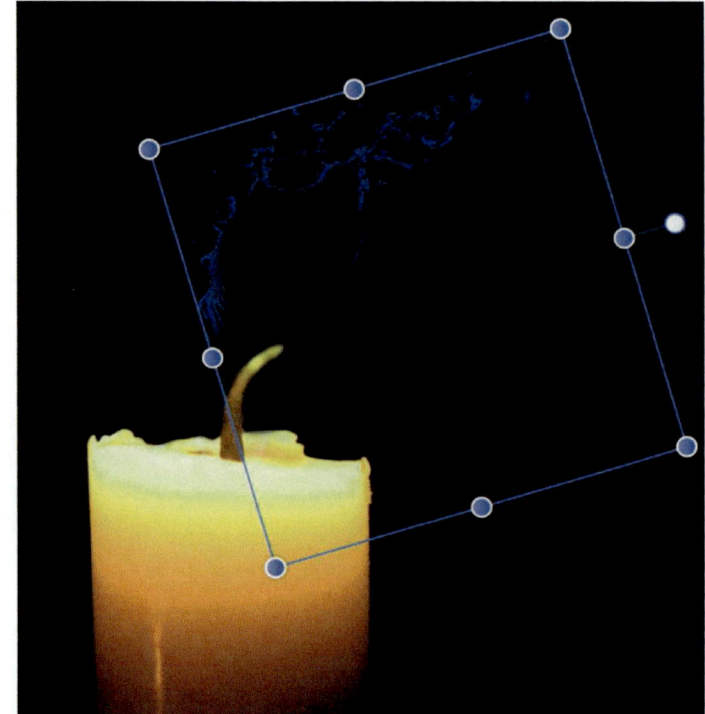

Now that we have the flame where we want it, let's change the candle's color to more of an **aqua-blue**.

To do this:

Click on the **Adjustments icon** & *select* **Recolor**.

Adjust the **Hue** to **190** & the **Saturation** to about **25%**.

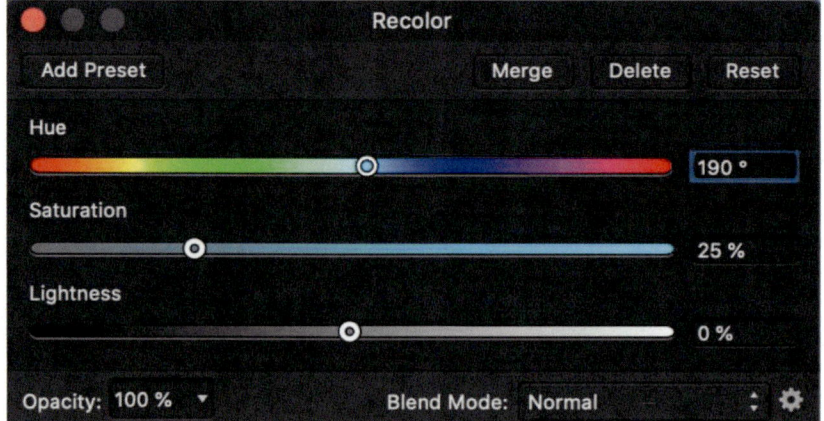

Using the **Recolor Adjustment** has affected the color of the splash, but we only wanted to change the color of the candle. So, we need to now move the top **Recolor Adjustment** layer so that is below-and-to-the-right of the candle layer. When you make this change, you will see that the candle's color stays the same while the water splash's color will go back to **blue**.

Click & *drag* the **top Recolor layer** below-and-to-the-right of the bottom Background layer (see yellow arrow for this action and necessary positioning).

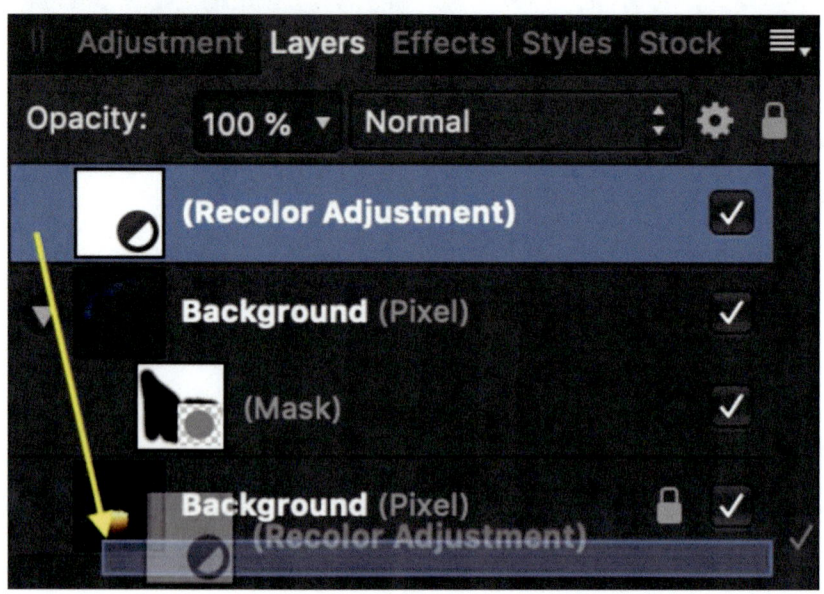

Note: Layers in this position are called Child Layers because they only affect the layer they're attached too, and no other layer in the Layers Panel.

The last thing we're going to do is add a light to our image to make it look like this candle is shining.

To do this you have to:

> *Click* on the **bottom of the Layers Panel** so that none of the layers are *highlighted* in **blue**.
>
> *Go* to the **Menu bar - Layer - New Live Filter Layer - Lighting**...

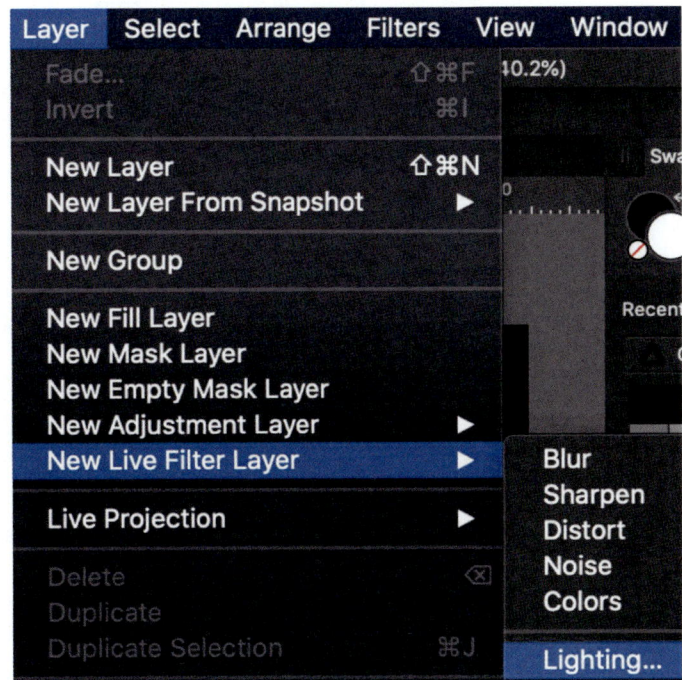

Note: Since none of the layers were highlighted in blue, the Lighting filter goes to the top of the Layers Panel. This is what we want.

This is how your Layers Panel should look like.

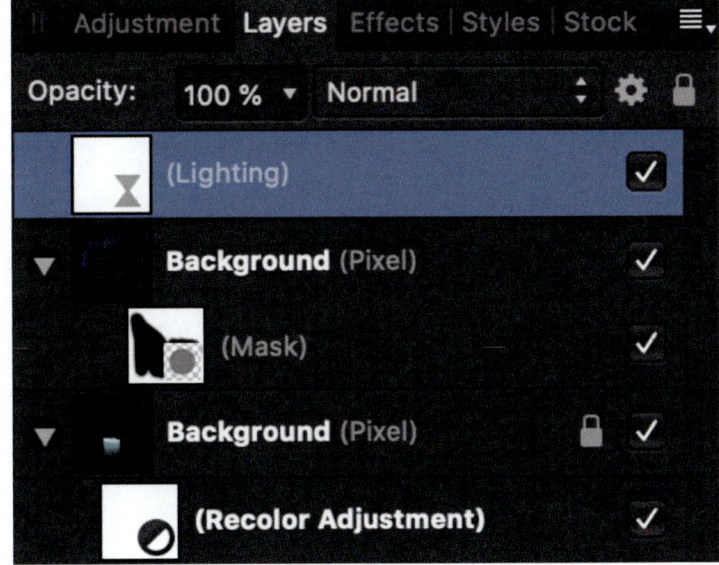

In the new pop-out window, there are many very useful things we can adjust to enhance our image. But, all we really want to do is add a glow to the middle of the candle's wick.

To add a glow to a specific place, we need to:

Change the **Type** of **Live Lighting** from **Spot** to **Point** (see **blue**-*highlighted* button).

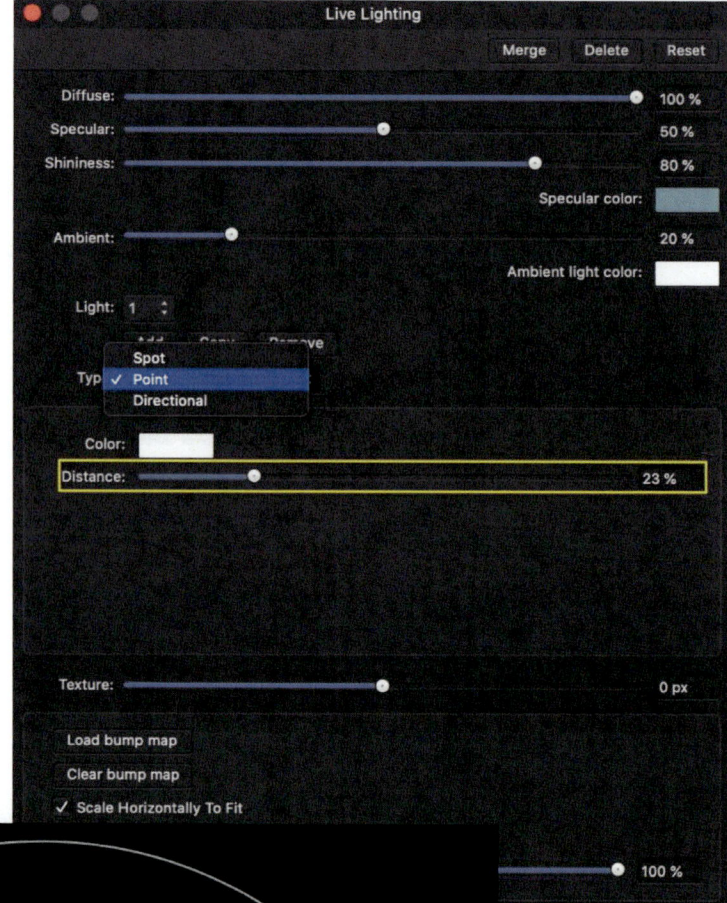

Adjust the **Distance** so the mid-point is in the middle of the wick and the circle just touches the outside of the water flame's edge. Perhaps the effect will be too bright.

Note: We placed the below image where it is on this page because the hidden information on the right image isn't important to this edit.

130

If it's too bright, we can *click* on the **Specular Color** rectangle (see **yellow** box) and *change* the glow color from a **white** to a soft **blue**.

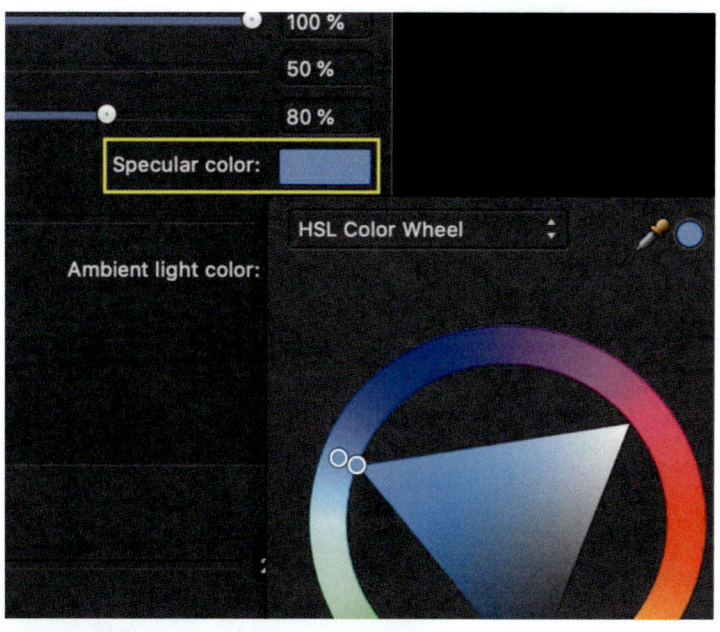

> *Click* on the **Specular color rectangle** and immediately the Color Wheel will appear.

> *Move* the **outside Hue node** to a nice soft blue color.

> *Press* the **red** button in the top-left corner of the pop-out window to close it.

Done. This is the final image.

Finished. This ends this tutorial.

Tutorial 12: How to Create a Face Swap

In this tutorial, we're going to learn how make a face swap.

Here are the webpages to the images we'll be using for this tutorial:

https://affinityrevolution.com/wp-content/uploads/2016/11/Girls.jpg

https://www.pexels.com/photo/baby-child-close-up-crying-47090/

Ok. Ready?

Upload these images to Affinity Photo and let's start.

First, we'll be working with the baby's face, so have that image in front of you.

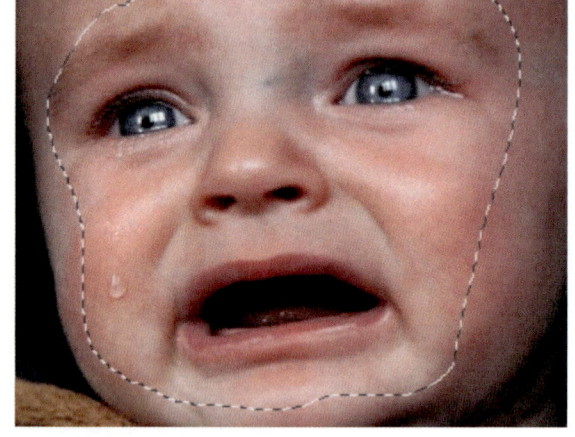

> *Select* the **Free hand Selection Tool** (looks like a Lasso). *Draw* a **selection** around the baby face - just above his eyebrows and down to his chin.
>
> *Click* on the **Refine** button on the Contextual Toolbar.
>
> *Make* sure the **Feather** is all the way up to **100%** (this makes the edges smoother).
>
> *Press* **Apply**.

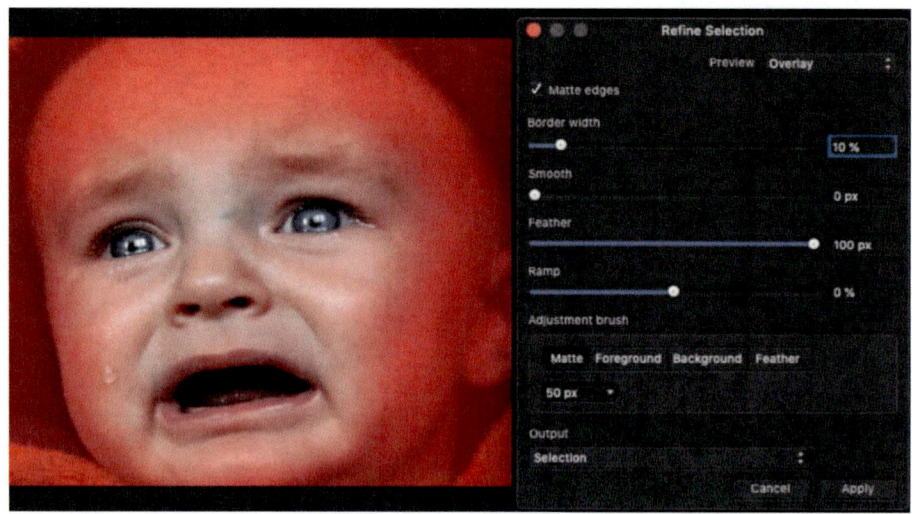

We are now going to *copy* this image of the baby's face & *paste* it on top of the image of the two girls.

Press **Ctrl/Cmd+C** (to *copy*).

Click on the **tab** with the girls' image (the different tabs are located directly above the canvas).

Press **Ctrl/Cmd+V** (to *paste*).

Make sure the top layer of the baby's face is *highlighted* in **blue**.

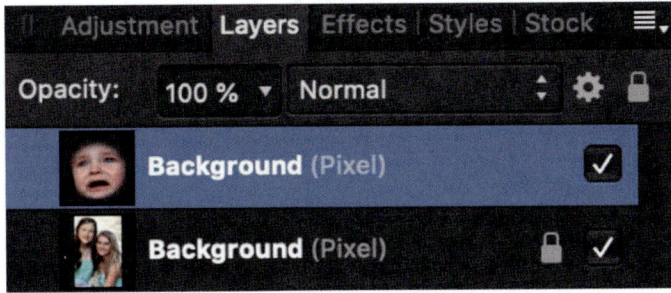

Change the **Opacity** to **70%** so we can see through it to the image below. This is an important step to do to be able to line up the top image perfectly on the bottom.

Hint: By *pressing* on numbers on the keyboard **1-0** you can quickly *change* the **Opacity** of the *highlighted* layer (**1 = 10%** and **0 = 100%**).

Select the **Move Tool** (or *press* **V**).

Move the **baby's face** over the face of the girl on the right so the eyes line up.

Resize & *rotate* the **baby's face** by using the **blue** dots around his face.

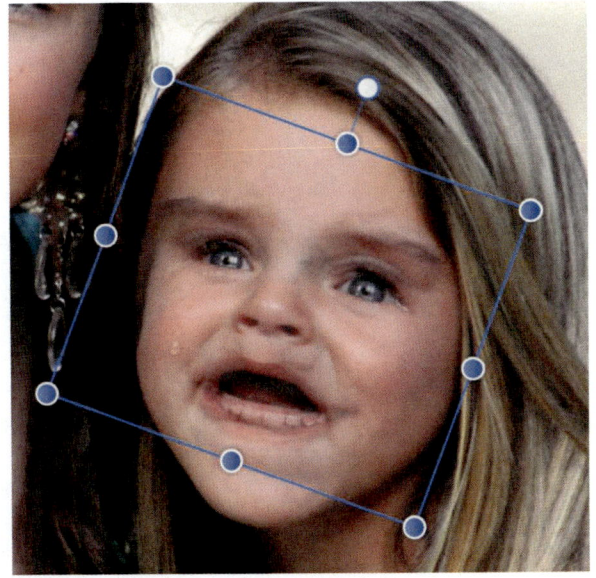

Change the **Opacity** to **100%** (by *pressing* **0** or by *clicking* on the **%** & *dragging* the slider all the way to the right).

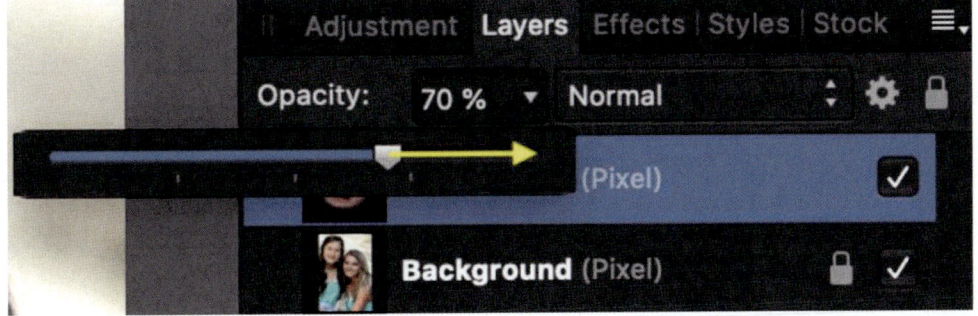

133

The result:

The image could look better because the image of the baby's face isn't blending into the girl's face as well as we'd like it to look.

In this next part, we are going to make the blending of these two images match as well as we can make them.

To match the skin tones:

> *Click* on the **Adjustments icon** & *select* **HSL**...

We only want the HSL Adjustment to affect the image of baby, so we need to move this new top layer down-and-to-the-right of the baby's face layer.

> *Click* & *drag* the **HSL layer** below-and-to-the-right of the middle background layer (see image for action).

Your Layers Panel should look like this:

We now need to see the **HSL** pop-out window again. To make it reappear (if it's gone), simply *double-click* on its **preview thumbnail**.

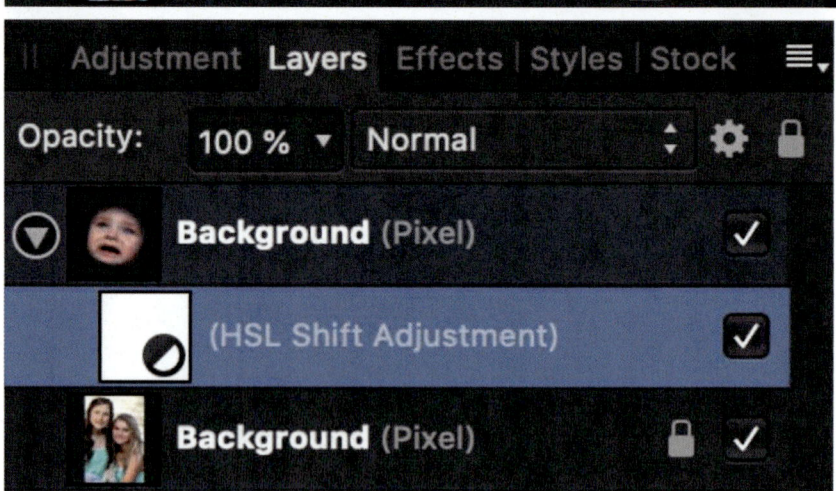

134

Once you have the HSL pop-out window open, these are the adjustments we recommend:

Slide the **Hue** slider to **-4°**.

Bring the **Saturation Shift** to **6%**.

Click on the **red button** in the top-left area of the pop-out window to close it.

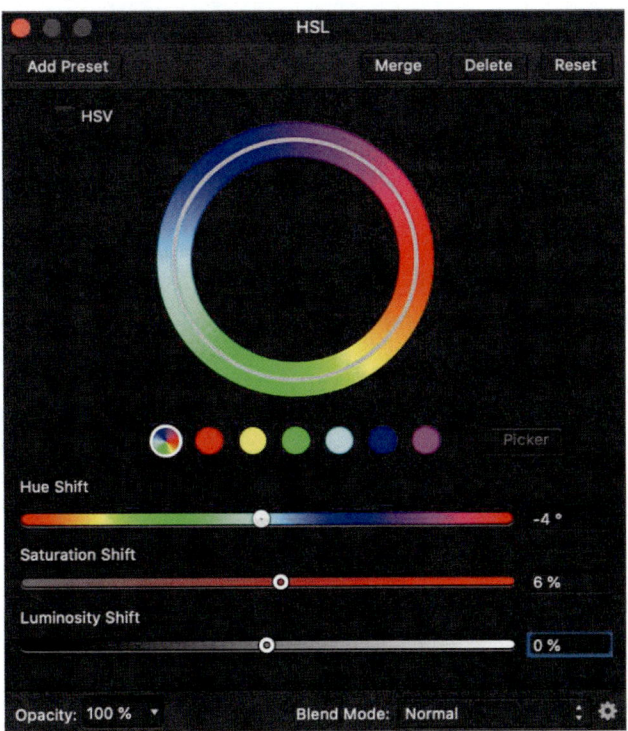

Now, we need to *change* the way the chin is blending in with the background image.

To do this:

Click on the **baby's face layer** so it's selected.

Click on the **blue nodes** around the face in the image and make the face a little longer vertically.

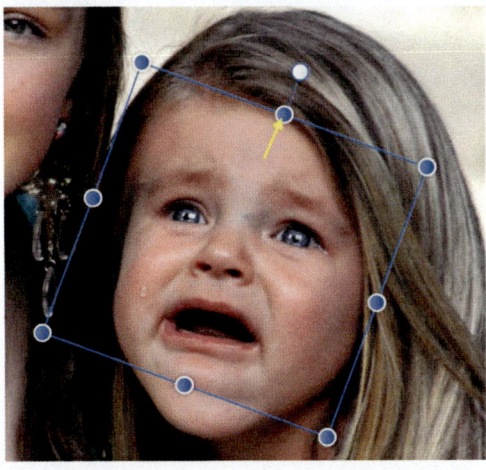

If the baby's face is bleeding off the girl's face, we are going to apply a **Mask**. When we paint to remove the girl's face, all we want to do is to gently paint over the area of the chin where there's a definite line.

To do this:

Click on the **Mask** icon.

Select the **Paint Brush Tool** (or *press* **B**).

Make sure your **foreground** is **black** (use the **X** to switch, if necessary).

Go to the **Contextual Toolbar** & *set* the **Opacity** to **50%**, the **Flow** to **100%** and the **Hardness** of the brush to **0%**.

Zoom in using **Ctrl/Cmd +** for precision.

Paint around **edges** of the baby's face.

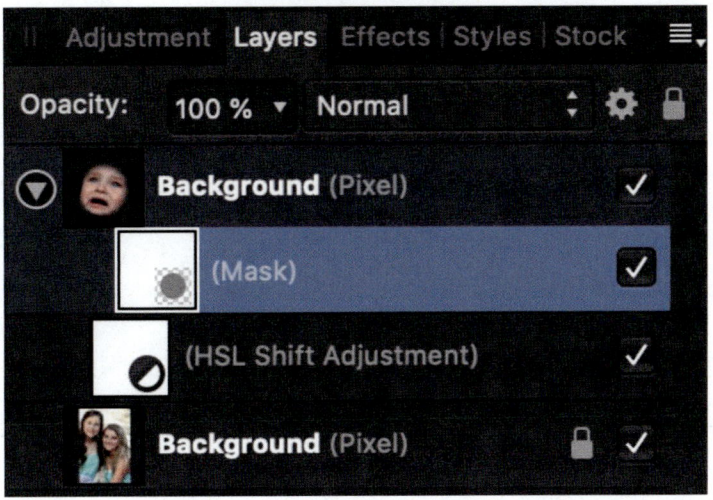

135

Here are our Before & After images:

Before **After**

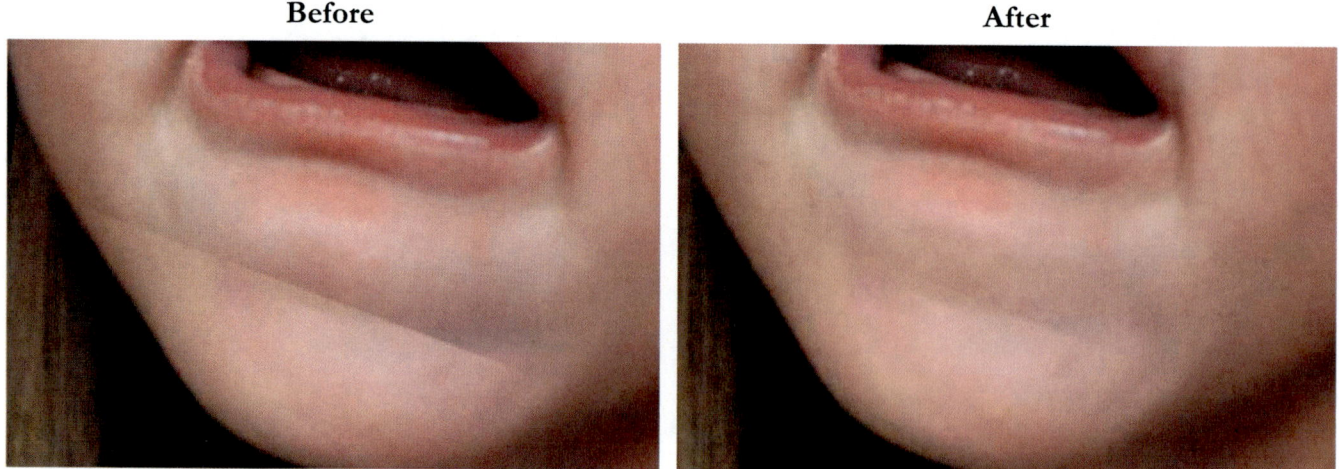

Done. This is our final image.

Finished. This ends this tutorial.

Tutorial 13: How to Crop an Image in a Circle Shape

Cropping images in different shapes is a creative way to create creative photo albums and collages, or to create family greeting cards. In this tutorial, we'll show you how to crop images in circle shapes, but you can also use what you learn here and crop in other shapes as well. The heart shape comes to mind for family cards for Valentine's Day, for example.

Here are the webpages to the images we'll be using for this tutorial:

> https://pixabay.com/photos/guitar-beautiful-music-instrument-944262/

> https://pixabay.com/photos/sunflower-vase-vintage-retro-wall-3292932/

Once you have the image of the girl uploaded onto the canvas, here's how you start (we'll use the sunflower image at the end of this tutorial to show you how you can add your newly-cropped image with another image:

Let's start:

> *Click* on the **small triangle menu icon** (yellow square) on the Rectangle Tool and in the pop-out window *select* the **Ellipse Tool**.

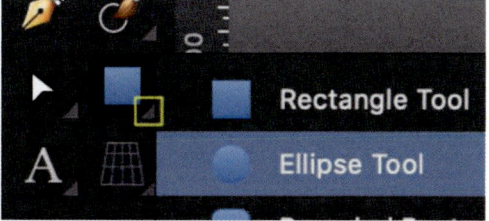

> *Hold-down* the **Shift key** and *click* & *drag* out a **circle** over the woman's head and shoulders (see our image for reference).

> *Click* on the **Move Tool** to *reposition* the white circle where you want it.

Hint: Holding-down the Shift key while you use the sizing nodes allows you to make perfectly symmetrical shapes. This holds true for your entire time working with Affinity Photo.

> *Go* to the **Layers Panel** & *click* on the bottom **Background** layer so it's highlighted in blue.

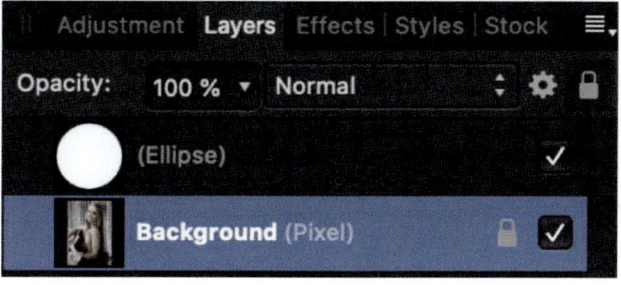

137

Move the **Background** layer underneath-and-to-the-right of the Ellipse layer. This will make it a child layer of the Ellipse layer.

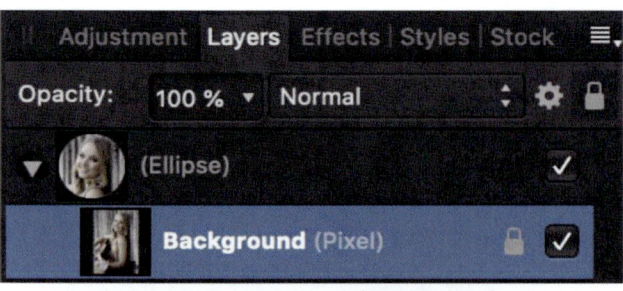

Your Layers Panel should look like this after this action. Notice how the bottom layer's preview thumbnail is positioned to the right of the preview thumbnail of the layer above it.

This is what our image should now look like:

We now have our image just the way we want it. But, we need to save our image as a .png file so that we can use this image wherever we want for current or future projects. Saving it as a .png file will keep the transparency in this image. If you don't know what that means, just follow along and we'll show you what we mean in a few steps from now.

To export our image as a **.png** file...

Go to the **Menu bar** - **File** - **Export**... (a pop-out window will appear with many choices).

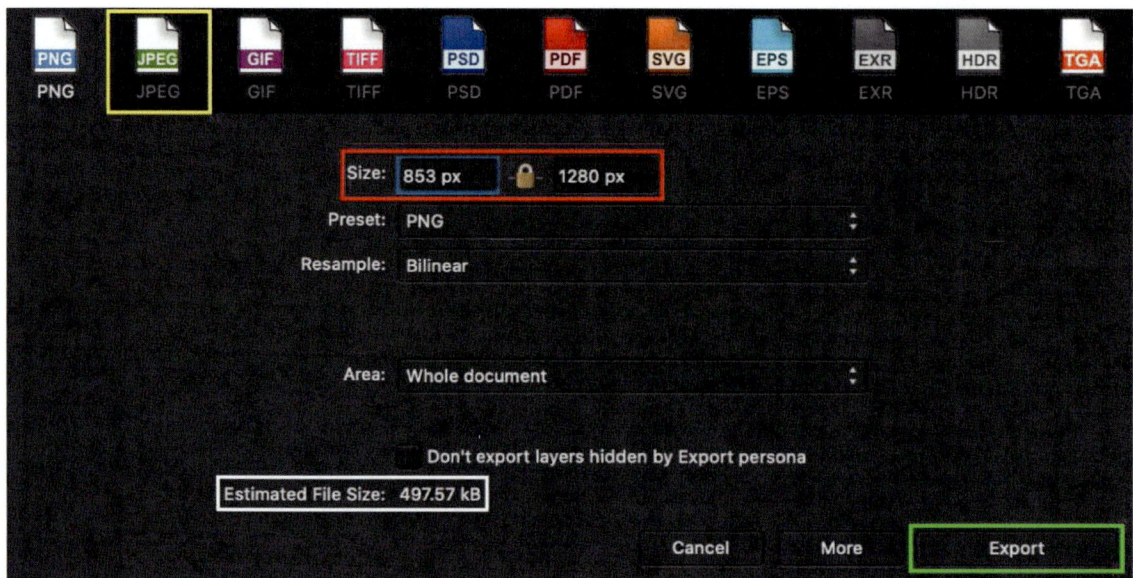

Yellow: Normally, when you export images they will be exported as JPEG's. So, this tab is usually selected with different, but similar options. You can tell the PNG tab is selected because it looks different from the other tabs.

Red: These are the dimensions of the image we want to export. If you click on one of these values to increase the Size, the other value will also increase. The Size of the image is reflected in the next marked area.

(continues on next page)

138

White: This is the size of the file you are about to send, which is directly related to the Red-marked values.

Green: Press this button when you're done making any changes to this screen.

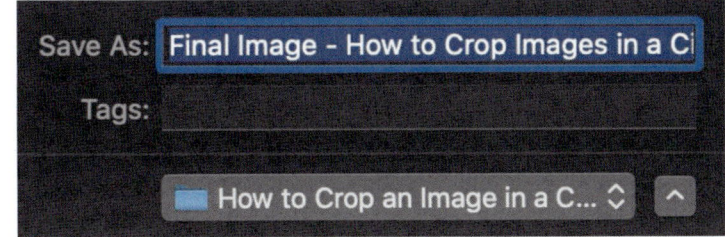

Save the **file** on your desktop or in any folder of your choosing. We created one called "How to Crop an Image in a Circle Shape" (see image above).

Note: Our image is now saved as a .png file, which means we can add it to any photo we want to create things like collages, greeting cards, etc. We recommend you also try this tutorial using the Heart Tool to create a similar effect.

Practical Example: Let's now use this circle-shaped image on top of another image. Since we've already downloaded the image of the sunflower in a vase, we'll use that. But, if you'd like to find any other image on Pixabay and try this out, please do so.

With our current image in front of us...

> *Click* **anywhere on the image** (transparent area or inside the circle) & *press* **Ctrl/Cmd+C** to *copy* it.
>
> *Click* on the **Sunflower Tab** so it's on the canvas.
>
> *Press* **Ctrl/Cmd+V** to *paste* our circle shape on top of this new image.
>
> *Select* the **Move Tool** & *reposition* our girl on the right-side of the sunflower image. Once you've found a good spot, we are now done.

Done. This is our final image.

Finished. This ends this tutorial.

Tutorial 14: How to Make a Realistic Shadow

Making shadows is a very important and subtle effect all good photo editors know how to do. There's nothing worse than adding an object to a photo and not take into account whether that object should be casting a shadow or not. When newly-added objects to a photo don't have perfect shadows, as you'd expect in real life, it's very obvious a photo has been manipulated. Master photo editors are so good at shadows and subtle alternations, you can't tell the original from the manufactured.

Here is the webpage to the image we'll be using for this tutorial:

https://pixabay.com/photos/burger-hamburger-food-lunch-meat-2018627/

Ready?

Select the **Selection Brush Tool** (looks like a paint brush with a dotted-circle at its tip).

Paint a **selection** across the cheeseburger, so the dancing ants surround it.

When you make selections of objects like this burger that have minute details around its perimeter, we often times have to use the Refine Selection Tool so the software can make a more refined selection than we can do with a brush.

Go to the **Contextual Toolbar** & *click* on **Refine...**

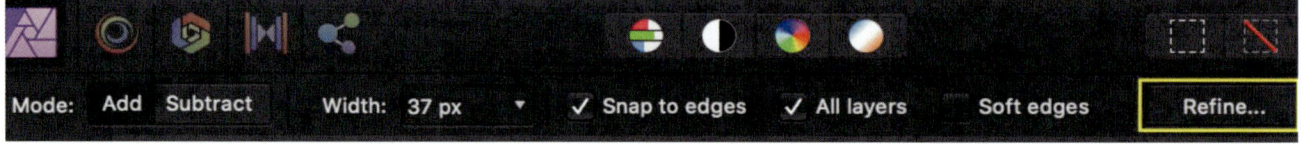

Paint a **selection** with the Refine Selection Brush (important that our burger is in full color while the background is Matt Red).

Press **Apply** when done.

140

Press **Ctrl/Cmd+J** twice to ***duplicate*** this layer.

Press **Ctrl/Cmd+D** to ***deselect*** the selection.

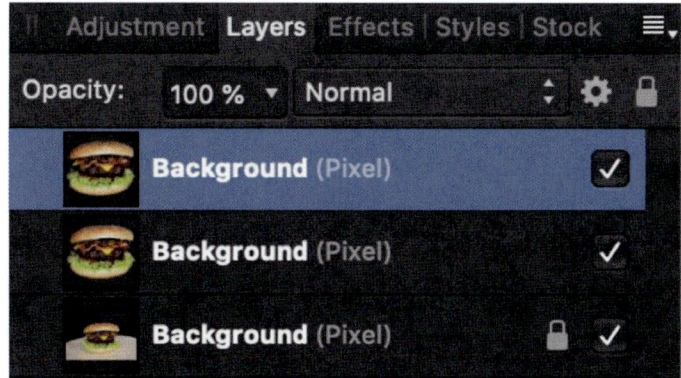

Select the **Perspective Tool** to *distort* the top layer of the hamburger. A pop-out window will appear. Make sure you click on Show Grid. It makes the next step easier to visualize what we are about to do.

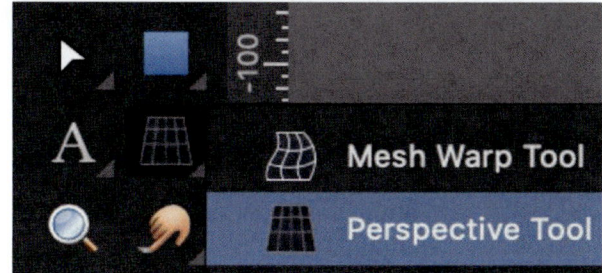

Click & drag on the **top two corners** of the tool and place the duplicated hamburger where you think its shadow should go.

Press **Apply** in the Perspective pop-out window (see above image for reference).

Move the **distorted top layer** and *place* it **above** the bottom layer so that its new position in the middle.

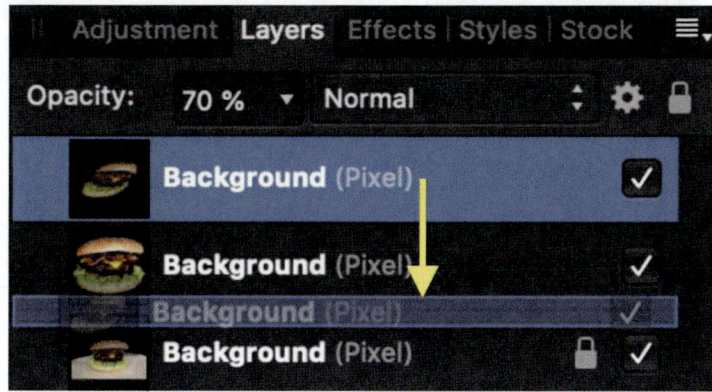

141

Make sure this is what you are seeing when you look at your image. If it's not, then you forgot to *press* **Apply** to the Perspective Tool's edit two steps above.

Make sure the middle layer is selected and highlighted in blue before continuing.

> *Click* on **Add Pixel Layer** icon.
>
> *Select* the **Gradient Tool**.

> *Click* & *drag* a **gradient** from the top-right of the distorted cheeseburger to the middle bottom of the original cheeseburger.

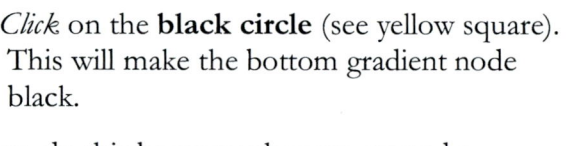

> *Click* on the **black circle** (see yellow square). This will make the bottom gradient node black.

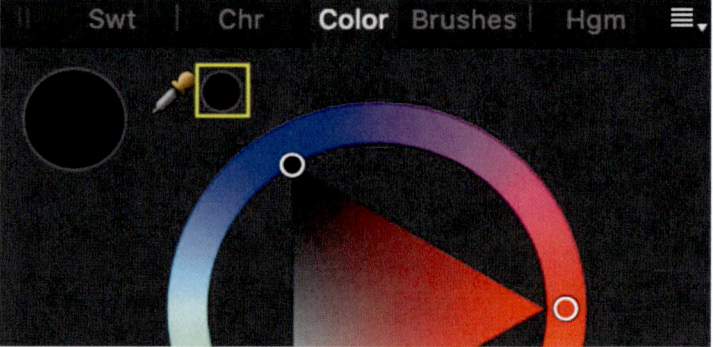

We can do this because when we created a gradient with our burger image (see image above) the gray node was selected. We know this simply because it's bigger than the white node. Because it was selected, just by pressing on this black circle marked with a yellow square, it changes the gray nodes color to black.

The result is the gradient goes from **white** to **black**.

Now that we have the gradient where we want it, we need to *move* the **Pixel** layer underneath-and-to-the-right of the layer beneath it - making it a child layer.

This will make the Pixel layer to be only applied to the middle hamburger layer.

> *Click* & *drag* the **Pixel layer** below-and-to-the-right of the layer beneath it (see yellow arrow for action).

> *Select* the **grouped layer** (see its circled triangle icon) and make sure it's highlighted in blue. This is what happens to a layer when you create a child layer - a layer that's below-and-to-the-right of its parent layer.

> *Change* its **Blend Mode** from **Normal** to **Multiply**.

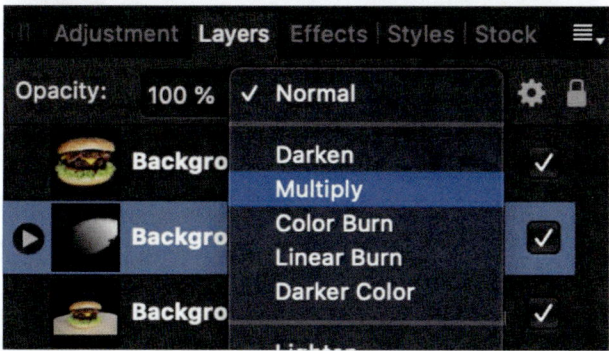

Our burger shadow is looking pretty good. The edges of the shadow do seem too sharp, though. So, let's correct this.

143

Let's add some needed blur to the shadow make it look more realistic. Make sure the middle-grouped layer is selected and highlighted in blue before we start:

Click on the **FX** icon and a pop-out window will appear.

Check **Gaussian Blur**.

Adjust the **Radius** slider to **7 px** (yellow rectangle).

Press **Close** to *exit* the pop-out window (white rectangle).

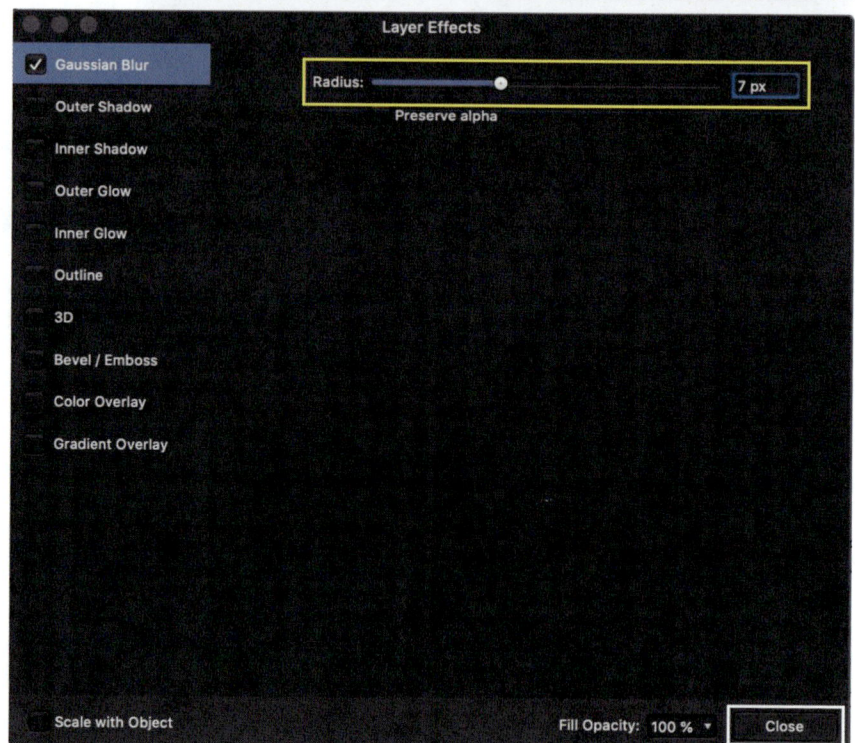

Select the **Move Tool** (or *press* **V**) to *reposition* the shadow if you'd like it in another position. We moved our shadow to the back just a bit so the shadow can't be seen in front of the burger.

Change the **Opacity** to **65%** to *reduce* the strength of the shadow. Changing the Opacity has a lot to do with the subject's surrounding and the overall lighting in the image.

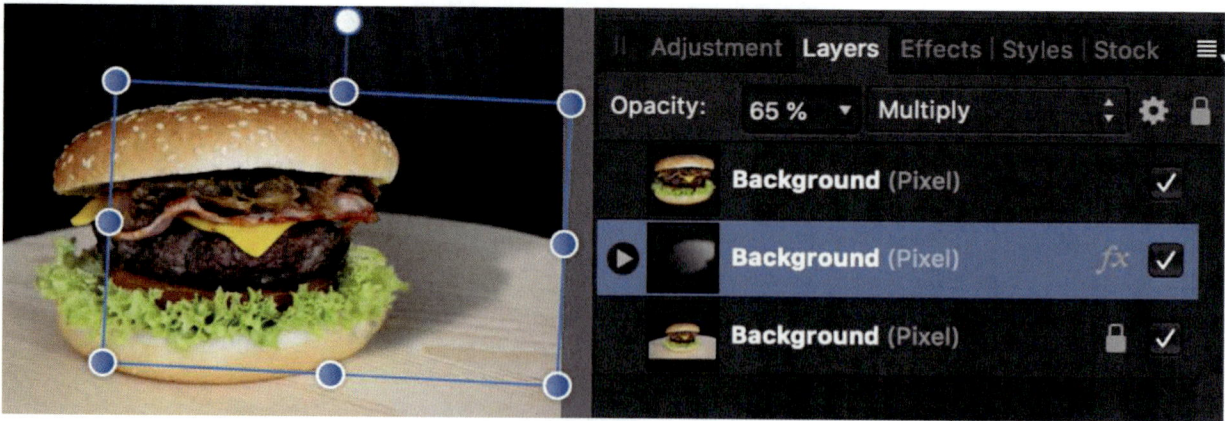

144

Done. This is our final image with its beautifully-created fake shadow.

Finished. This ends this tutorial.

Tutorial 15: How to Make a Transparent Clothing Effect

In this tutorial we're going to learn how to make a transparent clothing effect.

Here are the two webpages for the two images we'll be using in this tutorial:

https://pixabay.com/photos/t-shirt-red-man-plain-model-1710578/

https://pixabay.com/photos/road-red-rocks-rock-formations-1303617/

The first step we need to do before we start is to create a transparent background for the image of the man with the red shirt.

To do this:

Select the **Selection Brush Tool**.

Paint a **selection** over white area around the man. You will have to make individual selections around his fingers, between his legs and up on his sides. To do this, make the Selection Brush's Width very small so it fits into these areas. Take your time and go the best job you can do.

Press **Ctrl/Cmd+Shift+I** to *invert* the pixel selection onto the man and off the sides of the image.

Click on the **Mask** icon (looks like a Japanese flag).

Deselect the **selection** by *pressing* **Ctrl/Cmd+D**.

Your image should look like this now:

Note: You should be able to see the gray square-dotted transparent background all around the man.

The second step we need to do is to *copy* this image & *paste* it on top of the image of the desert road.

To do this:

Click anywhere on the image with the **T-Shirt**. This is an important step!

Press **Ctrl/Cmd + C** to *copy*.

Click on the image of the **road**.

Click **anywhere on this image** and use the shortcut **Ctrl/Cmd + V** to *paste* the T-shirt image on top of the road image.

Select the **Move Tool** (or *press* **V**) to *move* the man to the middle of the road.

The image on the canvas should look something like this:

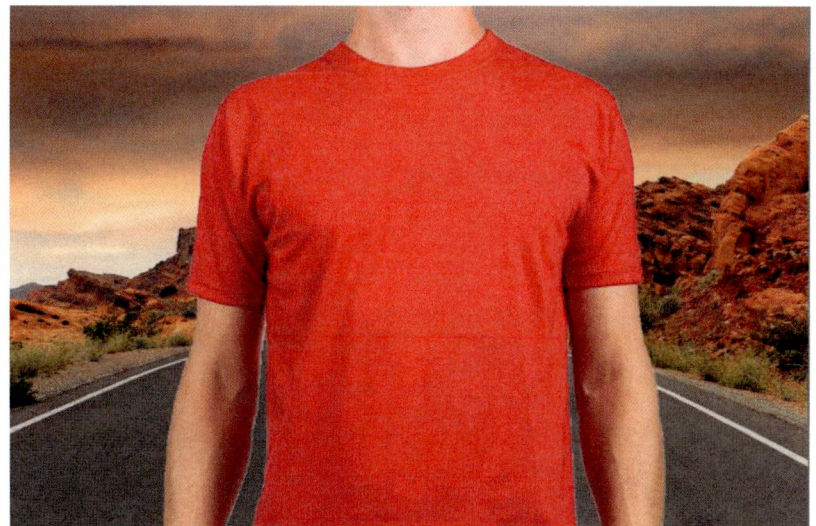

The third step is to make a selection of the T-Shirt to start the process of making it transparent.

Select the **Selection Brush Tool**.

Make a **selection** of just the red **T-shirt**.

Change the **Width** of the **Brush** by either using the right bracket key under the equal sign on the keyboard (or adjust the **Width** manually).

Our selection looks like this:

If your selection needs work, simply *press* **Refine** on the Contextual Toolbar and make the perimeter of the T-shirt's selection crisper.

If your selection looks good, *press* **Ctrl/Cmd+B** to bring up the **Grow/Shrink Selection** pop-out window.

In this pop-out, we want to adjust the **Radius** to **1 px**. This will cause the dancing ants to extend out 1 pixel away from the T-shirt.

Press **Apply** when done.

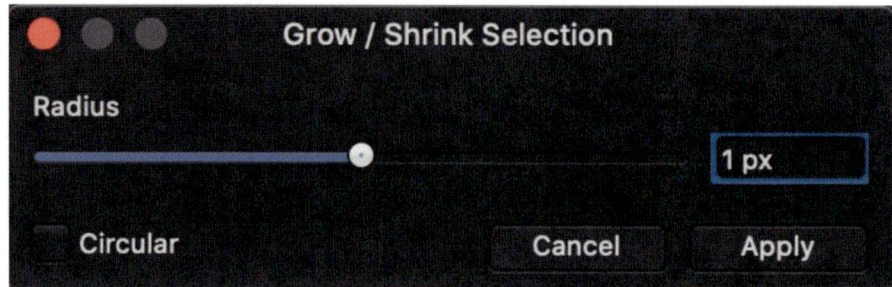

Press **Ctrl/Cmd+J** to **duplicate** the T-shirt layer.

Your Layers Panel should look like this now:

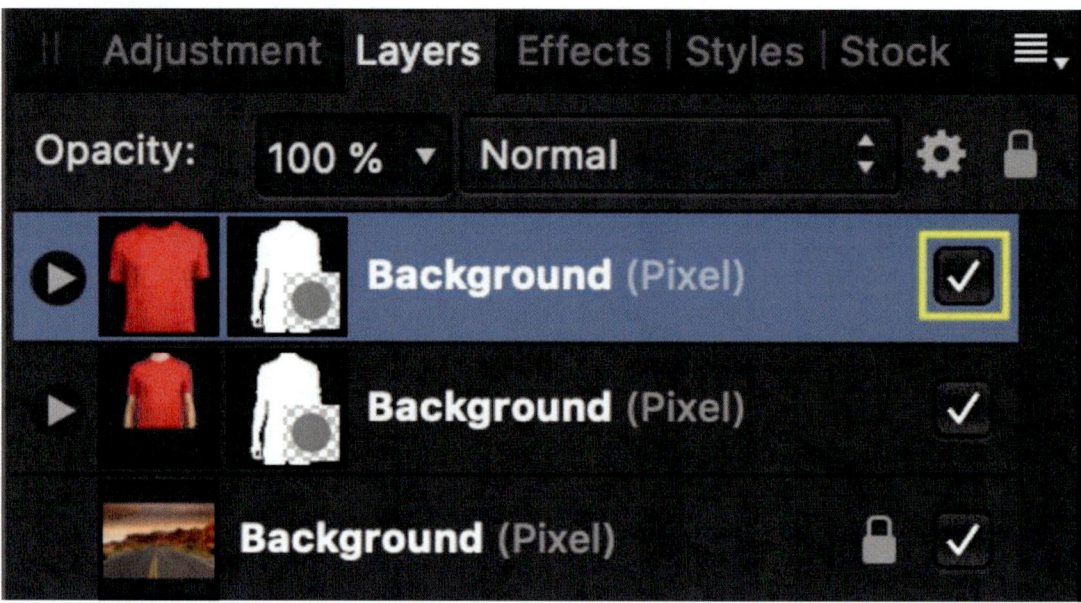

Turn off the **top layer** by *unchecking* the layer (see yellow box above).

Click on the **middle T-shirt layer** so it's *highlighted* in **blue**.

Click on the **Mask icon**.

The image should look like this now:

But, this is the exact opposite of what we want.

To fix this:

Press **Ctrl/Cmd+D** to *deselect* the dancing ants.

Click on the Mask's **preview thumbnail** located on the second mask layer on the current layer we are working on (see yellow square).

Press **Ctrl/Cmd+I** to *invert* this layer.

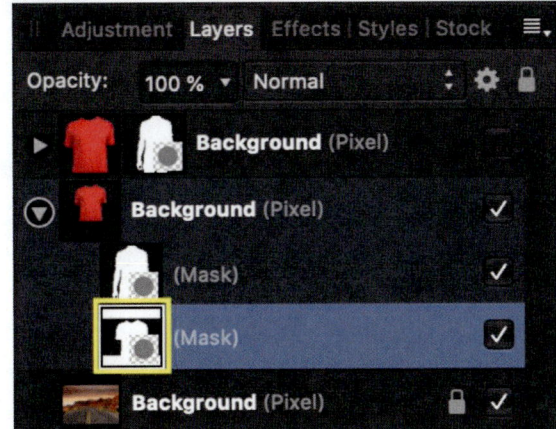

Note: Make sure you *click* on the layer and have it *highlighted* in **blue** before you **invert** it.

This is the image you should have on your canvas:

Note: A quick note about precision. If you look at the waist area of the man in the image we just worked on, you'll see a tiny white vertical line. We don't like seeing this. To correct it, simply zoom into the image and lines like these will disappear. If not, you can use the Erase Brush Tool (looks like the eraser-end of an old pencil) and erase away these annoying lines.

Now, let's look at the Layers Panel and *activate* the layer that is currently unchecked.

With the top layer active and visible, *click* on its **Blend Mode** (see yellow above) & *change* it from **Normal** to **Overlay**.

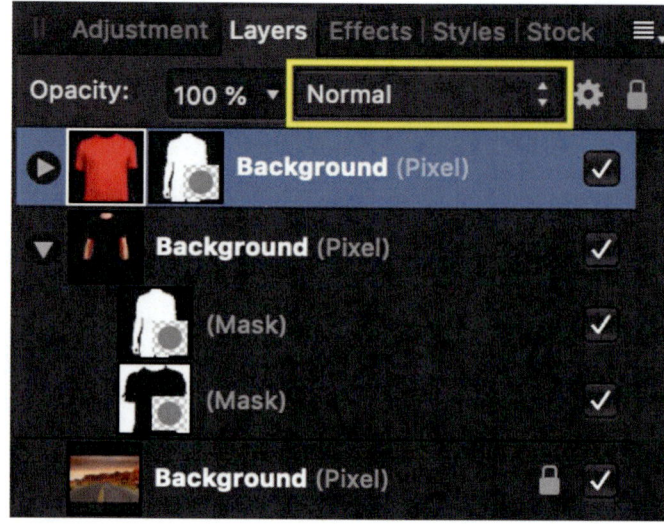

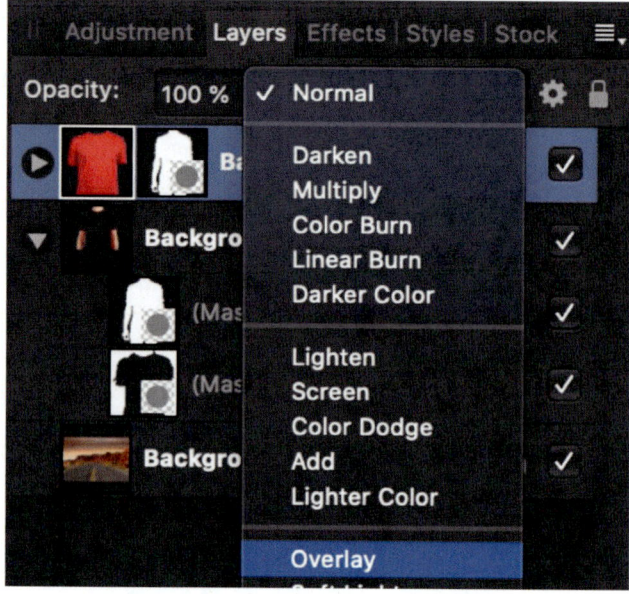

We can now see the background behind the T-shirt, but it's still red.

150

To fix this:

> *Click* on the **Adjustments icon** & s*elect* **HSL**.
>
> *Move* the **Saturation Shift** slider all the way to the left (see yellow rectangle in the image below).
>
> *Press* the **red X** in the top-left corner to ***close*** the HSL pop-out window when done.

This is how your image should look like now (we placed our image next to the HSL window).

You can see now that the HSL adjustment is affecting our entire image. This isn't what we want. We need to make it so that this HSL adjustment affects just the shirt.

Question: Do you know what a layer is called when it only affects its parent layer? It's called a child layer.

Let's make a child layer so the HSL adjustment layer only affects the top Background layer.

> *Move* the **HSL Shift Adjustment** layer in the Layers Panel underneath-and-to-the-right of the top Background layer (see red arrow for this action).

Movement of the HSL layer: What our Layers Panel should look like now:

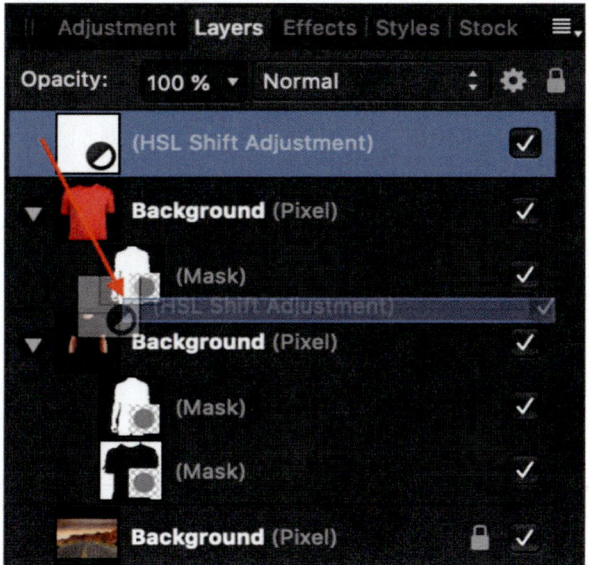
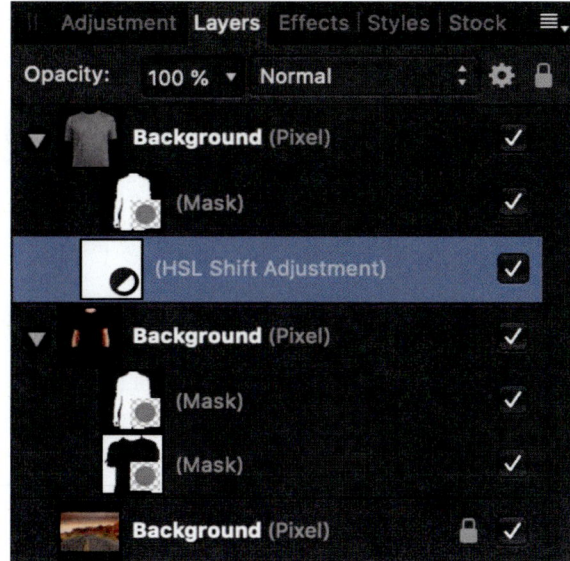

151

What our image should look like now.

Our effect is just about done, but let's make the man's T-shirt a little more visible at the top.

To do this we are going to apply a **Levels** adjustment.

    Click on the **Adjustments** icon & *select* **Levels...**

    Increase the **Black Level** to **13%**.

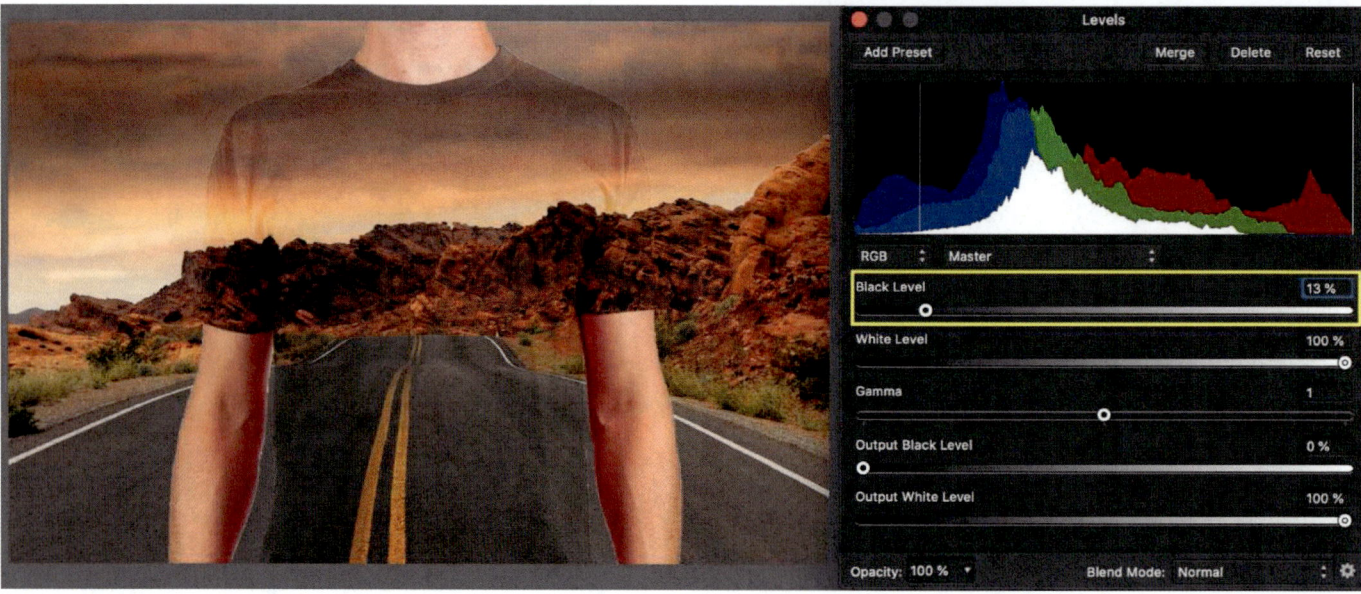

If you look at the shirt, you'll notice that it is definitely darker, but the road inside the shirt area is also darker. This darkening of the road isn't what we want. Here's how we'll correct this:

    Select the **Paint Brush Tool** (or *press* **B**).

    Set the **Foreground** color to **Black** to ***reveal*** the road layer beneath this new adjustment (see both sides of the man to see the color of road we're after here.

Paint over the **road** inside the man's shirt area to correct the color of the road.

Note: There are three primary ways to change the Foreground colors:
1. *Press* the **X** key to *alternate* between Fore-/Background colors.
2. *Go* to the **Colors Studio** & *click* on the **Black** circle to make it the Foreground color (yellow square).
3. *Go* to the **lower portion** of the Toolbar & *click* on the **Black circle** to make it the Foreground color (this only works if there are two columns of Tools).

Pro Tip: If you have different colors other than Black & White as the Fore-/Background, you can *press* the **D** key to instantly make the Fore-/Background colors Black & White and then simply *press* **X** to *switch* the color to your choosing.

Check out this screenshot of our work. We are partway done and you can see the area of the road we've painted over and the area we still have to paint. When you do this yourself, make sure not to paint above the height of the road. We've added a crude yellow border for you to see where you need to not paint above.

Continue painting over the rest of the road and when done, we are finished with this tutorial. Here is what our final Layers Panel should look like:

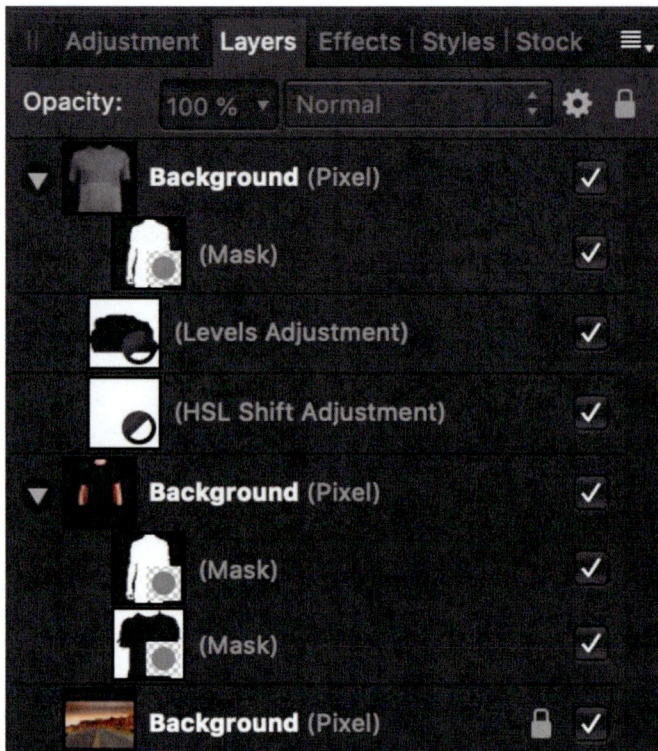

Done. This is our final image.

Finished. This ends this tutorial.

Tutorial 16: How to Put a Face on the Moon

In this tutorial we're going to learn how to put a face on the moon.

Here are the webpages to the two images we'll be using for this tutorial.

https://pixabay.com/photos/people-portrait-man-male-smile-1690965/

https://pixabay.com/photos/astronomy-full-moon-luna-moon-1869760/

Once you have the two images uploaded to Affinity Photo, first look at the image of the man.

The first thing we need to do is to make a selection of the man's face.

To do this:

Select the **Elliptical Marquee Tool**.

Click & *drag* a **circle** over the man's face.

Click **Refine...** on the Contextual Toolbar.

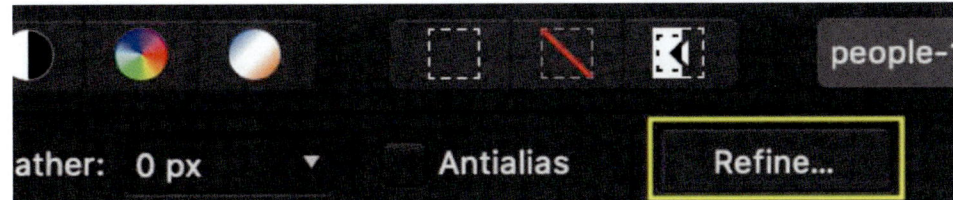

155

Adjust the **Feather** effect all the way up to **100%** (this will make the edges very soft - see image below).

Press **Apply** when done.

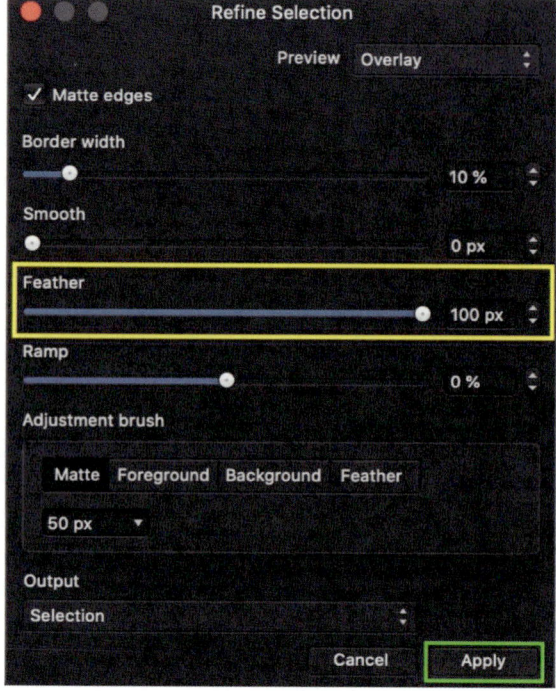

Notice how the red Matte color is not clearly defined around the man's face. This is what feathering does when we refine our circular selection around the man's face.

Next, we'll add the cut-out image of the man's face and place on top of the moon image/layer.

>*Press* **Ctrl/Cmd+C** to *copy* the man's face.

>*Click* on the **image of the Moon** at the top of the canvas.

>*Press* **Ctrl/Cmd+V** to *paste* the image of the man's face on top of the image of the moon.

>*Select* the **Move Tool** (or *press* **V**) & *position* the face in the middle of the moon.

Your image should look like this.

Note: Every time you use the Move Tool, these blue nodes that surround the face will appear if the image's layer in the Layers Panel is highlighted in blue. Once you click on the canvas around-and-not-touching our image, you'll see that the blue nodes disappear and the previously highlighted layer will no longer be highlighted (or active).

Also, check out the border of the man's face. Here you can see the feathering effect very well. The edges of the man's face are not distinct, but blurred. If we had not adjusted the Feathering in the Refine Selection pop-out window, then the man's face would have a very distinct separation from the moon's image, which would've killed this effect.

The next step is to make the man's face black and white to match the moon's image.

To do this:

    Click on the **Adjustments icon** and *select* **Black and White**...

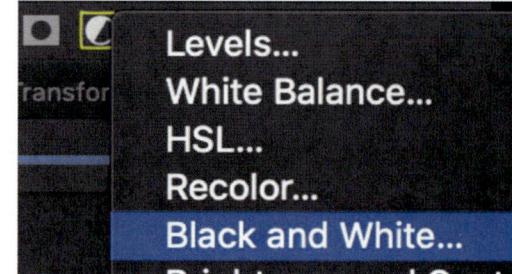

    Click on the **red button** in the top-left corner to close out of its pop-out window.

Note: Because the Black & White adjustment layer is located at the top of the Layers Panel, all layers beneath it will be in Black and White.

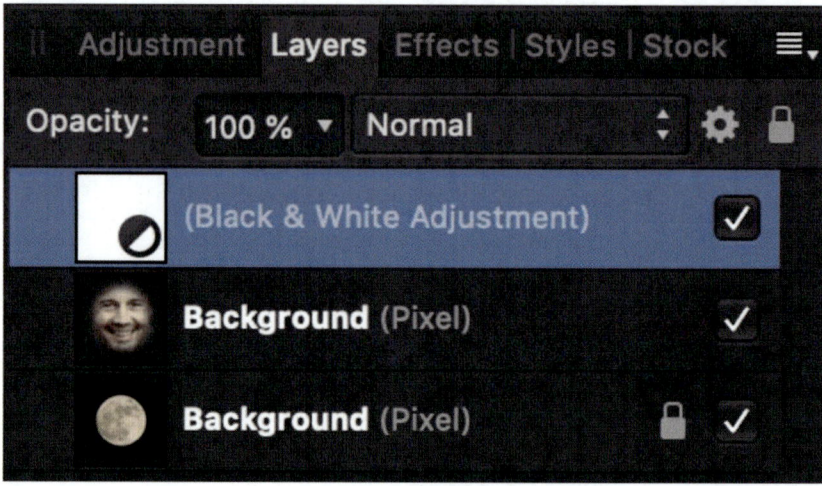

The next step we want to do is to blend the image of the man's face into the image of the moon so it'll look like they are more naturally melded together.

To do this:

    Click on the **middle layer** of the man's face so it's *highlighted* in **blue**.

    Change its **Blend Mode** from **Normal** to **Overlay.**

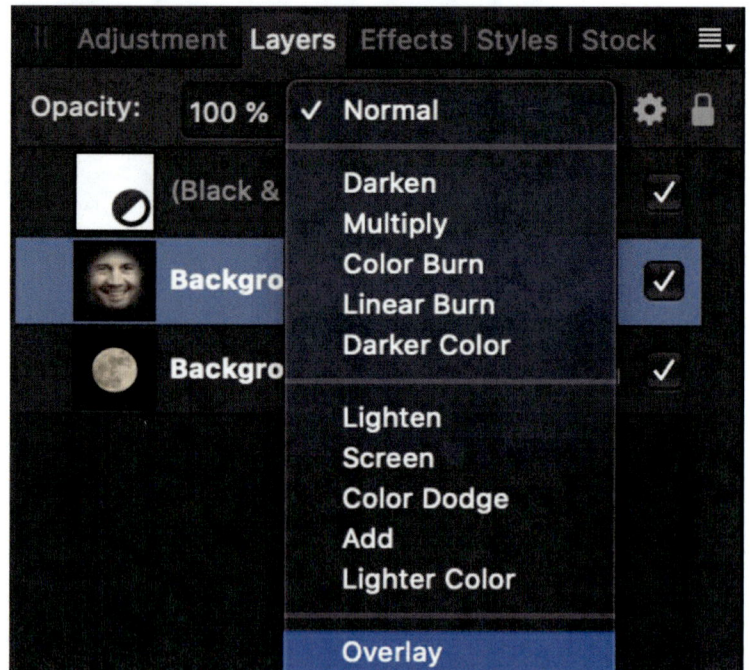

158

Press **Ctrl/Cmd+J** to ***duplicate*** this layer. When you do this, a new Background layer will appear above the layer you just duplicated. This image is showing the new duplicated layer.

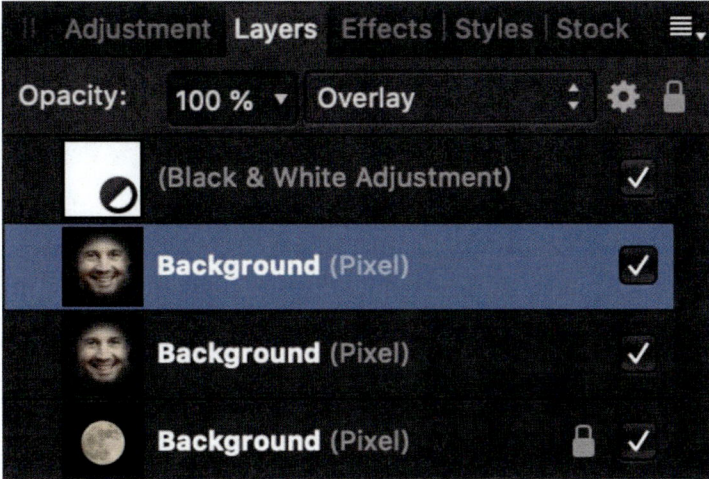

Note: Duplicating layers doubles the effect that layer had on the other layers in the Layers Panel and in our image on the canvas.

Change this duplicated layer's **Blend Mode** from **Overlay** to **Multiply**.

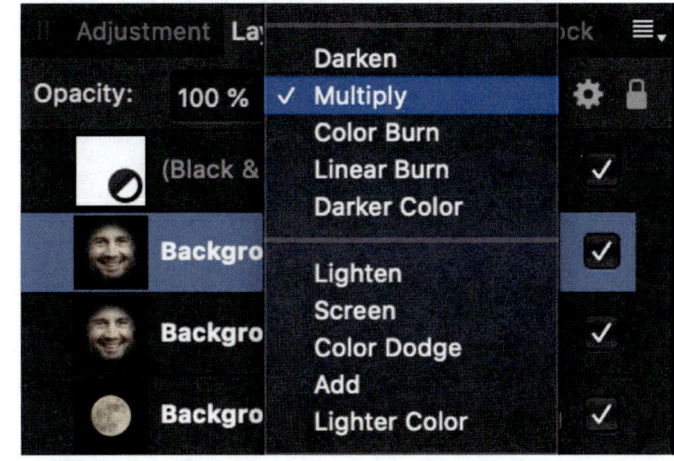

Hold-down the **Shift key** and *click* on **both layers** of the Man's face. This will make both layers highlighted in blue. Then, *press* **Ctrl/Cmd+G** to ***group*** them together.

Your Layers Panel should look like this now.

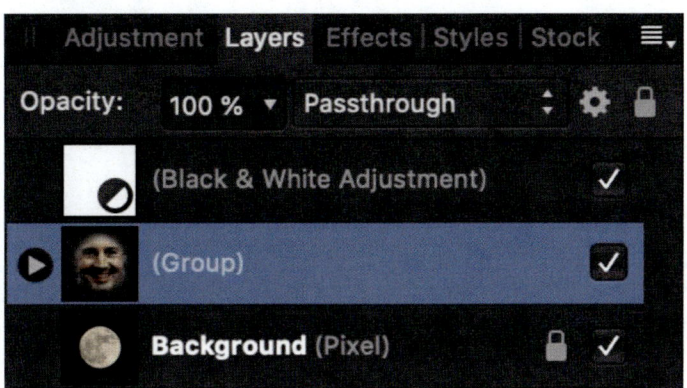

See the triangle in the circle on the left of the layer? This is the symbol for a Grouped layers. If you click this symbol the hidden layers will reveal themselves.

Right now, the man's face is a little too flat, so we're going to round it a bit.

To do this:

    Click on the **Live Filter icon** (looks like an hourglass).

    Select **Pinch/Punch Filter**.

    Increase the **Pinch/Punch** to **50**.

    Bring the **Radius** up to **300**. Watch the image distort the higher you go).

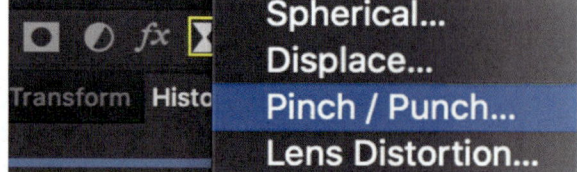

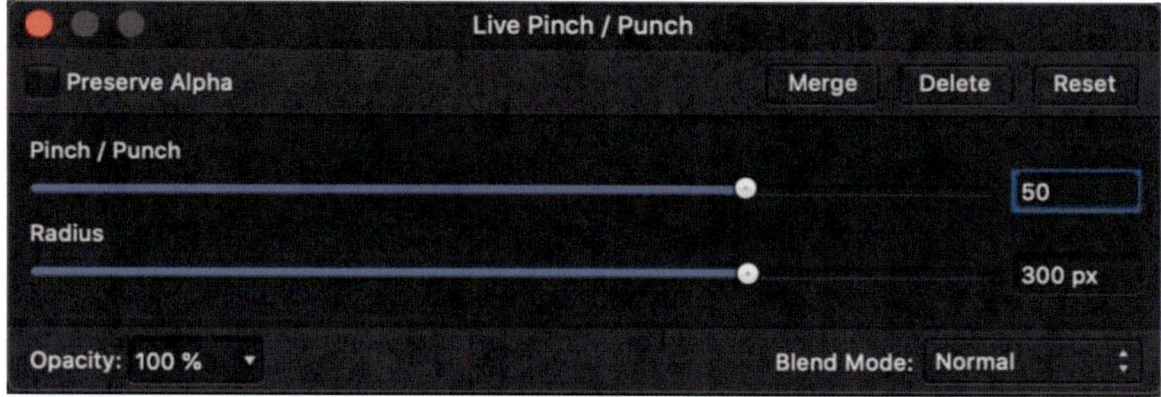

Now the face on the moon looks a little bit more rounded, as if it were actually on the moon.

Before we reveal the final image, let's take a look at our Layers Panel. This is what yours should look like now. If you want to go back and make changes to the Live Pinch/Punch effect, simply double-click on the preview thumbnail (just the white square) of the (Pinch/Punch) layer.

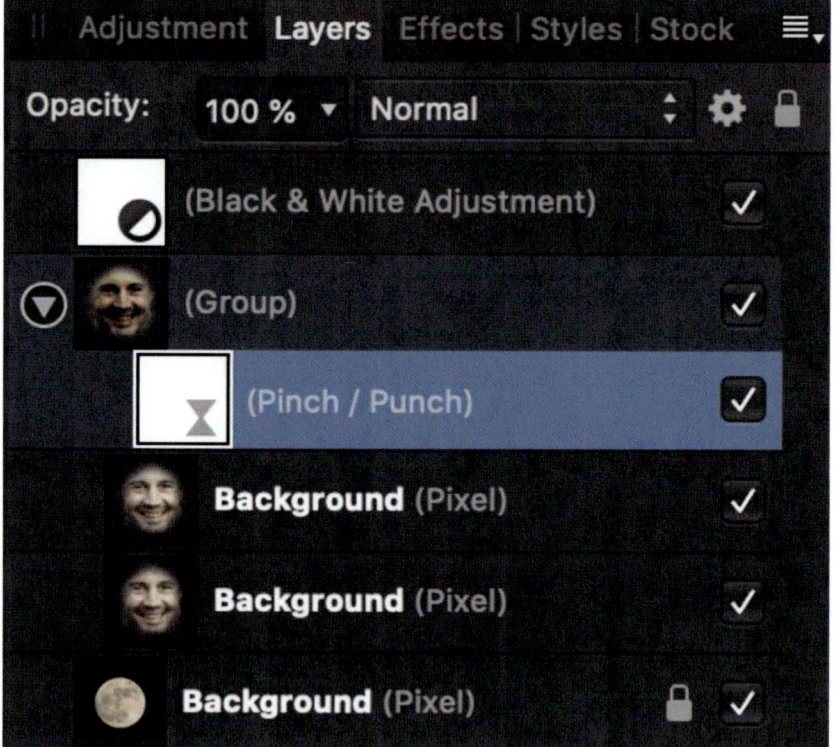

160

Done. This is our final image.

Finished. This ends this tutorial.

Tutorial 17: How to Make Realistic Reflections

In this tutorial, we are going to learn how to make a realistic reflections.

Here is the webpage for the image we'll be using for this tutorial:

https://www.dropbox.com/s/x432asw3tpikqsl/water-lily.png?dl=0

Once you have the image of the water lily on your canvas, here are the steps on how we can make a reflection.

Hold-down the **Ctrl/Cmd button** & *click* one-time on our image's **preview thumbnail** (see yellow square). This will create a selection around our image because the image is on a transparent background to begin with.

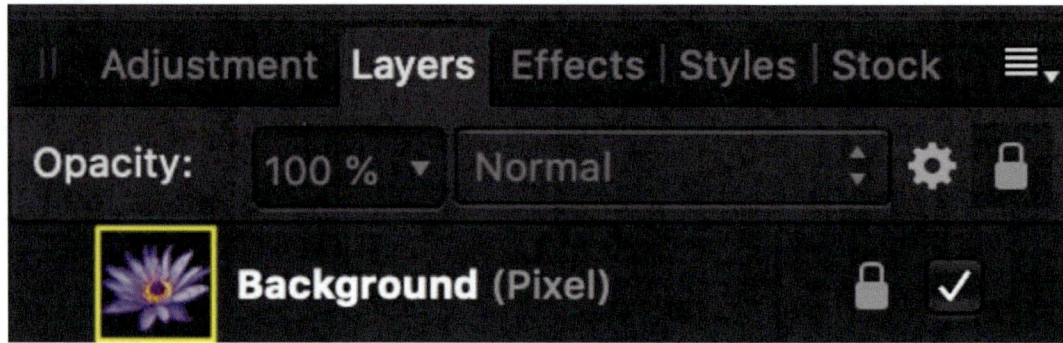

You should you now see the dancing ants, which means we have a selection of the flower.

Here are the next steps in this process:

Press **Ctrl/Cmd+J** to *duplicate* this layer.

Press **Ctrl/Cmd+D** to *deselect* the selection.

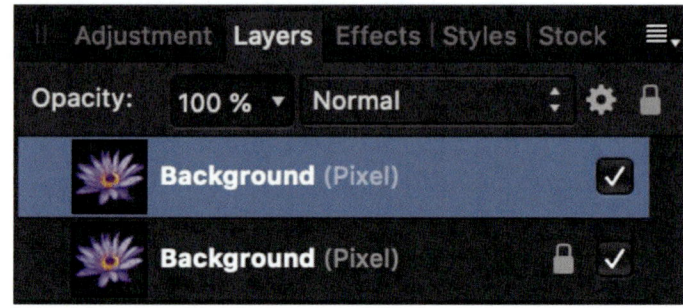

In the next steps, we're going to flip the perspective of the duplicated flower and adjust it so it'll appear as a reflection of our original flower. For future edits, this is the process you'll take every time when you want to create reflections or shadows of objects. Reflections & shadows are simply exact copies of the original subject, but located in different positions based on lighting and shadows.

Select the **Move Tool** (or *press* **V**) to *reposition* the flower. This will make the blue nodes surround our flower. This is what we want for our next steps.

With our object selected, we need to first flip our duplicated image to start the reflection effect.

To do this:

Right-click on the **flower** & *select* from the drop-down menu **Transform - Flip Vertical**.

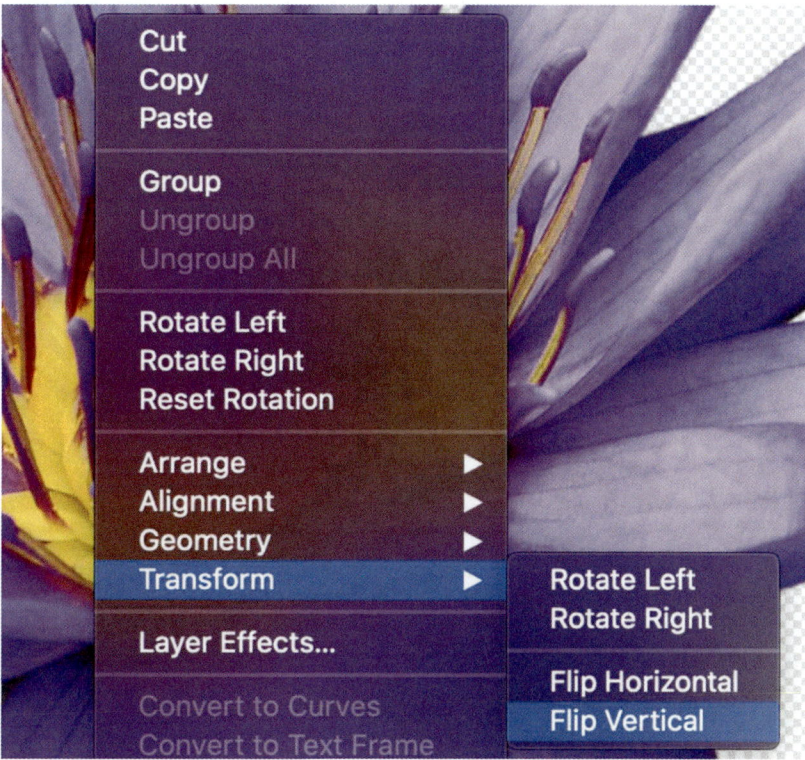

This is what our image looks like now with the duplicated image flipped vertically and on top of the original flower image:

Click & *drag* the **flipped flower** underneath the flower.

Don't worry if it disappears into the black area under our image (see lower portion of this image).

We'll fix that now:

> *Select* the **Crop Tool** (or *press* **C**).
>
> *Drag* out **some space** below the visible images that's below it-and-to-the-right.

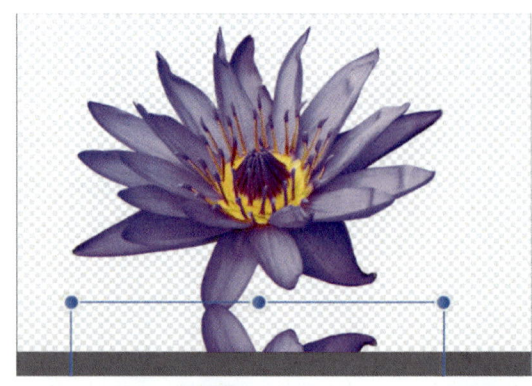

Try to match your image to look like ours.

> *Press* **Apply** on the Contextual Toolbar when done.

This is what our image should look like now.

164

Now, we need to rotate the bottom flower image a little bit so it's slanting to the right of the image above it.

To do this:

> *Select* the **Move Tool** (or *press* **V**).
>
> *Click* on the **rotation node** at the bottom (see black square) and make your rotation. Try to make your rotation so the bottom of the top two flower petals are touching the inverted two flower petals (or just make your image like ours).

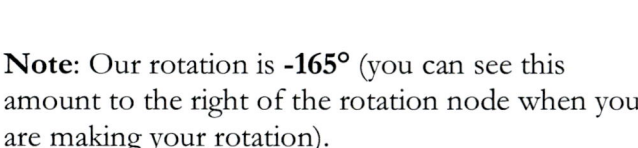

Note: Our rotation is **-165°** (you can see this amount to the right of the rotation node when you are making your rotation).

This is what we have so far:

Now that we have repositioned the lower flower, we need to now make it look like a reflection by having it slowly fade the further it is from the above flower.

To do this:

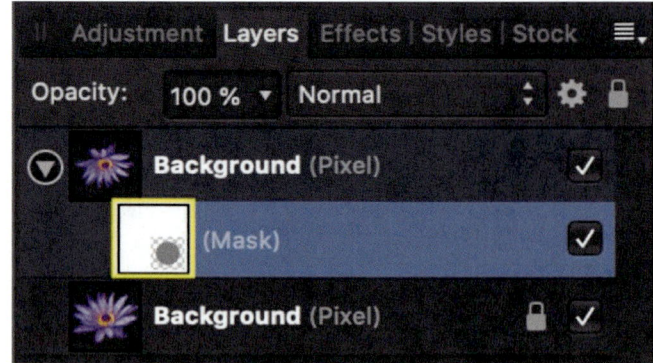

    Click on the **Mask** icon located at the bottom of the Layers Panel (looks like a Japanese flag).

    Click on the Mask layer's **preview thumbnail** (see yellow square).

    Select the **Gradient Tool**.

    Click & *drag* out a **gradient** starting at the top of the bottom flower and going to the middle bottom of the flower image.

This gradient will create the slow fade effect we are after.

The gradient is currently going to **gray**, which makes the flower only partially disappear. To create a better effect:

    Click on the **gray circle** located in the top-left corner of the Colors Panel (yellow square) and let's *change* its color to **black** by *clicking* on the **node** located in the inner triangle & *dragging* it up to the black portion (see white arrow for this action).

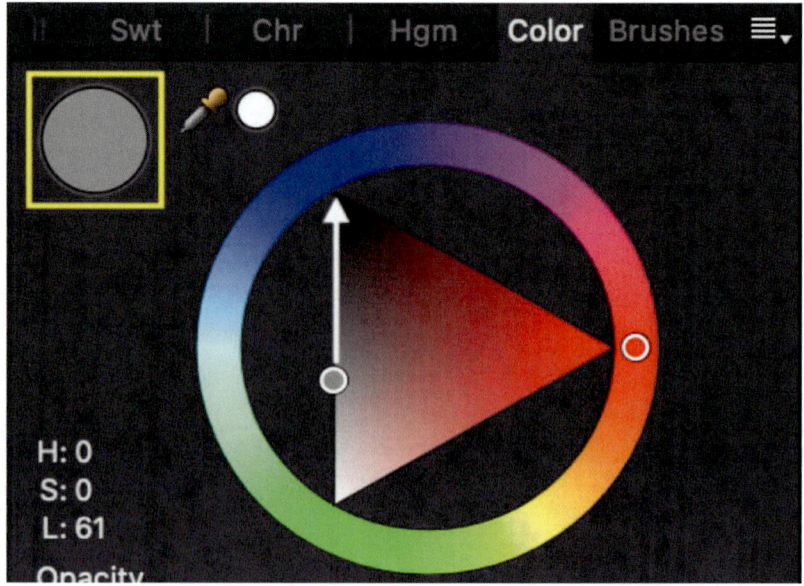

166

This is what your canvas should look like:

Now our **gradient** is going from **white** to **black** which is making our bottom image fade away.

The reflection is still too strong, so we need to correct that.

To do this:

    Click on the **top layer** so it's *highlighted* in **blue**.

    Lower the **Opacity** to **50%** (yellow square).

As a finishing touch, let's give our work a nice **black** background.

To do this:

    Select the **Rectangle Tool**.

    Click & *drag* a **rectangle** over the entire canvas (this image is showing what the rectangle looks like when placed over the image).

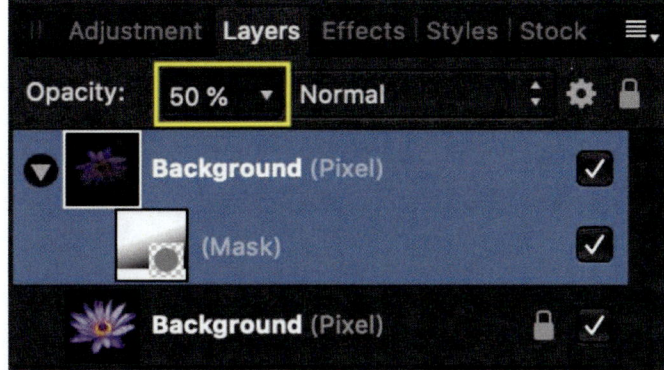

Go to the **Color Studio** and *click* & *drag* the **middle Color Wheel node** up to **black** (see yellow arrow for this action).

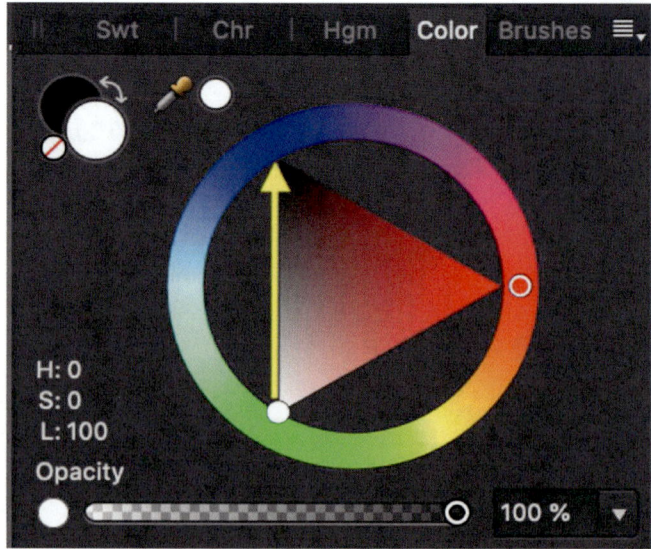

This will change the rectangle color to black because this layer is selected and highlighted in blue in the Layers Panel.

Here's the final touch to our image:

Click on the **top Rectangle layer** & *drag* it to the **bottom** of the layers stack.

This is what our Layers Panel looks like after this last step:

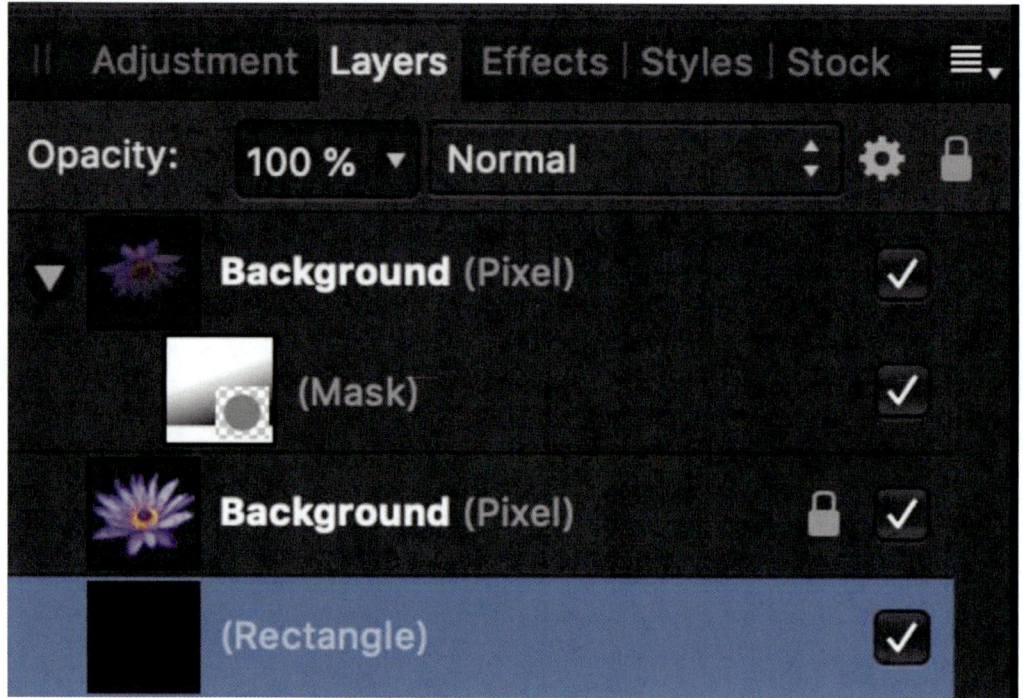

168

Done. This is our final image.

Finished. This ends this tutorial.

Tutorial 18: How to Restore Old Photographs

Ever looked at old photographs and wondered if you could make them look "newer" or better without all their creases, rips & tears? If so, then this lesson is for you. We will look at a few ways you can make improvements to your old photographs without sending them off to an expensive photo nerd for professional work.

Here is the photo we'll be using for this lesson:

> https://www.dropbox.com/s/nygb7kt4ay8zurt/How to Restore Old Photographs.jpg?dl=0

Ready to begin?

Upload the image.

Press **Ctrl/Cmd+J** to *duplicate* the layer.

Click on the **Adjustments icon** & *select* **Levels...**

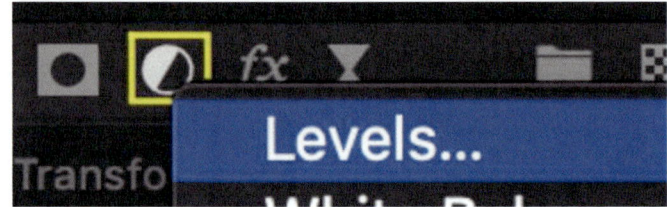

Adjust the **Black Level** to **10%** & the **White Level** to **85%**.

Press the **red button** to *exit* from this pop-out window.

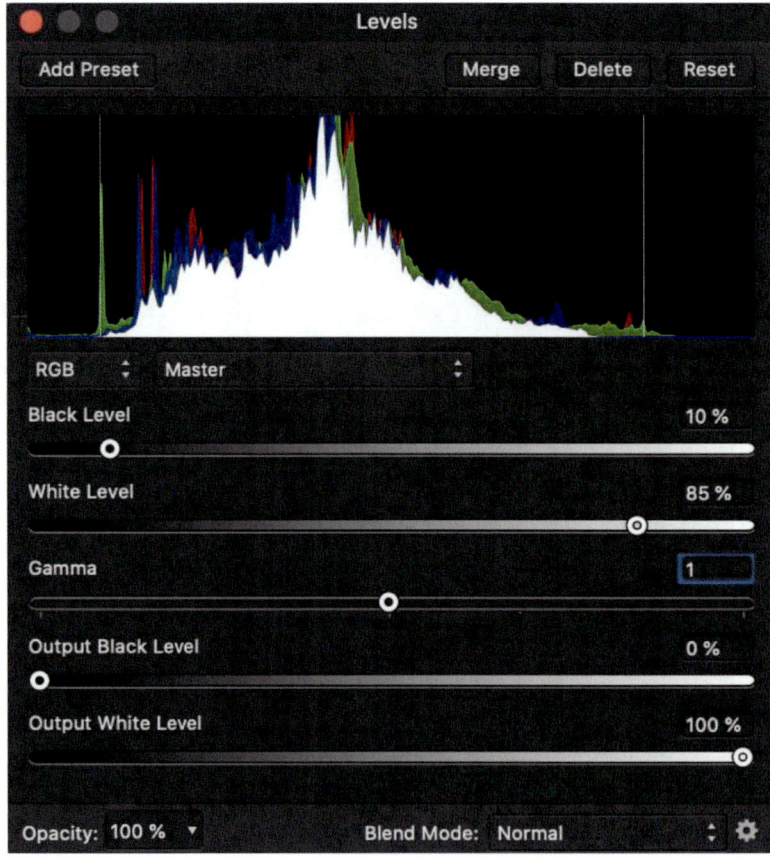

Some parts of the image have smudges & tears that we need to fix. We'll be using different tools to fix these different problem areas. The first area we'll work on is in the top-right corner of the image.

Click on the **middle Background layer** so it's highlighted in blue.

Select the **Inpainting Brush Tool** (or *press* **J**).

Paint in the **areas** shown in our image below. Notice how we didn't paint per se, but *clicked* **circles** of the Inpainting Brush Tool. Using clicks of the mouse keeps the tool from doing unnecessary corrections.

The next area we need to fix is the tear in the photo on the woman's right arm. To fix this, we'll use the Clone Brush Tool. Remember, with this Tool we set a reference point and then paint over the area we want to fix with the area represented by our chosen reference area.

Select the **Clone Brush Tool** (or *press* **S**) so it's activated.

Zoom in to the **image** by *pressing* **Ctrl/Cmd +** so the woman takes up the majority of our screen.

Go to the **Contextual Toolbar** & *set* the **Opacity** to 100%, **Flow** 100%, **Hardness** 0%.

Hold-down **Option/Alt** & *click* on the **woman's arm next to and below the tear**. Can you see the black cross? This is the reference point the Clone Brush Tool will use to copy over the damaged area.

Paint over the **tear area**, but be careful to paint only vertically up (& down if necessary).

Use **Ctrl/Cmd+Z** to *undo* any mistakes and go back and try again. This tool simply takes practice to master. Take your time and do your best. You can do it!

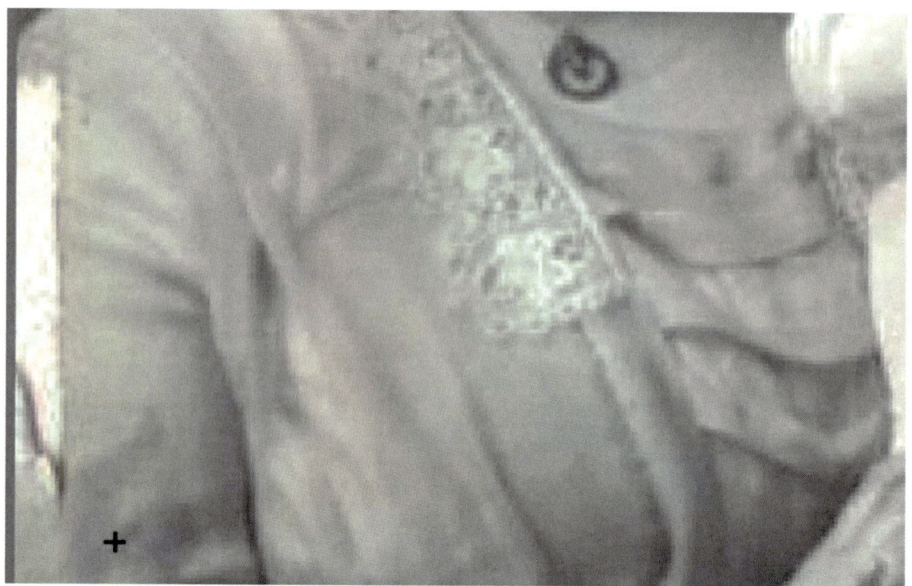

Done. This is our final image.

Finished. This ends this tutorial.

Tutorial 19: How to Transform Any Image into a Pencil Drawing

In this tutorial, we will learn how to transform any image into a pencil drawing.

Here is the webpage for the image we'll be using for this tutorial.

https://pixabay.com/photos/bridge-golden-gate-sea-sunset-1333645/

Ok, let's begin by opening the image we are going to use for this tutorial onto the Affinity Photo canvas. Once you have the image uploaded, here's what we do to create this cool effect:

Press **Ctrl/Cmd+J** to *duplicate* the image.

Click on the **Adjustments icon** and *choose* **HSL...**

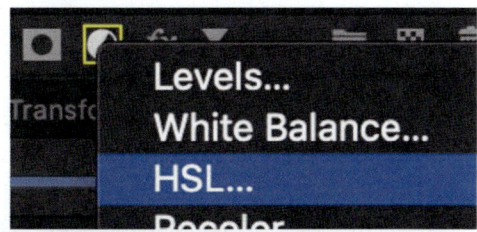

Bring the **Saturation Shift** all the way to the left to **-100%**.

Click on the **red button** to *close* the window.

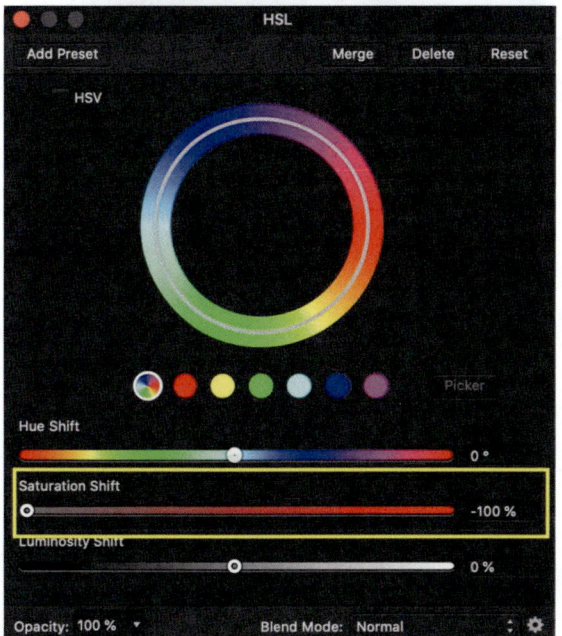

Click on the **duplicate** layer.

Change its **Blend Mode** from **Normal** to **Color Dodge**.

Press **Ctrl/Cmd+I** to *invert* the image (or go to **Menu bar - Layer - Invert**).

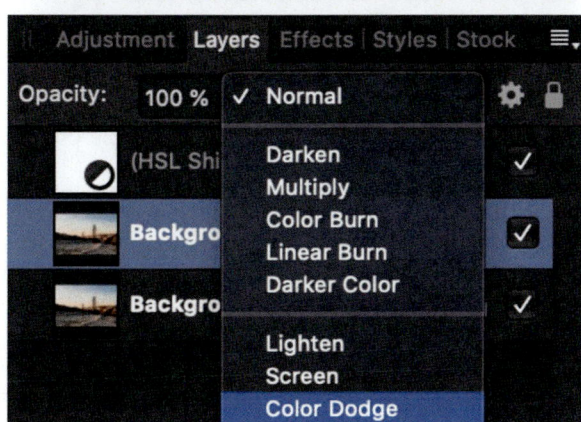

When you do this, your image will become mostly **white** and very grainy. Not to worry, we'll fix it next.

Click on the **Live Filters** icon (looks like a sand clock) and s*elect* **Gaussian Blur**... and a pop-out window will appear.

Adjust the **Radius** to **0.9 px** to give it a sketch-like look.

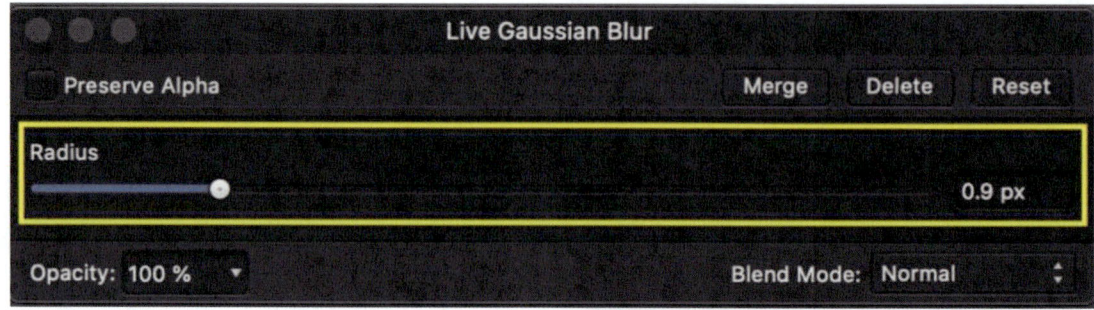

This is what your Layers Panel should look like:

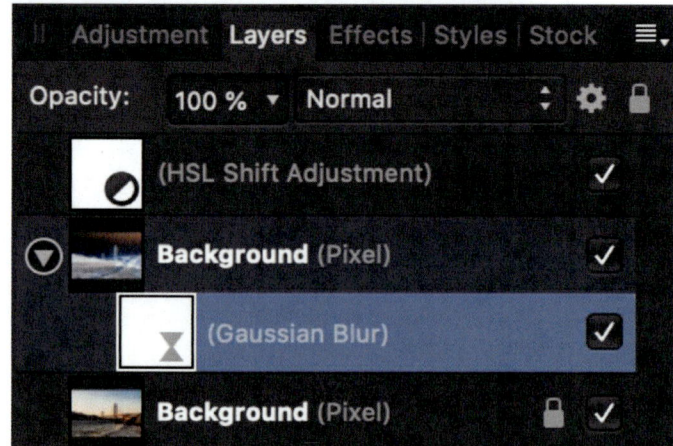

The last step in this technique is to adjust the **Levels** - this will add more contrast to our image.

Click on the **Adjustments** icon and s*elect* **Levels...** It's the first choice at the top of the drop-down list. The shortcut for Levels is **Ctrl/Cmd+L**

Adjust the **Black Level** to **60%**.

Press the **red** X **button** to *close* this pop-out window.

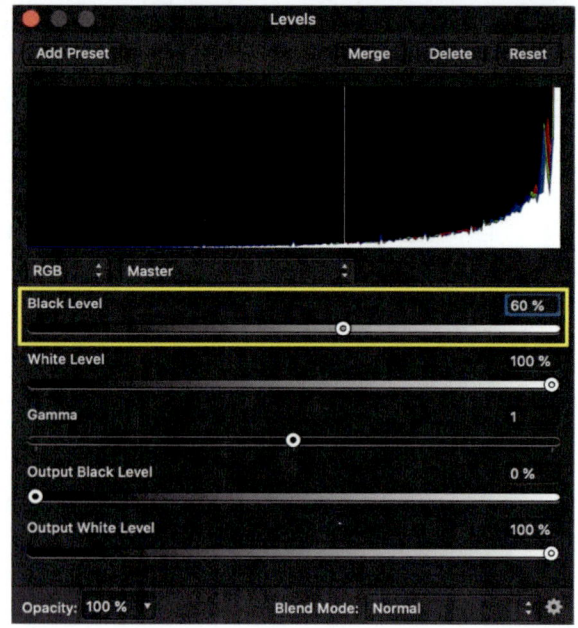

Note: The higher the **Black Level** is the darker the whole image will become. If you were to increase it to **100%**, the whole image would be a solid **black**.

174

This is what our Layers Panel should look like now.

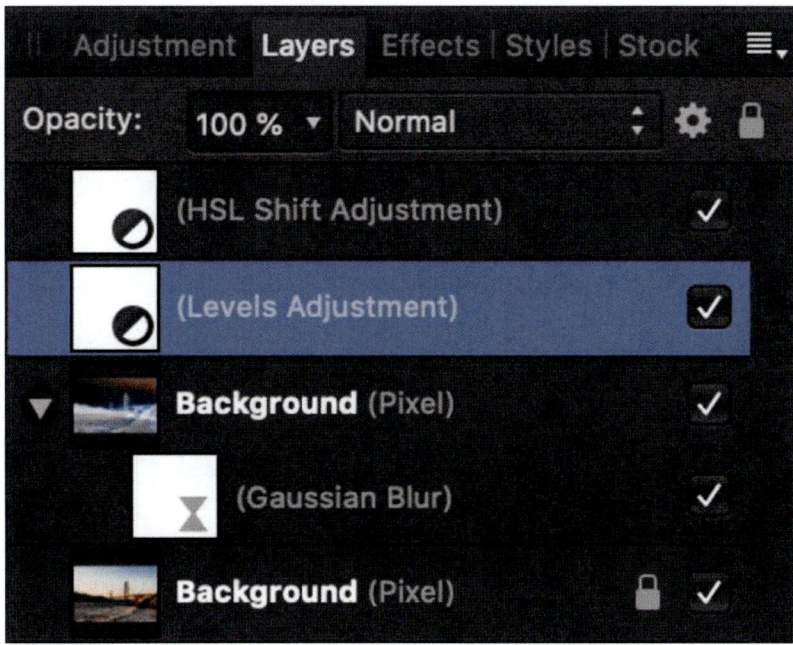

Done. This is the final image.

Finished. This ends this tutorial.

Tutorial 20: How to Create a Jumping Over Text Effect

In this tutorial, we are going to learn how to make a jumping over text effect.

Here is the webpage to the image we will be using in this tutorial:

https://www.dropbox.com/s/qf7p738esgduk6d/Jumping Man Pixabay Image.jpg?dl=0

Ready?

Ok, let's begin by opening the image we are going to use for this tutorial onto the Affinity Photo canvas.

The first thing we need to do is to make a selection of the man's legs.

To do this:

Select the **Selection Brush Tool** (looks like a paint brush with a dotted circle around its tip).

Go to the **Contextual Toolbar** and adjust the Width of the circular brush cursor so it fits within the inside of the man's pants.

Paint a **selection** on the legs.

Now, because we only want the selection on his forward leg, we need to remove part of the selection.

There are two ways to do this:

1. *Change* the **Mode** from **Add** to **Subtract** and *paint* over the **back leg-to-the-middle-of-his-belt-area**.

2. *Hold-down* the **Alt** button and *click* on the parts of the selection you want to remove. This is our preferred method as it's more intuitive and easier to do once you gain proficiency.

The image on the left is what our image should look like after we made a selection of the man's legs. The image on the right is what our image should look like now before we progress to the next step. Try to make your selection (i.e. the dancing ants) be in the same position as ours.

Now that we just have his leg selected:

> *Press* **Ctrl/Cmd + J** to *duplicate* this layer.

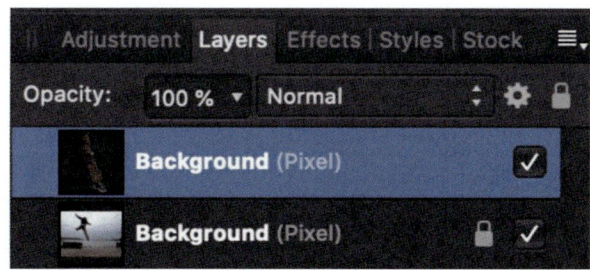

> *Press* **Ctrl/Cmd + D** to *deselect* the dancing ants.
>
> *Select* the **Artistic Text Tool** (or *press* **T**).
>
> *Change* the Font to **IMPACT** by either typing "impact" in the Font window (our image) or by scrolling down the massive list of Fonts until you find "Impact".
>
> *Type* out the word **Affinity**.

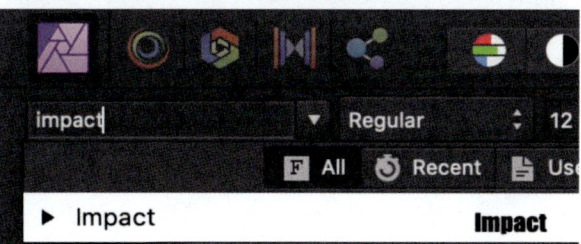

This is what our image looks like now. If yours is different, you can use the Move Tool & reposition your text to look like ours. We've gone over how to use the Move Tool in earlier chapters, so we won't explain how to do it here. If you need help, turn to Tutorials 16 & 17 for review.

Ready to finish this lesson?

> *Click* on the **top layer** so it's activated & *drag* it **beneath** the middle-duplicated Background layer in the Layers Panel.

This image shows this action of moving the layer.

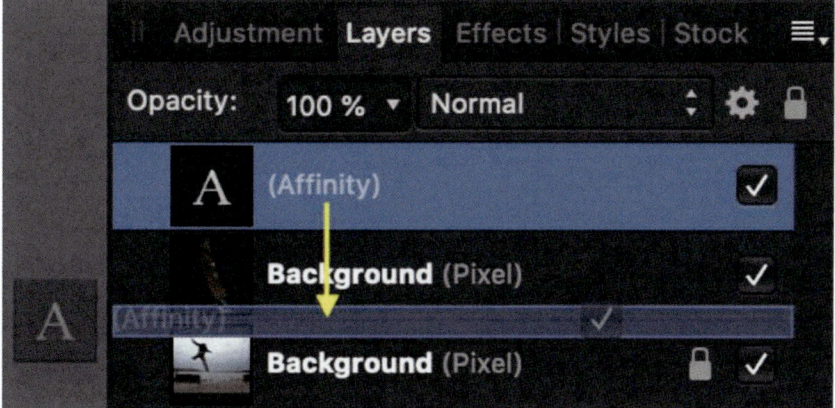

Note: Make sure the layer you move is not below-and-to-the-right of the middle Background layer. If that happens, *press* **Ctrl/Cmd+Z** to *undo* and try again.

Done. This is our final image.

Finished. This ends this tutorial and this book. Thank you!

List of Tutorials and Their Image Webpages

3 – How to Crop Pictures

    https://www.dropbox.com/s/3l42sx5yzashl2t/Cropping.jpg?dl=0

4 – How to Remove Imperfections from a Photo

    https://affinityrevolution.com/wp-content/uploads/2017/11/Jumping.jpg

    https://affinityrevolution.com/wp-content/uploads/2017/11/Ezra-1.jpg

5 & #6 – How to Use the Adjustments Layer / Masks (use the same image for both tutorials)

    https://pixabay.com/photos/seashell-shell-shells-sea-ocean-2821388/

7 – How to Make Selections

    https://pixabay.com/photos/moon-sky-night-moonlight-nature-2913221/

    https://pixabay.com/photos/purple-ship-sailing-ship-3054804/

Bonus Lesson: How to Make Selections Using the Pen Tool

    https://pixabay.com/photos/present-package-gift-celebration-1893640/

Bonus Tutorial: How to Create a Cool Transparent Text Effect

    https://cdn.pixabay.com/photo/2016/11/29/04/19/beach-1867285_1280.jpg

Tutorial 1: How to Create a Double Exposure Effect

    https://pixabay.com/photos/bald-eagle-raptor-head-close-up-2715461/

    https://pixabay.com/photos/zugspitze-alpine-summit-1048995/

Tutorial 2: How to Create a Color Splash Effect

    https://pixabay.com/photos/car-racing-motorsport-racing-car-4394450/

Tutorial 3: How to Create a Stylish Duotone Effect

    https://pixabay.com/photos/guitar-classical-guitar-756326/

Tutorial 4: How to Create a Matte Image Effect

    https://unsplash.com/photos/NOj7slD8qtc

Tutorial 5: How to do a Sky Replacement

    https://pixabay.com/photos/mount-rushmore-monument-landmark-902483/

    https://pixabay.com/photos/nature-sky-night-stars-2609647/

Tutorial 6: How to Create a High-Speed Effect

    https://pixabay.com/photos/architecture-building-infrastructure-2569760/

Tutorial 7: How to Create a Dispersion Effect

    https://pixabay.com/photos/clock-clock-tower-isolated-2939420/

Tutorial 8: How to Create a Face Warp

    https://pixabay.com/photos/model-female-girl-beautiful-woman-429733/

Tutorial 9: How to Create a Beautiful Pop Art Effect

    https://pixabay.com/photos/woman-model-young-model-fashion-2381628/

    https://pixabay.com/photos/kennedy-stone-background-ground-3740228/

Tutorial 10: How to Create a Pop Out or 3D Effect

    https://pixabay.com/photos/fitness-jump-health-woman-girl-332278/

    https://affinityrevolution.com/wp-content/uploads/2016/09/TV.jpg

Tutorial 11: How to Create a Water Flame Candle

    https://affinityrevolution.com/candle/2590837/

    https://pixabay.com/illustrations/water-splash-png-2748695/

Tutorial 12: How to Create a Face Swap

    https://affinityrevolution.com/wp-content/uploads/2016/11/Girls.jpg

    https://www.pexels.com/photo/baby-child-close-up-crying-47090/

Tutorial 13: How to Crop Images in a Circle Shape

    https://pixabay.com/photos/guitar-beautiful-music-instrument-944262/

Tutorial 14: How to Make a Realistic Shadow

    https://pixabay.com/photos/burger-hamburger-food-lunch-meat-2018627/

Tutorial 15: How to Make a Transparent Clothing Effect

    https://pixabay.com/photos/t-shirt-red-man-plain-model-1710578/

    https://pixabay.com/photos/road-red-rocks-rock-formations-1303617/

Tutorial 16: How to Put a Face on the Moon

    https://pixabay.com/photos/people-portrait-man-male-smile-1690965/

    https://pixabay.com/photos/astronomy-full-moon-luna-moon-1869760/

Tutorial 17: How to Make Realistic Reflections

    https://affinityrevolution.com/reflection/

Tutorial 18: How to Restore Old Photographs

    https://affinityrevolution.com/restore-old-photos/

Tutorial 19: How to Transform Any Image into a Pencil Drawing

    https://pixabay.com/photos/bridge-golden-gate-sea-sunset-1333645/

Tutorial 20: How to Create a Jumping Over Text Effect

    https://affinityrevolution.com/wp-content/uploads/2017/05/jump.jpg

The Five Areas on the Affinity Photo Screen

Every new software has its own screen set-up. Affinity Photo is no different. To make your learning as easy as possible, we have divided the User Interface (UI) screen up into five different areas.

During the course of the book we will often refer to areas of the UI like the Contextual Toolbar (CT), the Menu bar (MB), and the Layers Panel. If you are able to immediately and without thought know where these areas are, your learning will be greatly speeded up.

The Five Areas of the Screen:

Area 1:   Menu bar

Located at the very top of the UI - including File, Edit, Text, Document, Layers, Select, Arrange, Filters, View, Window, Help

Area 2:   Toolbar

Parallel line directly under the **Menu bar** - from L to R it starts with the **Photo Persona** icon and extends all the way to the right to an icon which looks like a **white** circle with its bottom right quarter in **blue** (or **Insert inside the selection**).

Area 3:   Contextual Toolbar

Running parallel and directly below the Toolbar. These options change depending on which tool you choose. Click on some of the different Tools to see the Contextual Toolbar change.

Area 4:   Tools

Located vertically on the far-left side of the screen below and to the left of the Contextual Toolbar. This is where all the tools are located.

Area 5:   Studios (this is where the Layers Panel is located).

The studios are located on the far right-side of the UI.

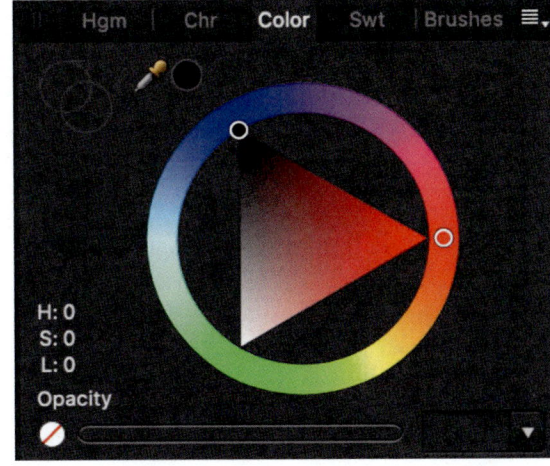

At the top of the Studios is the **Color Studio**. The tabs above the Color Wheel are Histogram, Character (for Text), Color, Swatches, Brushes. The four parallel lines at the far-right acts as a subcategory for each tab.

Click on this to see what happens when you're on Color.

Under the Color Studio is the **Layers Studio**:

The tabs are Adjustments, Metadata, Layers, Effects, Styles, Stock images. Again, the four parallel lines act the same as above. Below them is Opacity, Blend Modes, Blend Ranges, Lock/Unlock (a layer).

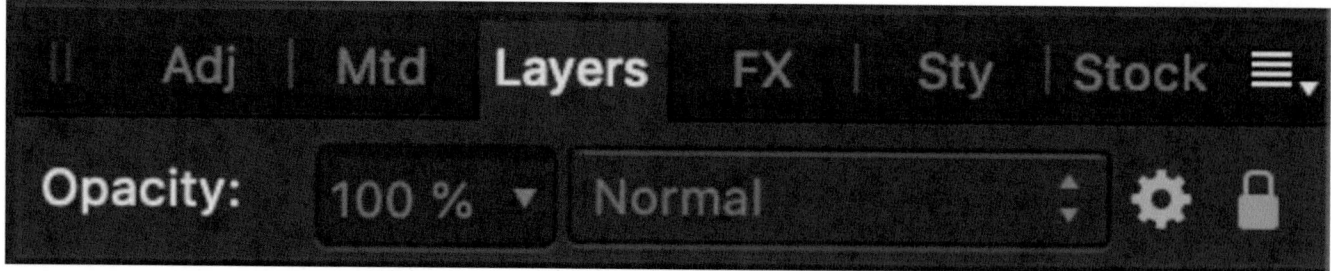

Below the Layers Studio are the **Layer icons** (left to right), Edit all layers, Masks, Adjustments, Layer Effects, Live Filters, Group layers, Add Pixel Layer, Trashcan. Below them are the tabs for Navigator, Transform, History, Channels.

Hint: We very often *click* on these different icons. We'll write things like "*click* on the **Adjustments** icon" and you'll need to know where this icon is located. Knowing this will help you tremendously.

The Most Common Shortcuts You Need to Know

To maximize your proficiency in using this software, we highly recommend you learn the shortcuts most often used. Knowing these will greatly increase your performance and speed. While there are many more to learn, these here are the ones you'll use the most. The "+" used below are not to be pressed, except when zooming in & out (to Undo, you will *press* **Ctrl/Cmd Z,** but we added the "+" to just show that in addition to *pressing* **Ctrl/Cmd** you also need to *press* **Z** at the same time).

There are many other shortcuts you'll learn along the way, but these are the main ones you'll need to know.

Windows Users:	Use **Ctrl** (not **Cmd**)
Mac Users:	Use **Cmd** (not **Ctrl**)
Undo	**Ctrl/Cmd+Z**
Redo	**Ctrl/Cmd+Y**
Copy	**Ctrl/Cmd+C**
Paste	**Ctrl/Cmd+V**
Cut	**Ctrl/Cmd+X**
Zoom in	**Ctrl/Cmd +**
Zoom out	**Ctrl/Cmd –**
Invert	**Ctrl/Cmd+I**
Duplicate	**Ctrl/Cmd+J**
Invert Pixel Selection	**Ctrl/Cmd+Shift+I**
Deselect	**Ctrl/Cmd+D**
Select All	**Ctrl/Cmd+A**

Dedication

This book is dedicated to one of the bright stars in my night's sky, my sweet friend Sandra Hanneson.

Thank you for being there when I needed someone to fill a part of me I thought was lost forever. Speaking with you for all those days and nights when I was struggling will always be one of the most-remembered moments in my life. I immediately fell in love with you because you were the woman I've always wanted to be with. But, as time went on, my feelings for you grew into a deeper idea of the word for friendship. Now, I am so blessed to be able to call you my friend. This book is dedicated to you because I am happy to tell the world about you.

Yours sincerely....

Made in the USA
Middletown, DE
29 June 2022